PRAISE FOR *IMPACT IMPERATIVE*

"Pam Ryan is an exceptional and remarkable person with a combination of intelligence and empathy. She is a force for good in the advancement of humankind in a challenging world."

—Bob Hawke, Prime Minister, Australia (1983–1991)

"Early on, Pam told me that Impact investing would become much more mainstream, and she was right. During her life, Pam's actions have positively impacted the lives of thousands. I am humbled to be among those individuals Pam Ryan has positively impacted."

—Jeanie Wyatt, Founder & CEO, South Texas Money
Management; Top Financial Advisor, *Barron's* magazine

"If there's anyone I know who cares about others, sees the world whole, knows that response is better than retreat, and is able to organize and motivate people toward a better future, it's Pamela Ryan. I've never stopped admiring Pamela's instincts and intelligence. *Impact Imperative* showcases this commitment to act, the vision of a better future, and principled practical ways to accomplish both."

—Dr. J. Patrick Boyer, Q.C., Author, Publisher, Lawyer,
Professor, and Canadian Member of Parliament and
Parliamentary Secretary for External Affairs (1984–1993)

"The concept that the world will be a better place because social entrepreneurs are out there working hard (and with technology, now working more cohesively and effectively) is amazing and hopeful. It's really changed how I think about the social ills of the world and helps me envision a more positive future for my kids and all the future generations. *Impact Imperative* needs to be read by many, many people."

—Sue Kolbly, Rideshare Driver, Accountant, and Editor

"If anyone can lead the way to transform our future in an enlightened manner it is the irresistible force of nature that is Dr. Pam Ryan."

—Kerry Heysen, Producer, and **Scott Hicks,** Dr. Honoris Causa (Flinders
University), Director, *Shine, Snow Falling on Cedars, No Reservations, Highly Strung*

"Dr. Pam Ryan has produced a master work for our time! Her breadth and depth of experience and extensive research and study give her the authority to provide us with prescient information, inspiration and strategic direction. *Impact Imperative* is of real value and inspiration, especially as we focus on present and future challenges that confront my country, South Africa."

—Merle Friedman, PhD, Organizational and
Clinical Psychologist; Principal, Psych-Action
in South Africa; Director, Psychology Beyond Borders

"This book is an inspiring achievement of serious thinking and concrete advice that has been years in the making. Pam Ryan has been drawn to sweeping ideas that could help provide solutions to deep-rooted structural challenges in human society, but those ideas must tangibly work. The Pam Ryan I have known is a unique blend of the visionary and the pragmatic, and this book is her important product."

—Mark Entwistle, Partner, Privus Capital;
Canadian Ambassador to Cuba (1993–1997)

"The stories we tell about the future are powerful shapers of the present. Pam Ryan is an innovative pioneer in helping to create different visions for our future and encouraging individuals, businesses, and governments to *act* on these visions now, so that we can meet the social and environmental challenges that face us. Because of its insights into both human activity and human psychology *Impact Imperative* has the capacity to trigger change at a very profound level."

—Betty Sue Flowers, PhD, Professor Emerita, University of Texas at Austin;
International Consultant for scenarios creation

"In this book, Dr. Pam Ryan makes a compelling case for why each and every one of us needs to act now if we are to have a positive impact on our future; the alternative is dire. Despite its weighty topic, *Impact Imperative* is easy and fascinating to read. It is a compelling call to action that no thinking person, after reading it, can ignore. We all need to become positive impactors. What kind of future do you want for yourself and your progeny? Dr. Ryan's book helps you answer that question. Run to your nearest bookstore and get this book! You cannot afford not to."

—dt ogilvie, PhD, Distinguished Professor of Urban Entrepreneurship, Professor
of Business Strategy, and Former Dean, Saunders College of Business, Rochester
Institute of Technology

"Increasingly, I'm asking a short question whose answer has immense consequences, 'Who Cares?' The answer to this question shows literally who has the power to make the difference for humanity's growth or brutal demise and that of Earth. *Impact Imperative* is crucial to understanding the shift *we must* make in order to having the privilege of choosing to enhance life and making an impact by simply saying *'I care.'*"

—**Gill Hicks,** Dr. Honoris Causa (Kingston University and London Metropolitan University), AM MBE, Founder & Director, M.A.D. Minds Agency and M.A.D. for Peace

"Pam Ryan's clarity of purpose around delivering impact is inspiring. She has particularly impressed me by bringing others—be it initially skeptical wealth managers or the next generation of foundation decision makers—*around* to that purpose by engaging them directly in the research and decision-making process. Importantly, this book now brings her approach to scale—by sharing the stories of role models, with a variety of approaches to impact, with a broader audience who can now find the best match for their own path to positive impact."

—**Kerry Rupp,** Entrepreneur, Venture Capitalist; Co-Founder, True Wealth Ventures

"With unparalleled insight, rigor, and passion, Dr. Pamela Ryan approaches a critical and timely topic in her important book, *Impact Imperative*. Ryan's decades of influential experience founding organizations across the globe provides her with a unique lens through which she crystallizes an urgent imperative—to save humanity through foresight and deliberative action. Bolstered by the insights of other innovators like herself, Dr. Ryan has prepared an immensely readable volume that should be of interest to thought leaders, business professionals, academics, and anyone who wants to be intellectually challenged, energized, and poised for action."

—**Roxane Cohen Silver,** PhD, Professor of Psychological Science, Medicine, and Public Health; Associate Director, ADVANCE Program, Office of Inclusive Excellence, University of California, Irvine

"Current political leadership is so short-sighted that we can be either seriously worried (and remain useless) or see those conditions as an extraordinary opportunity for non-partisans to propose new models urgently: from participative to collaborative, while being thoroughly innovative and entrepreneurial-based, Pam Ryan is trying to present us with a broad spectrum of such alternatives."

—**Pascal Vinarnic,** Innovator, Entrepreneur, Investor, Philanthropist; CEO & Chair of Fondation Demeter

"The Orana Foundation partnerships with Indigenous Australians show us the critical importance of thinking about the impacts we have in the present and how that will positively shape a future that is better for all. Like the ninja psychologist she is, Pam Ryan has challenged my thought processes and continues to do so through this *Impact Imperative*. Like Pam herself, this book is impactful, imperative, and draws light upon possible ways forward at this critical time. Read it, absorb it, and hopefully you too will make better choices."

—Jock Zonfrillo, Founder & Chair, Orana Foundation; Celebrity Chef and
Restauranter, Orana and Bistro Blackwood;
Winner of the 2019 Basque Culinary Prize and
Australian Restaurant of the Year 2019

"I have known Pam Ryan since 1989 and I can't think of a better scholar for providing an in-depth analysis of the interconnectiveness of social and environmental impact, and social and business entrepreneurship. *Impact Imperative* is comprehensive, informative, thought-provoking, and most importantly, inspirational. It is a must read for those who seek guidance in wanting to make a significant difference in our future."

—Janet Dukerich, PhD, Professor, Department of Management; Vice Provost for
Advocacy & Dispute Resolution, University of Texas at Austin

"I have worked with Pam Ryan over the past decade on several organizations featured in Impact Imperatives. Pam has a unique ability to survey the landscape, understand the issues and our key levers for creating a better future."

—Lance Fors, PhD, Founder & Former CEO, Third Wave Technologies;
Chair, Social Venture Partners International

PAMELA RYAN, PhD

IMPACT
IMPERATIVE

INNOVATION, ENTREPRENEURSHIP, *and*
INVESTING *to* TRANSFORM THE FUTURE

GREENLEAF
BOOK GROUP PRESS

Published by Greenleaf Book Group Press
Austin, Texas
www.gbgpress.com

Distributed by Greenleaf Book Group

For ordering information or special discounts for bulk purchases,
please contact Greenleaf Book Group at PO Box 91869, Austin, TX
78709, 512.891.6100.

Design and composition by Greenleaf Book Group
Cover design by Greenleaf Book Group
Front Cover images: Hands, Naruedom Yaempongsa; Hour glass,
VectorPlotnikoff; Black hand, Prostock-studio. Used under license
from Shutterstock.com
Harvard Business Review mockup (p. 274) reproduced by permission
of Harvard Business Review.
Contains images (p. 266, 271, 274) created by the Institute for
the Future.

Publisher's Cataloging-in-Publication data is available.

Print ISBN: 978-1-62634-665-9

eBook ISBN: 978-1-62634-666-6

Part of the Tree Neutral® program, which offsets the number of
trees consumed in the production and printing of this book by
taking proactive steps, such as planting trees in direct proportion
to the number of trees used: www.treeneutral.com

TreeNeutral

Printed in the United States of America on acid-free paper

19 20 21 22 23 24   10 9 8 7 6 5 4 3 2 1

First Edition

CONTENTS

Introduction

"We are in a world where a lot of great things are happening . . . the rules are changing . . . [our global] ecosystem could move one way or the other. . . . The need for leadership [now] is so potent."

—Pascal Vinarnic, French investment banker and
venture philanthropist

"We are a ticking time bomb . . . there is a dying and a birthing happening at the same time."

—Colleen Magner, South African consultant and educator

We are at an extraordinarily critical juncture—for humanity and the earth. Increasingly intense and frequent calamitous events like hurricanes, floods, droughts, earthquakes, windstorms, and bushfires propel us toward a tipping point in global consciousness. More and more people around the planet are experiencing the effects of these intense environmental jolts. The world's epicenters of financial and geopolitical power are experiencing seismic shocks of their own as nationalists and extremists rise. And without jolt or shock, the richest twenty-six billionaires on the planet have quietly assumed control of the majority of the world's wealth, while 2.2 billion of the poorest survive on less than $2 a day.[1] It is not surprising that some of the world's leading innovators—exceptional thinkers and doers—are among the growing numbers of people around the world tackling these issues.

THE TINGARI-SILVERTON FOUNDATION AND THE SEARCH FOR IMPACT INNOVATORS

Impact innovators or impact changemakers are fueling innovations in how to develop, organize, produce, distribute, and fund initiatives aimed at positively impacting some of humanity's toughest problems. Which is why our Tingari-Silverton Foundation (TSF)—in thinking about how to optimize our own positive impact—consulted more than 130 impact innovators like **Pascal Vinarnic** and **Colleen Magner**. Impact innovators know the world faces contrasting lush and bleak possible futures. They work at the leading edge of positive impact initiatives around the world, seeking to improve opportunities (education, health care, safety, access to clean food and water) for people and communities bearing the brunt of these global challenges. Yet impact innovators, despite positive developments, lament the continued hardships of people enduring the harshest predicaments—whether born of population shifts, socioeconomic inequities, conflict, or natural disaster. Their visions for our future cannot help but contain both hope and fear.

This book shares the findings from our conversations with many inspiring changemakers around the world and the ecosystems in which they work.

Talk of innovation and entrepreneurial ecosystems is trending among the world's decision-making elites. Prime ministers, presidents, state governors, and city mayors raise the specter of growing their own innovation ecosystems, hoping to create the next Silicon Valley or Austin, Texas. Ecosystems and systems-thinking encompass an awareness of the interdependence and interrelatedness of everything, including unintended and unforeseen negative consequences of good intentions somewhere else in the system. Leading impact changemakers understand that impacts can be positive and negative—that one small change in one part of the ecosystem can reverberate throughout the entire ecosystem.

This book illuminates not only the perceptions of changemakers about probable trends around the planet, but also the mindsets and actions they use to navigate unfolding global realities and still enact positive impact. This book also shares international research on the realities for life on our planet in the 2020s and beyond.

If there is one central message we have learned through our research, it is this: Our planet and all of its inhabitants face multiple possible futures, ranging from the dire to the flourishing. We—each and every one of us—can positively impact which of these futures becomes reality. The time for action is now. The imperative is here.

In the pages to come, we explore how we can all become positive impactors and reduce the harm we may inadvertently cause in our contributions to our communities and our world. How we can enact the mindsets and activities that contribute to better futures for everyone, not just the privileged few. All that prevents us from enacting our preferred collective futures are the fateful decisions we make in the here and now. Are we going to let our world stumble into a less than optimal future?

The TSF Quest for Optimal Positive Impact: A Research Journey

Tingari-Silverton Foundation's contemplation of this critical juncture for the future of our planet crystallized in 2012 when our board deliberated on the foundation's most desired future. Since our inception in the late 1990s, TSF—a small, private family foundation headquartered in Austin—has been intent on nurturing social entrepreneurial initiatives in communities around the world, communities where opportunities for people to achieve their potential were thwarted by circumstances—poverty, disaster, conflict, or postcode.

One of the foundation's key initiatives was a decade-long collaboration with the multinational accounting firm Ernst & Young to administer the annual "Social Entrepreneur of the Year" award. Our goal was to acknowledge, reward, and showcase standout entrepreneurial initiatives that positively affected disadvantaged populations. Each year, our foundation awarded a grant of $100,000 to the winner's organization. TSF did this while simultaneously administering a traditional grant-making program that funded social entrepreneurial initiatives in Texas and Australia, as well as in countries like Ethiopia, South Africa, Indonesia, and Sri Lanka.

In contemplating our foundation's preferred future, we decided to seek the insights of leaders in the impact field—thinkers, doers, innovators, and changemakers at the leading edge of the social enterprise movement. Our intent was to gather knowledge from the world's leaders in the impact arena; explore emerging trends relating to innovation, entrepreneurship, and investing for positive impact; and see how those trends might morph into positive futures for more people.

For nearly fifteen years, we were immersed in social impact, venture capital, and international humanitarian initiatives—experiences that imbued us with a reasonable awareness of the challenges facing humanity. Yet as our research progressed, we found scientists' extrapolations of life on our planet in 2030 and out to 2050 to be mind-reeling, almost blinding, revelations. The evidence screamed at us:

- Escalating climate events signaling the desperately precarious state of our planet—imminent threats to the access to clean air, water, and food, to the survival of all species.

- Escalating concentration of much-needed resources in the hands of the privileged few.

- Escalating tensions between the "haves" and "have-nots," between individualists and collectivists, internationalists and nationalists, elites and masses, high-wealth elites and high-education elites, extremists and mainstream populations.

- Escalating transformation of the global power landscape, reflected in indisputable population shifts.
- Escalating potential in an increasingly connected world for small acts to amplify impacts (positive or negative) around the globe.

The evidence confronting us ensured that we felt the weight of our planet and the dire plight of all of its inhabitants. We became agonizingly aware of the miracle our planet afforded us: to live, to breathe, to be granted another second. And another. Would our grandchildren and great-grandchildren be gifted the same miracle? Alarmist as it may seem, if we did not act now, this gift did not seem likely to endure. We therefore became driven by an all-pervasive impact imperative.

TSF Pivots Toward Preferred Positive Futures

We changed our trajectory with the aspiration to tip the balance toward hope. With this change our foundation became a virtual case study for putting what we learned during the research journey into practice.

Abolish Silos Between Business, Social, and Environment

We started by focusing on *impact*², dropping the term "social entrepreneurship." Like so many others, we had separated business and social entrepreneurship into two silos apart from the environment. Prior to our research, we had deliberately sought to support only *social* entrepreneurial initiatives, leaving environmental impact to others. Following our earliest forays into life on our planet in 2030 with changemakers around the world, the interconnectedness of social *and* environmental impact, of social *and* business entrepreneurship, along with the imperative to think and act around all three, became painfully obvious. The imperative to think in terms of impact within and upon the entire ecosystem was acute. So we switched. No more silos. Only interconnected systems.

Think and Act from an Ecosystems Perspective, Not Individual Agents

We amplified our ecosystems perspective and intensified our focus on entrepreneurs and organizations who are *ecosystem-changing innovators*—game-changing entrepreneurs rather than organizations engaged in social service delivery. Our foundation has always supported risk-takers and innovators, but now we support paradigm-shifting initiatives with the most potential to amplify impact on a massive scale using nuanced, complex definitions of scale.

Prioritize "The Greater Good"

We apply a *"do no further harm"* lens to all of our grant-making and investments. This lens guards against the possibility that in supporting an initiative in one part of the global ecosystem, we are inadvertently creating negative social or environmental impacts in another. Impact influencers **Danny Almagor** and **Berry Liberman** (Chapter 8) ask of every investment: "Is it good for people? Is it good for the planet?" To their mantra, we add: "Will it do further harm anywhere in the system, from local to global? Will this investment have a net positive impact for people in underserved populations? Will it have a net positive impact on our planet? Does it have potential for systems-changing, multiplier-effect positive impacts?"

Invest for Maximum Net Positive Impacts

We adopt a multidimensional, whole-of-ecosystem view of how we invest capital—grants, in-kind and pro bono, bridging or growth loans, mentor and role model capital, physical capital (office space), angel capital, crowd capital, network capital, venture capital, competition, and awards capital. We began assessing all the ways we invest resources, including all assets in our portfolio, for positive and negative impacts. For example, we wanted our investment in bonds going forward to be innovative, impactful systems-changing initiatives, directed at education, water and food security, natural disaster preparedness, affordable housing, and renewable energy in underserved populations. We allocated a portion of the foundation's portfolio for direct investing in entrepreneurial ventures deemed to be systems-changing innovations in products, services, or processes with the potential for positive impact on a massive scale.

We *apply impact criteria to assess our returns on investment*, asking piercing questions of fund managers and companies to optimize positive social, environmental, and governance impact without sacrificing financial returns. When we started these assessments, impact data were not readily available, so we insisted on proxy impact measures to assess whether a potential investment aligned with our mission. One of our proxy measures for a company putting into practice *any* positive social impact was the percentage of women or other minorities on their board and senior management teams. As data amassed demonstrating the positive impact on financial performance of women's involvement in senior management of any organization—from Fortune 500 companies, to start-ups and venture capital funds—gender became a critical measure, no longer a proxy.

Live and Breathe Positive Impact Values

Adding the Australian Aboriginal word *Tingari* (songlines) to our foundation name signaled our intent to ensure that the spirit of collaboration, respect, and stewardship lit our way forward. Songlines are the sacred spiritual and physical journeys of Aboriginal men and women across the vast Australian outback. These sacred spiritual singing journeys link current generations with past and future generations, as they have done for tens of thousands of years.

By embracing innovators who revolutionized positively impactful products, services, or processes for disadvantaged communities, we hoped to ensure that future resources nurtured paradigm-shifting positive impact initiatives. We wanted to amplify our impact. We wanted to focus on entrepreneurial innovators whose songlines, while already rich with empathy and compassion, respect, and collaborative mindsets, were particularly rich with audacity, boldness, and disruption.

THE GENESIS OF THIS BOOK

Our journey began with our collaboration with the Institute For The Future, a nonprofit think tank in Palo Alto, California, on an ambitious research initiative. Like the United Nations' Sustainable Development Goals aimed at eradicating poverty by 2030, we also aimed a decade or two into the future. Our journey led us to discover innovative thinkers and doers on every continent except Antarctica (although one of our interviewees, Pascal Vinarnic, ran a marathon in Antarctica). In fields as varied as biotech, civil and chemical engineering, health and other service delivery, microfinance, venture capital, impact investment, education, design, and venture philanthropy, these innovators have taken a decidedly humanistic approach to effect change for the greater good. Not seduced by visions of making their financial fortunes at the expense of all else, these changemakers are spurred on by visions of a world in which every human has equal opportunity to achieve their potential. These changemakers exemplify a long-term, whole-of-planet form of leadership, forging new frontiers in driving real results on how to "do business" while enacting positive impacts and minimizing negative impacts for the planet and its inhabitants.

Changemakers

Successful changemakers intent on positive impact are not constrained by the past. They think with a futures mindset. They are systematic about how they engage with and make sense of possible alternative futures.

These changemakers enact their own futures and shape possible futures for others. They understand risk, vulnerability, and creativity. They see the world as it is and is likely to be, and they set about changing that trajectory for the greater good. We knew from our first consultations that these impact innovators could provide important new knowledge and insights for all business and community leaders wishing to proactively author their organization's future rather than simply reacting to changing local and global business conditions.

The leading impact thinkers and doers we consulted represent the diverse roles that make up an entrepreneurial ecosystem and the behaviors necessary for an ecosystem to flourish. They model how to facilitate collaborative interrelationships within and across ecosystems. The research team spoke with designers, educators, and entrepreneurs from Texas to India to Chile, as well as incubators, funders, and investors from California, Venezuela, France, the United Kingdom, South Korea, Australia, and beyond. We wanted to understand what they were doing in the impact space, which pressing problems they were trying to address, how they measure the impacts of what they do, which crucial ingredients they draw upon to succeed, and what they think are the emerging trends for the decades ahead. During our consultations, we invited these impact innovators to conjure images of themselves and their organizations in the latter part of the 2020s and beyond.

These consultations revealed a comprehensive view of the global impact landscape—past achievements, emerging trends, as well as possible futures for impact—the optimistic, the pessimistic, and the in-between. They also revealed the dominant social issues being tackled now—and toward 2030.

To complement these conversations, we scoured trends analyses and surveys from diverse and respected sources such as The World Bank, United Nations, International Monetary Fund, and Institute For The Future, as well as insurance company research documents and academic studies—relevant rigorous quantitative and qualitative studies of social enterprise, entrepreneurship, and impact. We also searched media interviews and written works—blogs, academic and popular journal or magazine articles, and books. In many cases, the people we met offered these writings and even more insights.

We found that our journey of self-reflection and redirection paralleled an emerging global trend. Regardless of the terms people use to describe it—social entrepreneurship, social enterprise, impact investing, venture philanthropy, engaged investing, conscious capitalism, traditional philanthropy—the impact space is radically transforming. Enacting impact and investing in impact will radically influence business, organizational, and physical environments over the next decade.

Ever a leader in the impact arena, the UK government established the world's first independent impact investment wholesale body, Big Society Capital, in 2012, to spearhead this rising global trend toward positive impact. We interviewed inaugural CEO **Nick O'Donohoe**, who noted, "In 2008 no one used the 'impact investment' term. It is now common."[3] Governments, academic institutions, corporations, celebrities, and others are scrambling to join the movement, with millions of dollars flowing into the sector. As Sasha Dichter of the Acumen impact investment fund observed, "The sector is trendy. It appears glamorous. Everyone is paying attention. Lots of people want to do it."

The meteoric rise of impact in the global consciousness has been fueled by many of the visionary innovators we interviewed. They facilitate social innovation in a variety of roles that constitute the entire entrepreneurial ecosystem aimed at positive impact. One of the critical takeaways from our conversations with changemakers around the world was their awareness of and attention to the "system" in ecosystem, and all the parts of the system—the contexts for idea generation and development, for growing ideas into companies, the mentors, funders, and support service providers—were critical and synergistic. All elements of the system play vital roles in the mushrooming growth of the impact movement. Our book therefore shines light not just on the entrepreneur at the epicenter of any entrepreneurial initiative, but also on the interactive web of people who contribute to the entrepreneurial process from start to finish, the dynamics of relationships among them, as well as the end products—the ultimate impacts. Because this ecosystem thread permeates the mindsets and actions of virtually all of the leading impact innovators we consulted, an ecosystem framework—with a honed awareness of how one action or reaction impacts people, communities, and natural environments in all parts of the system—imbues the pages ahead.

THE STRUCTURE OF THIS BOOK

We organized what we learned on our journey toward a more positively impactful future around three areas of understanding, which constitute the three parts of *Impact Imperative*. The journey begins with an exploration of the nature of impact, positive and negative. Understanding how we negatively impact those we seek to assist—how we inadvertently do harm while trying to do good—is just as critical as how and what we positively impact.

Part One: Toward Clarity: Impact, Doing Good, Minimizing Harm

In the first section, we contemplate what thinking and doing positive impact means. We explore what can happen when, despite our best and most honorable intentions, the words and actions we enact to help individuals and communities enduring distressing predicaments inadvertently cause harm. We share insights on these issues from our conversations with impact innovators—the commonalities they share in their mindsets and actions. Inherently optimistic and aligning their actions and resources with their visions, many of these innovators foresee the world more like the most positive 2030 we envisage. They aim for a world in which substantive progress is being made against the most intransigent of the world's social problems. The social influencers we consulted articulated many cultural, policy, and program recommendations to bring about the most positive futures.

They see a 2030 in which impact considerations are mainstream, natural parts of all economic, political, and social activity. Such positive futures are characterized by omnipresent systems thinking, where most of us understand that impact can be positive and negative and that one small change in one part of the ecosystem can reverberate through the rest of the ecosystem. They see a 2030 in which old debates about how to measure impact are replaced by measures being understood on a spectrum—from esoteric self-questioning such as *"are we inspired?"* to concrete, but nuanced and codified measures across enterprises and sectors.

We also tackle existential questions about impact measurement and the challenges of determining if impacts have indeed occurred, whether positive or negative.

Part Two: Changemakers Inherent in Entrepreneurial Ecosystems

This section shares the stories of the inspiring people we met. We have categorized these changemakers in terms of the dominant roles they embody in the wider entrepreneurial ecosystem, although we see distinctions between social and business entrepreneurship as redundant by 2030. We highlight these specific people because they are exemplar thinkers and doers at the leading edge of the impact innovation and entrepreneurial ecosystem, embracing the new global realities and trends.

These impact changemakers navigate the global context with creativity, not only comprehending the nature and scope of the challenges ahead, but also mitigating them. They long ago pivoted toward positive impact trajectories, intent on contributing to the greater good. The lessons we learned from these changemakers about navigating rapidly changing landscapes and the future of impact entrepreneurship apply to individuals and organizations intent on shaping their own futures, rather than just getting ready for the future or building resilience to manage what the future might throw at them.

Part Three: Toward 2030: Which Future?

This section shares what we learned about the international context—the nature and scope of the challenges facing our planet and its inhabitants—that will form the global landscape as we journey through the 2020s toward 2030. This section is the result of our comprehensive, systematic wading through research from diverse and credible sources—from global institutions and think tanks to a rich lode of academic research. We analyzed tens of thousands of pages of data.

Research consistently shows that between now and 2030 there are several global trends that will continue, if not become amplified. We highlight those critical trends that will negatively impact our planet and the people on it. Only the degree of negative impact is unknown. How we—the collective human race—manage and navigate these realities will either exacerbate or mitigate the negative impact. Chapter 12 "2030: Four Alternative Futures," explores in detail global realities for 2030, such as trends in regional and world populations. We note that by 2030, 8.4 billion people will inhabit our planet, 61 percent of those in Asia.[4] India will outpopulate China by 2028, and as the populations of Association for Southeast Asian Nations member countries expand, there will likely be an accompanying shift in the financial axis of the world from West to East. The rich will continue to get richer as the wealthiest 1 percent increasingly monopolizes global wealth and the inequality divide intensifies.[5]

While many more on the planet benefit from economic growth, we share illuminating research about the devastating consequences of economic inequality, the single most consistent predictor of teenage births, infant mortality, low educational achievement, level of bullying, mental illness, homicides, and incarceration.[6] If these inequality trends go unchecked, we risk excluding millions from simple human rights—clean water, safe food, health, education, safe environments, and sustainable livelihoods—and possibly triggering challenging social and geopolitical challenges. One of the most alarming findings from these analyses was the escalating volume and intensity of mass global "loss events" through the next decade toward 2030 and beyond. An upward trend of ever-increasing environmental jolts is projected to continue through this twenty-first century—partly due to the rising temperatures of Earth's oceans and the overpopulation of disaster-prone areas. Add conflict and tension between extremists and moderates, between wealthy and poor (half the world's poor live in conflict-ridden areas), and the context for the world's poor remains dire in 2030.

These global realities will be juxtaposed against other trends like connective global technologies ushering in unprecedented transparency, accountability, and democratization of international agenda setting—all of which have the capacity to mitigate or exacerbate the consequences of the core realities. The degree to which other aspiring thinkers, makers, and doers wish to optimize positive impacts and minimize negative impacts in their own fields will depend to a large degree on how they detect, anticipate, and navigate these trends. Our research suggests that adept navigation of these trends will determine whether an organization survives or thrives.

To illustrate how the late 2020s might actually look for the planet and its inhabitants, depending on which trajectories the human race collectively enacts by the decisions made in the here and now, we present four specific, contrasting possible futures for our planet—set in 2030. Our research team was led on this part of our journey by the Institute For The Future, which conducted futures-facilitated roundtable group discussions. We also drew on the interviews with thought leaders, changemakers, and influencers. Few stories so clearly embedded in the future speak to the right now. Our alternative visions of 2030 do. These scenarios portray alternative futures ranging from a 2030 in which the capitalism juggernaut has escalated, to a 2030 in which global impact entrepreneurship has made only a small dent in alleviating the challenges of our planet.

We also describe a 2030 in which impact innovation is the norm—with high positive impact seen on a global scale. In this 2030, "doing" impact—thinking and breathing positive impact—is part of every organization's DNA and the dominant thinking of individuals and communities. These scenarios help us understand where we might be in 2030 depending on the choices we individually and collectively make today. How our choices today can lead to exacerbated inequities and potentially dark, unfulfilled lives for millions. Or not.

We conclude by turning toward the most hopeful 2030 and share the thinking and doing of leading impact changemakers on how to enact the most optimal futures. We explore likely developments in impact measurement as envisaged by many of the changemakers we consulted, and how our TSF is already putting into practice impact measures of tomorrow by combining highly customized assessments with readily available standardized measures.

TOWARD MORE HOPEFUL FUTURES

On this journey, our team vacillated between pessimism and optimism, between terror at what might befall all of us if we don't act now and hope that these impact changemakers are leading the way to positive and systemic change. At times, we felt consumed by a sense of urgency and deep concern that the work being done is insufficient—by too few people in too small proportions—and as a result, without definitive action soon, our planet and humanity was headed for doom. At other times—particularly in the aftermath of each interview with these amazing changemakers—our thinking became infused with hope, energy, faith. It is this hope, energy, and faith, along with the knowledges garnered from our research journey, that we invite you to consider in embarking on your own contemplation of alternative possible futures for you, your organization, and our planet. For humanity. We hope that the insights we uncovered in our journey about how to think and act like a positive impactor can inform your trajectory and your authoring of your preferred futures. We hope that in the process, you'll nourish the greater good, not just advance the privileged few.

PART ONE:

Toward Clarity: Impact, Doing Good, Minimizing Harm

Considering impact, enacting impact, and investing in impact are on the rise. Impact thinking and doing is increasingly influencing the organizational, socioeconomic, and political environments in which we live, work, and play. But what do we mean by "impact"? How do we know we are impacting? What if our impact is not what we intended? What if our "doing good" inadvertently causes harm?

Part 1 of *Impact Imperative* illuminates the multifaceted and inherently paradoxical nature of impact for the 2020s and beyond. We move from a focus on impact as a noun (a static "end") toward a more nuanced understanding of impact as a verb, as a dynamic process. The chapters ahead explore impact in all of its dualities—noun and verb, positive and negative, intended and unintended, micro and macro, immediate and long term. We hope our reflections trigger your reflections about the assumptions, language, and actions you and your organizations bring to impact.

We hope that in considering the dualities of impact, future acts of doing good will not contribute to or exacerbate inequities or distress in the very communities we seek to assist. We therefore invite everyone intent on doing good to constantly monitor and adjust their assumptions, frames, language, and actions—to do no harm.

We argue in the pages ahead that any contemplation of enacting impact must inherently consider both the negative and the positive, and how we ourselves contribute to the negative. The "do no harm" imperative is a necessary and equal partner to the impact imperative. This do-no-harm thread runs throughout the book.

CHAPTER 1

Impact? What Impact?

"If you asked me what the world looked like in twenty-five years,
I guarantee you that companies, all companies, will be reporting
not just financial metrics, but also impact metrics . . . Those things
will be driving part of their investment portfolios, and that will
effectively get companies to pay for negative externalities."

—Nick O'Donohoe, Big Society Capital

M etrics, measurement, evaluation. These terms have become familiar, almost ubiquitous and inescapable in the social enterprise world, although they can elicit trepidation and exasperation in equal measure. Yet there is nothing unfamiliar about the expectation that an organization, any organization, answers the fundamental question: Is the organization delivering what it aims and claims to deliver? The tricky part is how we can know the organization achieves its aims and unequivocally demonstrates its claims.

In the impact arena, exasperation derives from how specifically to measure the impact of enterprises whose positive impact missions are ahead of or equal to their financial missions. The social metrics that Nick O'Donohoe—who was appointed by the UK government as the first leader of Big Society Capital (BSC), the world's first institution established to facilitate a countrywide, even global, impact investment sector—sees as normal and universal in a decade or two are the source of debate and struggle as we enter the 2020s.

O'Donohoe noted how far the impact arena has come in just one decade. The G8 process raised the impact investing conversation to whole new levels, reflecting justifiable concerns and hype about reality. When leaders of the G8 (the "Group of Eight" of most industrialized countries—the United States, Britain, France, Germany, Canada, Italy, and Japan; Russia was temporarily suspended for its invasion of Ukraine)[1] gathered in Northern Ireland in June 2013 for their annual summit on global issues, then-UK prime minister David Cameron (president of the 2013 summit) convened a pioneering task force on social impact investment. A vocal champion of impact investing, Cameron backed his vision with political and other resources, including committing his Cabinet Office to be the task force secretariat for two years. This G8 task force was mandated with catalyzing a global market in impact investment to improve society, by facilitating global dialogue and action in the G20 and beyond. Initial members included all of the G8 countries, plus Australia and the European Union, both invited to join with observer status. Since then, O'Donohoe has witnessed seismic shifts, like the emergence of a critical mass of investors wanting to positively impact our world. More and more high-net-worth individuals and foundations are asking their banks about positive impact investments. Millennials are investing with their positive impact values and Baby Boomers are seeking alternative meaning and purpose to the financial drivers that may have dominated their lives so far. People are caring about both the positive and negative impacts of their own and organizational actions. They are increasingly paying attention to how they can contribute positively, not negatively.

Such client interest is nudging mainstream financial institutions into the impact space. O'Donohoe sees a significant majority of citizens wanting to do more and asking their banks how they can engage. Corporations, managers, CEOs, and boards of directors are seeking opportunities for impact investment—one of the fastest-growing investment strategies—and proactively embedding impact into their organization's culture and activities. Others are accessing this burgeoning source of financial and human capital, as individuals, family offices, philanthropic organizations, governments, institutional investors, and corporations embrace investing for positive purposes. In impact innovators' positive visions of global futures in the late 2020s, these positive impact values dominate entrepreneurial initiatives, investments, and consumer decisions. In the minds of today's impact changemakers, by 2030, these values are a normal part of operating an organization, of life.

What is "Impact"?: Impact as noun and verb, product and process

Conceptions of impact in the first two decades of the twenty-first century have mostly used the word as the end result of action. As a noun. The focus has been on measuring impact as the conclusion of a sequential set of organizational activities—a linear chain starting with an organization's mission and goals regarding social challenges and ending with impact. As a *noun*, impact belongs to the family of words that includes *effect*, influence, consequences, results, and conclusions. However, this dominant use of impact as a noun conceals elements of impact that are about force: impact as a collision or the striking of one thing against another. Impact as a verb.[2]

Most impact measures in the second decade of the twenty-first century focus on impact as a noun, only examining outputs and outcomes, the effects of an organization's activities. However, if only the products of an organization are examined, we miss a fundamental set of impacts. We focus on a finite end instead of ongoing evolution. We see only a problem to be solved within a specific time frame instead of a set of circumstances to be managed over time.

As a *verb*, impact is associated with words connoting "to affect"— the act of influencing, transforming, moving, shaping—but also, in some usages, the act of colliding with or slamming into. As Professor Karl Weick might say: If all incarnations from affect to effect, from influence to collision, have a tinge of impact to them, then determining what impact is and what it isn't, let alone measuring it, becomes exceedingly hard. But doable.

When our usage of impact comes to encompass its complexity—as both noun and verb, as product and process—we get close to articulating how impact and impacting, the doing impact and the measuring of impact, will evolve over the next decade or two.

Impact innovators we consulted foresee a 2030 in which common use of the word *impact* reflects its full meaning as noun and verb. This reflects the inherent intricacy of the extended and interconnected web of potential impacts (intended and unintended) of any organization. In 2030 the linear chain dominating pre-2020 impact thinking should be replaced by a collective understanding of the mosaic of relationship threads, and the multiplicities of relations among activities, processes, outputs, outcomes, and impacts—replete with feedback loops and circular cause-and-effect ramifications.

UNDERSTANDINGS OF "IMPACT" ARE EVOLVING

If contemplating all of these words feels like we are treading our way through a field studded with land mines, wariness is well warranted.

As the 2020s begin, battles still rage around the planet between shareholders and stakeholders, but the tide is turning toward a future where profit is not the only measurement of a company's well-being. The surge in demand for awareness and action toward net positive impact is being felt in the boardrooms of even the most profit-oriented corporations. Just ask the embattled CEOs of United Airlines or the Weinstein Company about the billion-dollar beating their financial bottom lines endured after public exposure of bad behavior (including delayed responses or cover-ups) that valued profits over people.

Leading thinkers and doers in the impact innovation arena, like

Nick O'Donohoe and *Stanford Social Innovation Review* editor **Johanna Mair**, believe that by 2030 technology-driven transparency and accountability will ensure that individuals and organizations enacting negatively impactful activities will be routinely called out, held to account, publicly shamed. So, by 2030, individuals and organizations will have no choice but to ensure net positive impact of what they do. By 2030, the debacles like Facebook's or Wells Fargo's public displays of disregard for customers' rights will be so last decade.

Despite the challenges of the 2010s, many impact thought leaders generally believe in a positive trajectory for impact from the 2010s' struggle to sift through all possible definitions and measures to consolidated understandings and clarity. When it came to impact measurement, our interviewees cohered around consistently salient themes. Impact innovators see impact metrics in the late 2020s reflecting a world where impact is *the* way, not a "third sector" or "fourth way." They see definitions of impact and measurement characterized by clarity and intent, transparency and accountability, forcing everyone into measurement. They see a 2030 in which conceptions of impact success are multistoried and customized, measures of impact are multistoried and customized, and definitions and measures of scale are multistoried and customized, with measures occurring at multiple levels. They see definitions and measures of impact reflecting evaluations of relationships and collaborations, processes and products. They see locals driving the impact measurement process with reference to global, sector, or other stakeholder measures, and impact definitions and measures simultaneously encompassing the short term and the long term.

For the remainder of this chapter, we examine the status of impact measurement in the 2010s, and then explore the challenges for measuring impact into the 2020s.

MEASURING IMPACT

How do we know when net positive impact has occurred? How do we measure impact? Designers, entrepreneurs, investors, and other stakeholders may have very different objectives and priorities. Some types of impact—for example, the number of farmers who use solar drying systems to preserve their produce, or the number of children with diabetes who use Jerry, the educational teddy bear, to learn how to monitor and care for their own disease—may be easier to define and measure than others. For example, how specifically the recipients of these initiatives were impacted, or how the entrepreneurs' lobbying efforts helped change public policy to enable government subsidies to farmers, or educational teddy bears being reimbursable on health insurance.

Forms of impact measurement that may capture more nuanced impacts—especially the gold standard, randomized control research designs—take time and specialized intellectual and research knowledge and skills. But a more nuanced approach to understanding impact is the key to unlocking proper measurement of it.

While virtually every impact changemaker envisages a future where impact measurement dilemmas have been solved by 2030, few have solved the measurement puzzle that might enable standardized comparable measures of impact across organizations, industries, and sectors. They were certain that by 2030, understandings of how impact manifests would be predicated on data. On evidence-based decision-making. They were certain that understandings of the nature, size, and rippling effects of impacts (both positive and negative) are much more advanced by 2030, facilitated by technology-enabled, real-time access to meaningful data. But measuring traditional returns or financial return on investment (ROI) is relatively simple and straightforward: Compare monetary income streams against monetary outlay streams, calculate the profits (or losses) and the consequent financial ROI, and explain in the annual report. Can social and environmental returns on investment, which are often social changes or quality-of-life improvements, really be measured in numbers? For enterprises intent on positive impact—whose missions dictate that their companies make a positive difference to societal challenges—the task of evaluating whether or not they have reached their impact goals is much more complex than a single or even triple bottom line of numbers.

Accurately capturing the multiplicity of impacts of an enterprise is often an illusive endeavor. Illusive because, as an *Economist* editorial asserted, defining what constitutes impact has been plagued by squabbles among impact constituents. Illusive because impacts are typically qualitative rather than quantitative, dynamic rather than static, long-term rather than short-term, complex rather than simple, and embedded in larger systems rather than existing independently. Impacts unfold indefinitely and are variable depending on contexts, timing, and levels of analysis. They are not adequately represented by reductionist monetary proxies.

IMPACT MEASUREMENT NOW

If the impact sector has been characterized by existential squabbles about what constitutes impact, determining how to measure potential impacts can be even more contentious. What is measured and how measurement occurs depends on a range of factors. Some of these factors seem simple: who is commissioning the measurement, where the measurement initiator lies on the donation or investment spectrum, and the goals of the positive impact initiative. Others are more complex, such as an entrepreneur's beliefs about how their product or service will make an impact; goals of impact measurement; type of enterprise; target population for the impact initiative; stage of development of the enterprise; risk appetites of donors and investors, and the degree to which they subscribe to a venture capital or other model of growth; the context in which an impact initiative is rolled out; and level of analysis at which measurements are targeted.

An example might illustrate the array of possible measurement options.

Case study in impact measurement: Grameen America

Our Tingari-Silverton Foundation was a first-mover investor in Grameen America's forays into Austin, Texas. Grameen Bank, with its rich history of funding women entrepreneurs in their pathways out of poverty, understood that its pioneering approaches to nurturing enterprise had potential to contribute to neighborhoods of the less fortunate in prosperous cities.

Austin is a city more known for its spawning of multimillionaires, people born to a postcode on the advantaged side of the digital divide, but as many Austin social impactors know only too well: "There but for the grace of the universe (or the postcode lottery) go I." Children born on the disadvantaged side of the digital divide, in poorer postcodes, often inherit more gloomy trajectories. Their futures can be limited and bleak. Many disadvantaged youth do not make it to their final year of high school. Some drop out when they give birth as a teenager; others get caught up in gangs and end up in prison, or become seriously ill or die before they should.

Grameen America launched operations in Austin in 2014. Since then, it has invested more than $10 million in women entrepreneurs in Austin's poorest communities. To help measure the success of these investments, Grameen America regularly sends reports to supporters and investors about its microfinance program in America, particularly in Austin. The organization relays its impact in terms of numbers: women "served," total loans dispersed and dollar values of loans, average credit scores of borrowers, total new businesses started, changes in numbers from previous years, and new members taking out loans since inception. Grameen America also tracks types of businesses that its microfinancing has supported: beauty and cosmetics (26 percent), clothing and fashion accessories (21 percent), food and beverage (20 percent), health products (12 percent), and so on. Grameen America's current focus on these measures is partly dictated by the fact that it only started in Austin in 2014, so by nature, its reportable results are short-term. Reporting other data, even if collected, is not particularly meaningful until several years of data show patterns over time.

We know from research in the microfinance industry that other impacts could be included in Grameen America's research and reports: changes in knowledge and skills around finance, business

management, budgets, and marketing; individual well-being indicators like self-esteem, sense of agency or control, happiness, and
life satisfaction; community-level health and well-being indicators
like numbers of children completing successive levels of education;
and domestic violence.[3] Even higher in the system is assessing the
impacts these new businesses have on less wealthy parts of the
wider Austin community.

DILEMMAS AND CHALLENGES FOR IMPACT MEASUREMENT

Nick O'Donohoe believes effective impact measurement starts with
impact enterprise measures that most reflect the positive changes the
enterprise is in existence to achieve. According to O'Donohoe, measurement should cover both the depth and breadth of impact (can assist
lots of people a little or some people a lot).

If investors pressure for more data, an impact enterprise usually tries
to deliver more data if it is financially feasible to do so. Examples of
available impact assessment tools include the European Venture Philanthropy Association's (EVPA) comprehensive guide on how to implement impact measurement in five easy-to-understand steps, at the
level of both the social investors and their investees. TRASI—Tools
and Resources for Assessing Social Impact—is a database developed by
the U.S.-based Foundation Center in partnership with McKinsey &
Company. With input from a diverse range of organizations, including social investors, foundations, nongovernmental organizations, and
microfinance institutions, as well as the Better Business Bureau, the
U.S. Agency for International Development, and The Center for Effective Philanthropy, the database is extensive and helpful for anyone trying to wade through the array of impact measurement possibilities.[4]

Massive progress has been made toward more nuanced and comprehensive measurement of impact during the 2010s. Examples include
B Corp's impact ratings systems; the social return on investment; the

Global Impact Investing Network's (GIIN) measurement initiative, IRIS; Ashoka's Measuring Effectiveness questionnaire; Social Impact Measurement of Local Economies (SIMPLE), developed by Social Enterprise London; Acumen's measures of immediate outputs; and the Bridges' Impact Scorecard. Yet most social enterprises intent on proving their impact on society's problems feel daunted by the task. As Johanna Mair noted, despite the plethora of methods available for measuring social impact and organizational performance, none has become widespread in the social impact field, and most users of these methods continue to struggle with the specific techniques for assessing social value.

To measure or not to measure is a fundamental question

Most of the impact thinkers and doers we consulted emphasized the benefits of measurement thinking and doing, quite apart from the results of those analyses. They warned of relying on measures or methods that reduce impact solely to monetary indicators. They alerted us to the dangers of disregarding the psychological and sociological impacts that an impact enterprise might have on the individuals and communities using its products or services. Some impact innovators argue that any one measure or standard is almost irrelevant. What is more important is how those measures or methods are used, why the chosen indicators were selected, what information about their own impact is expected from a given measure, and how those indicators might also disprove their own impact (i.e., play their own devil's advocate). Many of our impact leaders agreed that a key advantage of such measurement tools (including many listed in the previous section) is that they provide a starting point for the journey, even if a measurement journey is fraught with inherent dilemmas and challenges.

Australian businessman, investor, and philanthropist **Sid Myer** knowingly takes a controversial perspective on measuring impact:

[W]hilst I do think there is a place for some evaluation, I think lots of funds being used for evaluation would be better invested on seeking outcomes rather than evaluating over periods in which real outcomes are not able to be effectively measured. So evaluation, I submit, is not unimportant, but I suspect as an industry, philanthropy [and impact investing] places too much emphasis on evaluation. Evaluations tend to give comfort that the time or money invested ended up being spent or committed in a way you expected. But evaluations don't necessarily provide comfort as to what outcomes were real.

Myer explained how *some* "doing good" is warranted without monitoring and measurement with a telling example:

For many years, we [at The Myer Foundation] have worked hard to build strategy around what we do and don't fund . . . However, sitting separately from that, there is a football club in a town of three hundred residents in the middle of Victoria that needs a computer. And it just needs a computer. So where does that fit? Lumping it in with the small grants program is not really the answer, because the answer is born of the fact that some things are just *needed*. There is no strategy with them. It is not part of a business plan. It is simply somebody needs something to better their community or their people or their problem.

The football club computer forms a good example of potential ripple impacts throughout the wider community. A computer enables the club to be more comprehensive and systematic about how it recruits kids, provides information to kids and parents, and learn more from the internet about best methods for training and involving kids in football, and so on.

It is this dilemma in the 2010s—a showdown between financial and impact "returns"—that etches a deep frown on **Eli Malinsky's**

forehead. Now an associate director of The Aspen Institute leading the
First Movers Fellowship Program (which facilitates exceptional business leaders in achieving sector-wide positive impact), Malinsky was
the inaugural CEO of the Centre for Social Innovation (CSI) in New
York City. On assessing impact, he said:

> I think the push for metrics, quantification, and a little more rigor
> is very healthy and good and the sector deserves to be challenged
> on some of that. [But applying mostly business-world quantitative
> measures has a] downside [for] social enterprises. . . . It is not the
> same as a for-profit enterprise. Something gets lost in the picture
> when you apply one model to the other . . . I think also as much
> as the move toward metrics and quantification is good . . . there is
> a lot of quality to social impact work that does not render so easily
> into metrics that investors are most commonly familiar with, so
> some of the nuanced impacts get lost.

Impact entrepreneurs know these dilemmas only too well. They live
the tightrope between pleasing investors intent on financial returns and
investors intent on positive impact returns. And, as Malinsky pointed
out, if an enterprise is down to the sustainability wire, it may choose to
please the investors with the deepest pockets and allow financial metrics to take precedence over more qualitative impact measures. In the
2010s, these investors were likely to be the financiers.

Myer shares concerns about money trumping impact. He sees some
worthy causes missing out (like the simple need in a rural town for a
computer or a toilet):

> There is a point where risk return in solving a wicked problem
> becomes unviable when matched with an opportunity to invest
> in a problem that is not as wicked. And so with respect to wicked
> problems: Is that really the place for philanthropy? Is it the place
> for social impact investing?

Other impact thought leaders challenge the growing demand for impact measurement as fait accompli: for example, Abigail Noble, former head of impact investing initiatives at the World Economic Forum and head of Africa and Latin America for the Schwab Foundation for Social Entrepreneurship, and now CEO of The ImPact. While not diminishing the crucial information provided by evaluations, Noble echoed similar sentiments when she noted: "Many donors and philanthropists are moving too far toward impact investing (and all the measurement that entails) and too far away from traditional grant funding. Some causes just don't make dollars."

Many investors *do* want comfort that their donated or invested dollars are having the positive impact the entrepreneur aims and claims to deliver. When choosing among potential enterprises for their investment, evidence of actual impacts may sway their decision. However, as Sid Myer says, many philanthropists and impact investors are, like him, willing to take a leap of faith (often informed by instincts honed through years in the impact arena) that positive benefits will be reaped. They invest regardless of measurement because they believe investing in that issue is the right thing to do.

A whole host of other challenges in impact measurement baffled 2010s investors. Determining what specifically will be measured to demonstrate the aimed-for impacts or the type of measure—quantitative, qualitative, monetary, or nonmonetary—has caused many a headache for entrepreneurs, investors, and researchers. Abigail Noble reflected these concerns with her worry that onerous donor and investor reporting requirements can divert organizations away from core missions. Myer and Noble have voiced concerns that the process of impacting can be diminished or restricted by measures that favor validation rather than usefulness or reporting rather than actual positive impact. Acumen Fund's Sasha Dichter warns social enterprises of the traps involved when funders' demands for short-term evaluations may not fit the organizational growth model appropriate for the business and impact model of the enterprise. Dichter's concerns are echoed by

NESsT's Loïc Comolli, who observed that many funders only fund short-term. So, for enterprises whose positive impacts are—by the very nature of the issue being tackled and the program implemented to tackle it—long-term, typical short-term indicators may fall short in capturing any meaningful change.

What should be the time frame of impact measurement?

Paralleling Comolli's consternation around measures being able to capture impacts over the life cycle of a social innovation, Sid Myer argues that real impacts are not readily evident in the short term. Indeed, real, meaningful impact may take years, even decades, to reach maturation. Myer says, "It takes time to actually see the outcomes or for the outcomes to be achieved . . . often way in excess of the time frames in which the evaluations are usually conducted." Many substantive impacts do not occur within annual reporting or election cycles, so the *when* of impact measurement greatly influences what is found.

The *when* may be affected by the stage of the enterprise's or ecosystem's development, or by the market or sector in which the enterprise operates, even the region or country of its target population. Myer's sentiments are shared by other positive impactors. Abigail Noble observed that most foundations ask for reports from their fund recipients with short time horizons (for example, those results reported in annual reports). She asserts that strong positive impacts take five to ten years. Impact investing is called patient investing for a reason. So, in conducting impact measurements, entrepreneurs, investors, and researchers must decide how far out they are willing to go beyond short-term measures of outputs and outcomes to more comprehensively measure the ultimate impacts of the impact enterprise's actions.

What is the appropriate level of impact measurement?

Just as the timing of measurement can influence which impacts are found, many leading impact thinkers and doers are well aware that impacts vary according to the level of the ecosystem at which measurements are taken. Kurt Peleman, former CEO of EVPA, stressed the importance of measuring impact at multiple levels of the global ecosystem: regions, nations, communities, sectors, industries, organizations, families, individuals. Peleman believes that true impact is often reflected in "big level measures including quality of psychological life," like Bhutan's Gross National Happiness Index.

In Bhutan—nestled in a remote region of the Eastern Himalayas—quality of life is measured by this pioneering index. The comprehensive happiness measure reflects an ethos of environmental sustainability, cultural preservation, and "holistic" civic contentment. It surveys citizens on a range of individual contentment indicators from quality of sleep, physical vigor, and neighborly interactions to societal issues like Bhutan's role in the world. Bhutan's head of the Ministry of Information and Communication, Kinley Dorji, told *The New York Times*: "Happiness itself is an individual pursuit. Gross National Happiness then becomes a responsibility of the state, to create an environment where citizens can pursue happiness . . . to create the conditions for happiness."[5] Just as Bhutan routinely surveys citizens to determine collective contentment, Peleman wants epistemological data routinely collected more globally (e.g., at each census) on community well-being questions, such as: Are people happier? Are people less depressed? Are there fewer suicides?

What assumptions about impact and measures exist?

Measurement criteria and methods can be greatly influenced by assumptions made by an entrepreneurial team, its impact investors, researchers, or other stakeholders. One massive assumption made by impact entrepreneurs and investors alike is that the enterprise's activities directly correlate with the impacts being claimed—that the enterprise's activities are the *cause* of the impacts being measured (often called the "Attribution Assumption"). This direct linkage may not be true. It is critical for evaluators and researchers to consider other influences. For example, in the Grameen Austin case, what might the number of small businesses started in Austin have been over the same time period had Grameen America not entered the Austin market? Are there other reasons for the growth in jobs—such as the fact that Austin was consistently one of the fastest-growing economies in the United States during that time? What might the women entrepreneurs have done without those microloans? Have those microloans resulted in sustainability of those businesses over the long term? Were there psychological and sociological impacts in this Austin community—either positive or negative?

Social return on investment (SROI) can be dramatically affected by small changes in assumptions. Later changes to any calculations for a program can result in very different levels of SROI.[6] These questions are why randomized control design (RCD) research is the gold standard for measuring these kinds of impacts. RCD also controls for other possible causes of positive impacts—for example, changes in the economy, changes in the political climate or policy (a government pursuing a social justice agenda), or demographics like age, education, and gender.

What impact measurements should be funded for optimal understandings?

Most impact measurement tools and methodologies require substantial funds and time. These resources are often prohibitive for impact enterprises operating on a shoestring.

In the 2010s, investors and donors did not typically allocate enough funds to measure impact in systematic, comprehensive ways. Such challenges ensure that accurately measuring social impact remained elusive. While many of the measures available by the late

2010s attempt to overcome these challenges, some impacts are not easily captured. Importantly, measures that reduce impact assessment to monetary analyses in an attempt to be comparable with financial ROI may fall short of the scientific method's validity and reliability criteria. Nick O'Donohoe's use of the terms "financial metrics" and "social metrics" conveys the continued reliance on quantifications.

Yet, as The New School's **Mariana Amatullo's** research shows, qualitative measures may be more telling, such as her groundbreaking use of psychological measures—well-being, self-esteem, sense of agency, who a person sees as in control of their own fate—as well as sociological measures like levels of domestic violence, suicide rates, and levels of community happiness. These qualitative measures can provide richer, more nuanced and meaningful understandings of impacts—on the individual human psyche, on the collective, and on the complex dynamics of relationships that make up ecosystems. For these more nuanced measures to be done responsibly with validity, they need qualified researchers like Amatullo to design, implement, and interpret them. The impact innovators we consulted understood the need to build these research funds into operational budgets.

SOME MEASUREMENT INITIATIVES MEASURE THE WRONG THINGS

Several impact leaders we interviewed, including Sid Myer and Kurt Peleman, were acutely aware that even with research expertise, impact measurement initiatives might measure the wrong things. Peleman worries about social enterprises and impact investors focusing heavily on financial ROI at the cost of social returns. One consequence of this skewed financial focus may be the inadvertent creation of more problems—for example, shortcuts in essential programs including research—sacrificing true positive impacts.

Given all of these challenges, we cannot lose sight of the imperative to demonstrate (with rigorously collected evidence) that impact initiatives are delivering what they aim and claim to deliver. We must also be realistic. Donors and investors alike must put their money where their demands are and specifically include funds disbursed to help impact entrepreneurs adequately measure an enterprise's impacts over the short term and long term, and hold the enterprises to those commitments. As Harvard researchers Ivy So and Alina S. Capanyola argued in 2016: "It is crucial to identify when it makes sense to measure impacts and when it might be best to stick to outputs—especially when an organization's control over results is limited, and causality remains poorly understood."[7]

ENTREPRENEURSHIP FOR IMPACT INSIGHTS SUMMARY

Behind the ultimate measures of impact success is the staying power of the enterprise, the sector, the ecosystem. The Skoll Centre for Social Entrepreneurship's **Pamela Hartigan** said at the 2015 Skoll World Forum: "If we don't have a planet, all this impact talk will be for naught." Impact changemakers believe the impact sector will not only contribute to solving some of the world's most pressing problems, but will do so as part of an escalating movement of global impact thinking and doing. As the impact movement becomes mainstream by 2030, impact monitoring processes and measures become equally mainstream.[8] The result: The third decade of the twenty-first century will usher in positive changes in evolving impact indicators—from the customized local enterprise level to the standardized, including those for global sustainable development goals.

CHAPTER 2

Intending Good.
Doing Harm.

"Social enterprise and impact investing are about intention . . . *to make dollars and change the world. [In social enterprise and impact investing], intention is the most significant element of the organization's mission. The* why *behind the organization's existence. In the process, the organization can deliver positive impacts on the lives of individuals and on the environment . . ."*

—Danny Almagor, Small Giants, Australia

There are many reasons to sing the praises of social entrepreneurship, social enterprise, and impact investing, particularly in the wake of the seismic political shakeups of the 2010s. The notion of doing good, facilitating good, and investing in doing good makes those of us in the throes of such activities also feel good. But are we in danger of global altruism in overdrive? Are intentions to do good inadvertently imbued with latent forces that ultimately do harm?

Monsignor Ivan Illich certainly thought so in 1968. At a conference in Cuernavaca, Mexico—way before the terms *social entrepreneurship* or *impact investing* were widely known—he delivered a stinging critique of voluntary service when enacted without conscious reflection of motives and impact.[1] Illich lamented the paternalism and condescension often inherent in service, urging those in service to reflect on how these practices might negate their intentions and actions. He questioned motives, values, and the capacity to "do good," especially in any international service "mission."

We are still learning about the dangers of good intentions. We know from studies of well-being and trauma in the aftermath of large-scale events like natural disasters, terror attacks, or conflict that the best of intentions by laypeople and professionals alike can indeed do unimagined further harm. The impact entrepreneurship field is no different. Whether installing innovative water wells in Africa, giving shoes away in Central America, or funding microfinance initiatives in Asia, many social entrepreneurial initiatives may have inadvertently caused harm.

In this chapter, we draw from the insights of the visionary changemakers you'll be introduced to in Part 2 of this book, along with research, to explore how the impact arena can avoid the traps of altruism in overdrive. We describe some of the potential harmful consequences that can ripple through an entire global impact ecosystem—often triggered by one small action. We relay what visionary impact changemakers think and do to minimize negative social and environmental impacts while maximizing the positive.

This chapter is not intended to lambaste those of us trying to do good with the best of intentions. It is intended to stimulate self-questioning and critical analyses of potentially harmful behaviors. It is a call to honestly consider how we might be using our privilege in potentially harmful ways, and to harness those good intentions with less detrimental, more functional mindsets and actions. With the rise in global conscience, the worldwide surge in purpose, and the burgeoning of impact investments, with all of these noble intentions, how can doing good possibly go wrong?

WHITE SAVIORS?

Acutely attuned to the latest trends, venture capitalists and entrepreneurs alike have seen the global and local signals, the demographic shifts in attitude. Many are asking themselves: Is this a trend we want to ride? Can we still maximize financial ROI if we take into account the soft stuff? Entrepreneurs are asking: How can we tap into this capital?

Skeptics see this wave of interest in impact as marketing: being *seen* to do good, not necessarily about doing actual good. Still other observers worry that this new wave of investing is just another way that rich white people use their privilege to reinforce stereotypes of the "poor," the "broken," the "downtrodden"—perpetuating narratives that diminish recipients and elevate the power of the disbursers with their wisdom, money, and resources. A different form of colonialism at play—financial imperialism by the wealthy over the "needy."

Discussions of this sordid dark side of volunteering, missionary work, financial colonialism, or imperialism is not new. Rudyard Kipling's castigating words in *The White Man's Burden*—"Take up the White Man's burden, In patience to abide . . . To seek another's profit, And work another's gain"—were echoed over a half century later in the stirrings of philosophers Jean-Paul Sartre, Noam Chomsky, and Argentinian revolutionary Che Guevara. These sentiments found vocal force in Ghanaian president Kwame Nkrumah, who popularized the term *neo-colonialism* in the early 1960s to describe the socioeconomic and political control that can be exercized economically, linguistically, and culturally by multinational companies. Ivan Illich applied the themes to "voluntourism" soon after.

Public debate about "white saviorism" has gathered steam in mainstream and social media around the world during the 2010s. In March 2012, Nigerian American author Teju Cole unleashed a series of tweets:

1. *From Sachs to Kristof to Invisible Children to TED, the fastest growth industry in the US is the White Savior Industrial Complex.*

2. *The white savior supports brutal policies in the morning, founds charities in the afternoon, and receives awards in the evening.*

3. *The banality of evil transmutes into the banality of sentimentality. The world is nothing but a problem to be solved by enthusiasm.*

4. *This world exists simply to satisfy the needs—including, importantly, the sentimental needs—of white people and Oprah.*

5. *The White Savior Industrial Complex is not about justice. It is about having a big emotional experience that validates privilege.*

6. *Feverish worry over that awful African warlord. But close to 1.5 million Iraqis died from an American war of choice. Worry about that.*

7. *I deeply respect American sentimentality, the way one respects a wounded hippo. You must keep an eye on it, for you know it is deadly.*

Cole's words were retweeted and reproduced in multiple languages across the globe in various media forms, including *The New York Times* and *The Atlantic*[2]. *The Atlantic* later published Cole's expanded analysis of the "white savior industrial complex." In that analysis Cole describes his observations of well-intentioned, yet naïve and privileged white Westerners who work in development, particularly in emerging economies. His piercing comments are a twenty-first century echo of Kipling's.[3]

Western countries offering aid cannot always understand the complexities and nuances of the predicaments they try to fix. According to Cole, unlike the people actually experiencing the disaster, people on the outside cannot connect the dots or see the patterns of power behind the isolated disasters. Cole provides examples of patterns of power that create systemic, often intransigent issues not fixable by Band-Aid-style aid. These include "militarization of poorer countries, short-sighted agricultural policies, resource extraction, the propping up of corrupt governments, and the astonishing complexity of long-running violent conflicts over a wide and varied terrain."[4] Other African and Western writers have added their voices to the growing call for a halt to white savior mindsets. James Schneider of *New African* magazine urges people cooperating across borders and coming together to do good in regions not their own, to not patronize, overpower, or warp local understandings and efforts. He laments: "Africa is now, and has been for at least 250 years, struggling against different forms of white saviourism."[5]

American author and journalist Courtney Martin attributes the call to white saviorism to the "reductive seduction" of other people's problems. She acknowledges that heeding the calls to do good is "psychologically defensible." Who would not be seduced by the chance to solve other people's exotic problems in exotic locations? Martin points to the entire voluntourism industry and this tendency to be seduced by others' problems is "not malicious, but can be reckless." And, at times, harmful. Many in the industry nurture and facilitate these "desires and delusions."[6] Jacob Kushner, an independent journalist who writes about East and Central Africa, affirmed these concerns in his long-form article, "The Voluntourist's Dilemma." Kushner laments the problems that surface when well-intended, often naïve volunteers stay at orphanages to help care for children. He argues that this practice, when not appropriately managed, can, in some cases, leave at-risk children with attachment disorders and encourage orphanages to purposefully keep them in poor conditions to attract more volunteers.[7]

In the last few years, *The Guardian*'s "Secret Aid Worker" section has related anonymous true stories about the dark side of doing good in the humanitarian aid and development industries. One aid worker describes the enormous costs and disruption of celebrity visits. Others expose the lack of diversity in boardrooms and senior management ranks, or the unthinking use of images of people in distress for visual marketing purposes.[8] One aid worker described the age-old trade-offs when a social enterprise accepts much-needed funding from the very companies who may be contributing to the systemic problems in the impacted communities. Money and white Western "help" can be seductive. Most large-funded nongovernmental organizations (NGOs) are financed and patronized by aid and development agencies, which are, in turn, funded by Western governments, The World Bank, the United Nations, and some multinational corporations. Even with knowledge of such pitfalls, Western-infused solutions might feel like a positive shot in the arm in places like Haiti, with its history of earthquakes, political corruption, and myriad other problems.

White saviorism and impact investing

Statistics give credence to the flourishing of white saviorism in the growing impact investing arena. Two-thirds of the world's impact investment funds emanate from North America and Europe, and two-thirds of the world's impact investment funds are distributed to emerging economies, particularly those in the Southern Hemisphere. Some analysts see this trend as a troubling reincarnation of colonialism in financial form.

British researchers Firoze Manji and Carl O'Coill provide compelling evidence that social impact NGOs—particularly in sub-Saharan Africa—have come to occupy the same cultural niche previously occupied by Christian missionaries. Many impact NGOs share internationally accepted principles of "good" development with the same religious zeal with which missionaries shared the tenets of Christianity. Manji and O'Coill condemn aid for shoring up those forces that "subjugate and immiserate the majority" in the communities they seek to help.[9] Intent on spreading the "Development Gospel," many aid workers travel to a country with "The Answer," essentially ignoring local contexts, local resilience, and local ideas and actions.

In 2016 the call for critical reflection of privileged white Westerners lording over others less fortunate morphed into satire with the emergence of Barbie Savior. Beaming images and insights of white voluntourist Barbie's "blessed" experiences in Africa appeared in the form of Instagram selfies (cheekily labeled "slumfies"),[10] and Barbie Savior quickly garnered global attention. The two anonymous creators of Barbie Savior were frustrated by what they had witnessed in their own international work: false callings to duty, dishonest appeals to emotion, and the viewing of oneself as uniquely qualified to bring necessary information and change to the global poor. The frustrations of Barbie Savior's creators stemmed from the "fetishizing and over-sentimentalizing" of experiences by those who are voluntouring without the altruistic desire to serve. Barbie Savior's messages highlight erroneous perceptions that problems in poor communities, particularly in developing nations, are easily solvable. The self-lacerating satire exposes the dangers of reverence for claims to "alleviate the suffering of the poor" and bring "joy to the disadvantaged." Barbie Savior's Instagram bio says it all: "It's not about me . . . but it kind of is."[11]

As Barbie Savior's creators openly admit, those of us who have worked in the humanitarian and impact sectors a long time are not immune to white savior tendencies, no matter how self-reflecting and honest we are. Despite our intentions to do good, along with our sincere attempts at empathy, people living in communities who suffer from white saviors' efforts to solve local problems remind us that we cannot truly know another's experience, especially in a context of dramatic power differences.

DOING GOOD. DOING HARM. LET US COUNT THE WAYS.

In a spirit of trying to reduce our own white saviorism tendencies and practice critical reflection and self-examination, this next section examines how blatant financial power differentials can inadvertently influence those of us drawn into the heart of impact work, particularly as investors.

Microloans, anxiety, and other potential rippling negative impacts

In 1976 Muhammad Yunus loaned $27 to a group of fledgling village women who were entrepreneurs, thus pioneering microcredit throughout Bangladesh and beyond. Yunus's model specialized in giving small loans to some of the poorest people on the planet and led to the founding of Grameen Bank. Grameen means "rural" or "village" in the Bangla language, reflecting the bank's initial targeting of rural communities. The Grameen model of microfinance became an exemplar for the world, earning Yunus a Nobel Prize.

These days, microfinance and financial services account for 40 percent to 45 percent of global impact investment funds (followed by energy at 11 percent, housing at 8 percent, food and agriculture at 8 percent, and health care at 6 percent).[12] The microfinance model is praised and emulated across the planet, and key aspects—group involvement, work outside the home, skill development, independent income stream, and so on—are believed to be critical to positively influencing psychosocial well-being, including self-esteem and a sense of personal empowerment and agency.

Our own research into the psychology of microfinancing, however, revealed that microfinancing is not as universally beneficial as the dominant narrative suggests. Carrying debt can have negative psychosocial impacts, such as increased stress and even depression, as women take on more work responsibilities inside and outside the home. In some communities, particularly patriarchal cultures, microfinancing to women can inadvertently change the power structures in families and communities, leading to increases in domestic violence as men feel disempowered and that they are losing control.[13]

PlayPumps, TOMS, and unintended negative impacts

Many other social innovations aimed at "helping" the plight of the poor have had even more troubled histories. Take the "PlayPump."[14] Developed in the first decade of the twenty-first century, PlayPump was a merry-go-round-type device connected to a water pump. As children move the merry-go-round, water is pumped from its natural source into a storage tank and is then available on demand. Installed across Mozambique, among other countries, the pumps were intended to aid water supply to communities while the kids had fun.

These days, many of the pumps sit idle or have been replaced by a hand pump. Ghosts of well-meaning inventors and investors who may not have understood the complex issues of water in the Mozambique context. How might such a well-intended innovation do harm? First, many critics have questioned the inherent assumptions about children's "work" versus "play" to create water flow. Further, the PlayPump may have been a solution imposed for the wrong problem. If water scarcity rather than water flow was the issue, then no amount of "play" by the children can make clean water accessible. What happens when the water is not available? If water supply is low and demand is high, children can be exploited by expectations that they toil away, often in the heat of the day, to produce community water.

Potential harm also comes from the opportunity costs of hundreds of thousands of dollars spent on PlayPumps that could have been spent on more viable water strategies. The PlayPump *did* succeed in providing learning for others embarking on social innovation journeys about the need to design and implement with locals, taking into account nuanced local contexts.

Similar caution is warranted around business models intended to have a positive social impact. TOMS's initial business model—buy a pair of TOMS shoes and the company gives a pair to an impoverished child—attracted controversy. By late 2016, TOMS had gifted sixty million pairs of shoes. Despite the face value of this act to do good, critics point to the many ways handouts can do harm. Acts such as these can depress or even replace local industries and markets, creating a need where one may not have existed, increasing the risk of spending money on things people neither need nor want, fostering a culture of aid dependency.

To its credit, TOMS commissioned a study by the University of San Francisco to determine whether the company's strategy was having a positive impact. Researchers used a randomized control research design across a thousand households in El Salvador. They found that TOMS's "gift" of shoes negatively impacted future shoe purchases. Worse from an impact perspective, the free shoes had no effect on over-all shoelessness in the local population, shoe ownership, general health, foot health, or self-esteem. More troubling, the researchers found that almost 70 percent of the children who were *not* given the shoes agreed that "others should provide for the needs of my family," reflecting grow-ing expectations of a handout.

TOMS and PlayPump illustrate that sometimes impact initiatives are driven by what white Westerners perceive to be "the problem," which may not be perceived to be a problem at all by locals. For children who are poor, shoes may be one of the last items on their need/wish list. Or, more basic: Western assumptions that shoes are a "need" may even be erroneous. Communities who have for generations trekked barefoot through the bush have feet conditioned to such conditions compared to Westerner-provided new shoes. What happens when the new shoes wear out and little feet have become accustomed to covers that are no longer available?

Smart Focus Vision and creating markets through charity

Similar questions might be applicable in another example, this time relating to eyeglasses given to children in poor communities in Asia. One social enterprise, Smart Focus Vision (a spin-out from Stanford University), is an impact initiative that brings an integrated approach to eye care, desperately needed in rural areas of Asia and Africa. A self-described "high-growth company" headquartered in California, Smart Focus deploys innovations in eye care and service delivery to reach children in rural China. There is no doubt about the positive impacts of improved vision—whether through health care or the provision of glasses. (Stanford studies have shown that eyeglasses not only improve the welfare of children but also lead to potent—greater than 20 percent—gains in school performance.)[15] Smart Focus provides the first pair of glasses for free as well as fee-for-service treatment and eyewear.

Cynics might say that giving away the "first pair free" is not charity—that this single gift builds access to the huge and untapped Chinese rural market by the eyeglasses manufacturer. Again, the questions can be asked: Is provision of free glasses causing any harm in the local ecosystem? What happens when the free glasses are broken or lost, or no longer right for the patient? Is the money spent on providing free glasses better spent on other aspects of the wider eye health/vision issue? The most positively impactful social enterprises design their organizations, products, and services to counter against such potential rippling negative impacts.

INVESTING MORE CONSCIOUSLY

These examples of impact-intended initiatives in microfinance, water security, health care, manufacturing, and retail point to the need for product and service designers to build in safeguards against such harmful impacts, and for supporters and investors to be highly deliberative and selective about how and where to invest. Such potential unintended harmful consequences suggest that optimal investment strategies need to be based on rigorous evidence about potential negative and positive impacts, regardless of the dominant "doing good" narrative.

Investing more reflectively and consciously with ecosystem awareness may be counter to some of our own natural human tendencies, where personal stories and anecdotes, especially those backed by vivid images, sway our judgments. Calvert Impact Capital CEO Jennifer Pryce noted that their impact investing clients "signal loud and clear that the narratives of the impact—the stories, photos, and videos of how the capital is helping empower people and communities—are more engaging for them," with social impact metrics playing a secondary role.[16] Even fewer investors take into account negative impacts on the wider ecosystem, whether local, regional, or global. Countering these biases is a must if we are to optimize positive impacts.

Nowhere is the juxtaposition between the intention to do good and the potential to do harm more poignant, or potent, than in humanitarian aid and development. Those of us in the growing impact arena can learn from the still-nascent self-reflection in this area. For our discussion of how we do unintentional harm while meaning to do good, we draw on the pioneering work of development economist Mary B. Anderson, Columbia University professor Michael Wessells, and the Psychology Beyond Borders research team in their exposés of inadvertently doing harm, particularly in the humanitarian arena.[17] These insights and observations are offered not in denigration of so much positively impactful work being done all over the world, but in a spirit of constructive reflection aimed at contributing to a more positive trajectory for impact. The ultimate aim: to maximize positive impacts and minimize negative impacts for the people the impact communities seek to assist.

Ways we inadvertently do harm

The likelihood of causing harm can be exacerbated by multiple characteristics of the context one is operating in and the nature of the work: uncertainties about fundamental impact goals and orientation, the power differential between outside agencies and local people, the complexities of local culture and politics, the complexities of emerging impact investment politics, and the lack of training about the impact of initiatives for people (social entrepreneurs, impact investors, venture philanthropists, government, and nongovernment) working in the area.

As in the humanitarian aid arena, our presence (or our financial presence) in impact initiatives can and does cause harm. With almost 70 percent of impact investment funds coming *from* Europe and North America and almost 70 percent channeled *toward* emerging markets, the impact arena is ripe for unintended harm, defying the very intentions to do good that compel impact entrepreneurs and investors in the first place. When engaging in impact work, whether directly or through funding, we can inadvertently do harm when we:

- Make erroneous or short-sighted assumptions.

These errors come about when we do not sincerely and honestly analyze our own motives for doing what we are doing. While most impact entrepreneurs and investors have the best of intentions, they may also have other motives for being involved. Self-reflection is critical. Do our own motives contribute to harm? What about our conclusions? Have we jumped to conclusions about the source of problems—which may generate the wrong strategies?

These assumptions can also appear in the "solutions" that organizations offer, if they have not thoroughly researched the problems with extensive collaboration, consultation, and research. Or when "solutions" are offered without knowing which tools the local communities have already generated or tried and which local strategies worked or did not work.

- Look at the wrong scale.

We must think about the big picture, ecosystems, and local, regional, and global systems. We must consider our own work in the context of the larger macro geopolitical and socioeconomic context of a country or sector, as well as the field of impact investing and development. When we are not aware or deliberative about the nature and scope of our own impact in a particular context, we can set up a social enterprise or invest in one area with too little knowledge of local culture, customs, and ways of doing things and end up duplicating existing impact work.

- Introduce strategies that require far greater resources than the local community can muster after we are gone.

For example, wells, toilets, solar panels, or Western educational or art supplies. This can happen when we do not take into account the nature of local infrastructure and resources, or enact strategies that do not contribute to local capacity, infrastructure, or resources.

This is also true for strategies that do not allow for adequate follow-up. For example, providing products, services, or programs without ongoing supervision or support to the community impacted. It is vital to look at projects not only in the appropriate scale in the process but also in the effects: If we focus on short-term results without taking into account the impacts and needs for the long term of the affected population, we can do great harm.

- Don't truly listen to the individual, the family, or the community we hope to positively impact.

When we "colonize" with our Western concepts of "poor," aid, and well-being, we often create the most harmful impacts.[18] Even well-intentioned events can appear to be entertainment or adventure for the "givers." For example, one United Nations agency advertised to its members: "Come on the adventure of a lifetime" so they could ride bicycles across Vietnam to advocate for female victims of abuse (marketing one group's distress as another's adventure). Such moves not only reinforce racial and socioeconomic stereotypes while reaffirming the achievements, the comforts, and the compassion of the privileged, often white Westerners, but they also negatively impact local communities.

Westerners' ignorance can have harmful effects. We may use other people's tragedy for our own ends, for example, marketing. So many impact enterprises use photos and videos of people in tragic predicaments to raise funds. By giving interviews to media and using names, stories, and cases, we can hurt the person, the group, or the community involved.

- Disempower the local community.

When we impose strategies without locals leading the decisions, we can greatly diminish local power structures. For example, privileged visiting investors deciding on a school curriculum for a model school to be built in a community in need of a school. If a community does not co-design and own a strategy, how can they sustain it?

By excluding or changing local power and economic and social structures, we diminish existing community enterprise, markets, support networks, and infrastructures rather than building on them. This happens when we:

- Select a local group with whom to align. For example, when we as resourceful NGOs turn up with supplies, money, and people, and choose to align with a particular local group (we may already know them, they can speak English, they appeared well credentialed and connected), that partnership can bring extra wealth, status, and power to the chosen group. They, in turn, can do unintended harm as a result of our giving them resources that they are not equipped to "run" with.

- Hire locals in ways that distort the local economy and social networks (pay or provide benefits that cannot be matched by local employers).

- Buy local goods and services, leaving little left for local consumers, adding to scarcity and inflation. For example, in Haiti, one large, well-endowed NGO paid far more for everything (food, transport, shelter, wages) than other NGOs, leading to inflation of prices and social tensions.

- Turn people and communities into dependent victims and ignore how they daily exhibit their own resilience and ingenuity (not often detected or understood by the privileged).

- Create security risks for the local people, our local partners and hosts, just by being there.

Professor Mike Wessells, who has long warned about the potential to do harm in the humanitarian arena, sees this potential to harm as systemic, requiring concerted awareness and action at multiple levels and among a diverse array of stakeholders. He urges sweeping changes to training and preparation so the next generation of humanitarian workers (and others intent on doing good) are infused with "ethical awareness, cultural competencies, understanding of historical and social forces, and technical skills they will need to respond [to emergencies] in a productive, appropriate manner. . . . Above all, there needs to be stronger norms of self-reflection and critical thinking."[19] These same words can be applied to those of us doing positive impact work on any continent.

UNDERSTANDING THE IMPACTS OF OUR WORDS

At a most fundamental level, for those of us intending good, words matter. They can bolster or diminish. They can infuse a life force or break a spirit. They can be therapeutic or debilitating. We can spew out words conveying our own labels, or we can listen to the words the "other" uses instead. Our words are our tools of reduction—the means by which we are seduced into thinking we can fix other people's problems. Our words—labels, clichés, catch phrases, buzzwords—may stop us from truly listening and seeing. Any psychologist versed in the traps of selective perception will warn us: We see what we already believe. We see what the words in our head tell us to see. If we categorize a group of people as working poor, victim, oppressed, poverty stricken, that is all we see. And in only seeing the label, the designated name, the buzzword, we strip those people of all the other aspects of who they are. They may also be entrepreneurs, creators, survivors, leaders, warriors, team players, and so on.

When joined together in themes, words create narratives—which can buoy, invigorate, buttress. Or, conversely, undermine, constrict, curb, and blunt. The do-gooder narrative—in which the hero is usually a well-funded, privileged white Westerner—conveys the message that well-funded, privileged white Western people have the unique power to uplift, edify, and strengthen.[20] The do-gooder narrative perpetuates the belief that "solutions come from without, are top-down, and flow from male dominated panels in the conference rooms of the Western world."[21]

This narrative was particularly evident in Haiti in the aftermath of the devastating 2010 earthquake. Voluntourists, missionaries, and NGOs of every size, nature, and nationality flooded stricken Haiti. Few examined their motives for being there. Few comprehended that their very presence could inadvertently do more harm than good. Few considered the message sent to the local people when a white privileged outsider flew in with a team of other white outsiders and—wielding celebrity power—set up a huge white tent on the fringes of one of the largest displaced-persons camps, ultimately becoming the leader of that camp. Were no Haitians capable of such a role? Did anyone try to find out? Even though the humanitarian teams who descended on Haiti were generally noble and well intentioned, their very intentions and subsequent actions had unintended impacts—negative and positive, visible and invisible—across Haiti and beyond. Noble and good intentions are meaningless if they inadvertently steal resources, jobs, experience, opportunity, and dignity from the very people the hero seeks to "save."

ENTREPRENEURSHIP FOR IMPACT INSIGHTS SUMMARY

Muhammad Yunus long ago smashed "doing good" misconceptions and dominant narratives. The work of Yunus and the Grameen Bank shows the power of solutions coming from within, from the "bottom" up, and flowing from local communities. He says: "In my experience, poor people are the world's greatest entrepreneurs. Every day, they must innovate in order to survive. They remain poor because they do not have the opportunities to turn their creativity into sustainable income."[22] The millions of everyday entrepreneurs around the world who started with a Grameen microloan are living proof that enduring life under the poverty line need not diminish the person.

It is imperative that changemakers intending good consciously use knowledge and research on possible negative ramifications to collaboratively tailor products and services to avoid inadvertent diminishing impacts.

CHAPTER 3

Doing Good.
Minimizing Harm.

How can we avoid the pitfalls of our own beliefs? The inadvertent harm set in motion by our own good intentions? Most of us involved in "doing good" often start with the best of intentions, yet we unwittingly do harm. How do we counter our own often-unconscious biases and minimize harm?

We can start by abandoning defensive rationalizations or other forms of self-protection and adopting a critical, self-reflecting, devil's advocate mindset. We can confront the dehumanizing effects our labels can unwittingly have on the people and communities we seek to assist.

This chapter is informed by our work at Psychology Beyond Borders (PBB). At PBB, in parallel with our psychosocial service delivery, research, and policy advocacy, we spent a decade self-examining, observing, and critically analyzing how we might do better in our attempts to assist those living through difficult circumstances.[1] As we approach the 2020s, with a worldwide surge in intent to do good, it is imperative that we understand how we do harm in our impact work, and equally important, how to minimize harm.

DECIDING WHETHER OR NOT TO "DO GOOD"

To ensure that we enact the good we wish to do, impact innovators and changemakers must be conscientious in how they embark on their entrepreneurial initiatives. The following steps are essential:

- Clearly and comprehensively define raison d'être.

By thinking deeply about the core mission of our organization, why we are in existence, and if our unique skills and knowledge can positively impact the identified impact challenge. We may determine that we are not the right organization or people for the task. Ask the following questions when ruminating on your raison d'être:

1. Why us? Why not locals?

2. Who constitutes the population or community our product or service aims to benefit?

3. What impacts will our product or service have on this population? On people and the planet beyond the targeted population or community?

Thinking about potential positive and negative impacts at all layers and levels can help us better understand the scale of the needs being addressed and hopefully focus the processes adopted to address them.

- Think of impacts on systems—from local to global.

Many of the impact influencers we interviewed from different parts of the planet act from understandings that everything and everyone are connected. In the late 2020s, they see widespread consideration of the multiplier effects throughout the entire global system of every action or inaction—that one change can lead to change in the whole system. An increased awareness of positive and negative impacts up and down the chain (a systems approach) dominates the impact area by 2030. There is also widespread appreciation that when any enterprise is launched, it may have unintended and unforeseen negative consequences somewhere else in the system.

Impact innovators consider the planet in a holistic way, as one huge system with many other systems embedded within. All parts of the system, no matter how mammoth, are interrelated to all other parts of the system. A systems approach invites impact changemakers to consider how actions they set in motion will affect other parts of the system, at all levels of the system. In the impact context, the relationships among the individual, organizational, community, state, national, and international systems, as well as the global system as a whole, are crucial for how impact activities are designed, enacted, and evaluated. Serial entrepreneur Tony Boatman summed up this approach: "Putting it together as an ecosystem and platform with a procurement system and [considering] the whole thing as a package."

It is systems thinking that can help us avoid doing harm to those we seek to assist. We can use it to help build on and enhance relationships among existing community institutions, nongovernmental organizations, or government programs with similar missions/goals. By thinking of the entire ecosystem, we can ensure that initiatives can be meaningfully replicated by locals in the future by collaboratively supporting or designing, delivering, and evaluating impact initiatives together.

Collaboratively supported or designed and delivered impact initiatives:

- Cultivate relationships and practices that can benefit stakeholders long after discrete impact projects are completed.

- Build on indigenous ways of doing things.

- Help build a critical mass of local skills for use in future similar situations.

- Help facilitate more connected local networks that the people now linked by this work can use to support each other in future similar situations.

Impact initiatives must be transparent and include information about process and likely timing of exit. This way, impact initiatives have equal partnership with locals in ways that are meaningful to locals long after the visiting team is gone.

- Practice narrative humility.

We advocate awareness of words and narratives, and having critical consideration of the roles our words and narratives suggest for impact initiatives and those with whom we work. We draw on the Sidekick Manifesto, where economics professor Shawn Humphrey urges people involved in impact work to develop skills of "sidekicking" rather than heroism, of joining with locals and following, rather than leading. Humphrey admonishes: "I cannot know another's story of material poverty. I don't know how it began or how it will end. It is not my story. Before sharing it with others, I will seek permission: No more stolen stories."[2]

Part of decentering ourselves from the narrative involves making sure we are amplifying local voices and actively seeking their involvement in collaborative initiatives. This means asking (in sensitive ways) trusted confidants about cultural norms and practices that are crucial for "foreigners" (and we can be foreigners in our own country) to know and abide by (for example, men and women wearing clothes with appropriate covering). These consultations should be meticulous, detailed, and comprehensive—covering situations from greetings and dining, to perceptions of women, perceptions of men, religion, and "outsiders."

We must abide by local customs for social interactions and education, and take into account local religious, ethnic, and other practices—we are a part of the local story, not the other way around. Often, impact initiatives fail to investigate ways that locals have approached such issues in the past. Instead, we must ask them what has and has not worked for them in previous challenging predicaments, and based on that past experience, what they think will work best now.

By learning their narrative, impact changemakers can investigate ways that the targeted issues and impact strategies manifest in this community; how the locals describe this to themselves, to each other, and to outsiders; as well as how they view outsiders (especially those from other countries or socioeconomic backgrounds who are there to "help"). Prioritizing local perspectives will help entrepreneurs and investors avoid words, actions, or programs that disempower or diminish local strengths and resources—especially existing social networks or capacities to assist fellow humans in need.

We must also take care to ensure that the narrative's conclusion does not disproportionately benefit outsiders, particularly those implementing or investing in the products or services.

- Do the homework.

It is so easy to visit another community with the supreme confidence that the products and services we know to be effective in our own contexts will work in another. We understand from psychosocial research that some impact initiatives can do more harm to some people when enacted without a comprehensive, evidence-informed understanding of the negative and positive impacts of specific initiatives.[3] Doing homework involves reconnaissance, due diligence, and assessment of how communities, families, and individuals are impacted by the initiatives we design, implement, or support.

Such reconnaissance is our first opportunity to do no further harm during our initiative's work by:

- Learning as much as possible about customs, cultures, and critical events from hard sources (government and nongovernment reports, especially the World Health Organization, the United Nations, your own country's department of foreign affairs, the local country's departments of health and education, reputable journalists' articles about the country, etc.).

o Speaking with key informants in and from the communities being impacted through extensive oral and written communications.

We must support or co-design and deliver impact initiatives (not automatically assume the role of providing direct products and services to locals) through meaningfully working with locals in all phases, especially building capacity to enhance local skill bases for service delivery. We can do this by:

o Partnering and collaborating with local entities—government and nongovernment.

o Using rigorous qualitative and quantitative methods to investigate the local situation—the extent and nature of the predicament facing this community and these individuals and families.

o Incorporating research to both the process and content of in-country work.

o Ensuring that we don't immediately jump to provide instant assistance (the "solution" may prove to be the wrong one once all data are collected).

It is an imperative for all impact thinkers and doers to ensure that the products and services we design, implement, or support facilitate the positive impact we profess, without contributing to harm, anywhere in the entire system.

The comprehensive approach to initial information gathering described above should, in turn, inform a more detailed, comprehensive reconnaissance and collaborative needs assessment. When conducting and analyzing needs, assessments must be comprehensive, culturally sensitive, and ongoing. We must *listen*. We cannot learn from the "other" if we as impact workers do all of the talking or fill the time with our own chatter.

- Ensure impact initiatives are collaborative, culturally appropriate, relevant, and validated.

It is easy to assume that adding a few indigenous words or local case studies can suffice as cultural adaptation of white privileged approaches. Applying knowledge of cultural differences and attitudes to the design and implementation of products and services is a great starting point for ultimate efficacy.[4] But we need to do more. As with initial reconnaissance, the impact initiatives themselves must be collaborative, culturally sensitive, with ongoing calibration as contexts change.

- Include evaluation of impacts in planning and budgeting.

When urged to conduct an evaluation of his training workshop in a tsunami-affected third-world country, one psychosocial worker said: "I know the answers. We always get top ratings for our programs. People love us." People "loving us" is vastly different from concrete evidence using objective indicators of improved psychosocial health and how particular products and services affect people in given contexts. How do we know we are not doing harm if we do not rigorously research and evaluate the impact of what we are doing? This means including research and evaluation in initial strategizing and budgeting (and not just self-report surveys).

- Minimize further harm after the impact initiative is complete.

Too many impact workers and organizations make forays into a domain—perhaps characterized by dire conditions and extreme need—deliver their product or service, and then leave without long-term monitoring of impacts. Referred to by some in the humanitarian arena as "parachuting," this kind of provision of impact products or services can inadvertently create multiple problems for locals.[5] Adequate ongoing follow-up would include:

o Long-term monitoring of impacts at all levels.

o Regular, consistent, and as-needed communications with designated liaison personnel on the in-community implementing team, preferably using videoconferencing, which would allow physical cues to be part of the conversation.

o Communicating with partner agencies regarding ongoing commitments and projects—with regular and consistent follow-up consultations, providing product or service adaptations as needed.

o Communicating findings and giving documentation to stakeholders in a format that is beneficial to them and the community, as well as disseminating results and lessons from monitoring and evaluation activities.[6]

o Setting up regular weekly discussions—then phasing to biweekly, monthly, and semiannual discussions—of how implementation and follow-up are proceeding, specifically including debate about all possible previously unanticipated or unimagined impacts.

o Checking in periodically with local liaison personnel once regular supervision meetings are phased out to let them know you are "there," available, and accessible for ongoing issues.

o Keeping meticulous records of feedback discussions, especially concerns regarding positive *and* negative impacts that have implications for changes to the work being done.

EXAMPLES OF MINIMIZING HARM: LOCAL-CENTRISM LIGHTING THE WAY

Across the world, visionary social innovators and impactors are enacting entrepreneurial processes and products in ways that maximize positive impact while minimizing harm. For centuries, the indigenous Huichol women of Jalisco in the Sierra Madre region of western Mexico have been weaving textiles on backstrap looms. Like the Aboriginal songlines in the vast Australian outback, this western Mexican weaving tradition has been passed down from mothers to daughters since pre-Columbian times. Like Aboriginal songlines, weaving—integral to each woman's identity—holds forceful spiritual, emotional, and historical meaning for the weavers and their families.

In the twenty-first century, weaving has taken on added meaning and purpose. In a collaboration that includes the Huichol communities, University of Michigan students and staff, and the Boston-based architecture firm Kennedy & Violich, the weavers, led by local Estella Hernandez, weave solar, nanotechnology LED lighting into traditional bags that they carry by day.[7] Because the light units are woven or sewn into regularly used, everyday items (clothing, bags, or blankets, using local materials), they are neither cumbersome nor culturally improper, and are easily integrated into rural or nomadic communities. During the day, as these items are worn or used, the photovoltaic technology woven into the item's fabric harvests the sun's energy to produce a surprisingly bright white light at night. Each textile generates enough electrical power (about three hours' worth) to charge small electronic devices like cell phones. In the Sierra Madre villages of Mexico, these textile-embedded solar panels provide direct, reflected, or diffuse lighting in homes and cottage-based industries like community tortillerias, sandal making, weaving, beading, and repair work. Adding to their practicality, individual lighting units can be linked together as a group through digital communication protocols, creating solar energy for cooperative community projects. These portable, not prohibitively expensive lighting units can be customized according to a community's needs and traditions.

Since these Mexican beginnings, the Portable Light Project has partnered with local communities in other countries, including Kenya, Madagascar, Venezuela, Guatemala, Ghana, Brazil, and South Africa. In Nicaragua, portable solar lighting is enabling local employment in biodiversity initiatives to save endangered turtles in isolated areas. In KwaZulu-Natal, South Africa, the Portable Light Project has collaborated with the Integration of TB in Education and Care for HIV/AIDS program (iTEACH) to provide solar light blankets to rural patients suffering from HIV and drug-resistant tuberculosis. These blankets, while providing much-needed warmth, power patients' lighting and devices to enable at-home medical treatment, whether self-administered or by families. This power source is particularly critical for their treatment regimen at night, when light or power is often unavailable.[8]

On the streets of South Africa's third largest city, Durban (eThekwini in Zulu), another exemplary social innovation resulted from local leadership and grassroots collaboration. Mauritian/South African architect Doung Anwar Jahangeer and street vendor Moses Gwiba joined forces to adapt the popular 1960s coffee carts, "café-de-move-ons," to the Spaza-de-Move-on. The Spaza-de-Move-on is an efficient, durable metal cart designed to give street vendors a more comfortable, convenient, effective way to earn their livelihoods. A community collaboration with CityWalks, an initiative of Durban's sustainable city planning program, Spaza-de-Move-on is one of dala's livelihood initiatives that facilitate informal livelihood and entrepreneurial networks.[9] An interdisciplinary creative collective in Durban, dala facilitates creative collaboration among practitioners—architects, researchers, performers, urban planners, designers, the municipality, and the people and organizations who live and work within and around the city—on impact projects.[10]

Similar community-embedded social innovations—in process and community engagement—with net positive impacts can be found in Asia. In North Jakarta, Indonesia, the Penjaringan community is no stranger to natural and human-made disasters. When fire struck in 2007, destroying a hundred homes, ten thousand people living under a newly constructed raised toll road were evicted from the area. The residents living in the surrounding neighborhoods created the Development of Community Under Elevated Road Group and joined forces with the Focus Cities Research Initiative.[11] Using an innovative collaborative process, the groups developed sixty-five scenarios depicting diverse options for using the space under the toll road, including recreational green areas, communal and market gardens, mobile vendors and small shops, cultural event spaces, pedestrian and public transportation, as well as infrastructure for water, drainage, sanitation, waste management, and security.

In the small West Indian city of Sangli—known as the Turmeric City and part of the sugar belt of India—about 15 percent of the city's half-a-million people live in slums. Several years ago, Bandhani, an informal federation of poor women and men, joined with Shelter Associates, a consortium of architects, social workers, community workers, and geographic information systems analysts, to involve people living in Sangli's slums in designing ways to improve living conditions. They were able to engage 3,800 families—almost 50 percent of the poor across twenty-nine slums—to participate in Sangli's slum-development and housing initiatives.[12]

One of the organizations promoting local solutions to local problems is IDEO.org, the nonprofit arm of the world-renowned design firm IDEO. When we spoke with IDEO.org's CEO, Jocelyn Wyatt, she explained the organization's passion for spreading the ethos of human-centered innovation in the social sector. Wyatt is a staunch advocate for local approaches to local issues, where the complexity of local contexts is best understood: "We realize that there is no single solution . . . Instead, [our IDEO work] is really about having a better understanding of the communities we are serving, and then designing solutions *with* them that really benefit their needs rather than thinking that there is this golden bowl and a single solution—that it all has to be one way or another way, but actually it is about . . . understanding and sort of leaning into the complexity of that and designing solutions that really meet that."

These local-centric, community-embedded collaborations for impact innovation are an evolution from the "user-centered design movement" that gained momentum through the first two decades of the twenty-first century. This next iteration of more egalitarian design is reflected in the work of Ezio Manzini, professor of Industrial Design at Milan Polytechnic and director of CIRIS (the Interdepartmental Centre for Research on Innovation for Sustainability). Vehemently believing in and living his conviction that the main activity of designers is social innovation, Manzini exemplifies collaboration in positively impactful ways. He asserts that the work of the designer is not to solve the problem with a perfect object or service, but to create a platform for co-designing with individuals in context within their local community. That is, local stakeholders should be directly involved in designing strategies to counter the problem.

In these more egalitarian approaches to tackling society's tough challenges, there is a place for both local knowledges and (sometimes external) expertise. Manzini distinguishes between *diffuse design* (performed by everybody) and *expert design* (performed by those trained as designers). Both diffuse and expert designers collaborate to enable all people involved to use their capabilities and enjoy their part in the solution, rather than passively consuming the end product. Manzini calls these *enabling solutions*. An evolution of product service systems, enabling solutions go beyond meeting customer needs to allowing individuals or communities to achieve their own results with their own skills and abilities.[13]

The examples cited above, as well as numerous ones documented by Manzini in his books—such as collaborative housing in Milan, Italy; community-supported agriculture in China; interactive storytelling in India; and digital platforms for medical care in Canada—provide rich examples of the fruitful outcomes of intentional local and expert partnerships. All of these tech and non-tech social innovation processes, products, and services illuminate how considered and deliberative collaborations can trigger and support meaningful social changes. Like Manzini, we urge those intending to contribute to positive impact to upend old mindsets to enable egalitarian, local-centric, systems-oriented thinking and doing around the toughest challenges facing many people on our planet. This kind of collaborative thinking and doing represents a paradigmatic shift. Rather than jumping to solutions for problems, this local-centric, systems-oriented approach is embedded in a respect for and determined understanding of local capabilities and knowledge. It is an encouragement and facilitation of diversity and the free flow of people and ideas.

Leading impact innovators of the 2010s decade see these new approaches as mainstream by 2030. They see today's typical design and development of impact products and services based on top-down processes rendered a relic of the past. Instead, they see a consolidation of a new generation of services emerging from collaborative, largely bottom-up, design and implementation processes. Today's leading impact innovators know that white savior tendencies may be a natural outcome of our upbringing, our education, and our experiences. They know, too, that inserting considered reflection, deliberation, respect, collaboration, and co-design intent into impact work can minimize more negatively impactful do-gooder tendencies.

ENTREPRENEURSHIP FOR IMPACT INSIGHTS SUMMARY

As we look toward 2030, with a widespread release of the shackles of Western white saviorism, we hope to witness a celebration of the capacity of all human beings to shape their own destinies, with acknowledgment that locals know their own circumstances better than those of us on the outside looking in. Rather than letting our fellow do-gooders eddy down into a dark chasm of history repeating itself, may we heed the call of Ivan Illich to examine our good intentions in all their nuances—from the best to the worst. Let us hear the words of Muhammad Yunus: "Everything that is given to the poor makes them poorer. We never have to give. We can accompany the poor in their suffering, but not give them money. One of the blunders that rich countries make with Africa is giving to them; that's why today they are poorer than before."[14] Let us all be accompaniers, not parachuting leaders in our efforts to make a positive contribution to humankind and our planet.

PART TWO:

Changemakers Inherent in Entrepreneurial Ecosystems

E xemplary impact changemakers bring an aura with them. Something invisible, like the atmospheric shift that precedes a mighty storm. Impact changemakers are only too well aware of the cocktail of factors that could tip our planet and its inhabitants toward doom. These impact innovators approach this critical juncture in our planet's and humanity's future with a calm and piercing scrutiny. Positively contributing to the greater good is their beacon.

Impact changemakers see contrasts in opportunities for health and education, and the potentially crippling ramifications for quality of life, livelihoods, homelessness, and mortality. They see people at risk of marginalization, of falling prey to peddlers of extremism and terrorism. And they are a part of bold, audacious action—a "youthquake" and an "agequake" fueling unprecedented intention to do good—combined with stirring recognition of the critical need for understanding and accounting for impact (positive and negative) in the entire global ecosystem. They see a beguiling gateway to our best decade yet for innovation, entrepreneurship and impact. But only if more of us heed the imperative. In this section, we showcase exemplary changemakers who are critical contributors to the entrepreneurial ecosystem aimed at the world's toughest challenges. As a preface, we define ecosystems in more depth.

> **e·co·sys·tem** (noun):
>
> 1) A biological community of interacting organisms and their physical environment (in general use) 2) A complex network or interconnected system.[1]

"Ecosystem" is a term derived from the combination of "eco," or "of ecology" (the branch of biology that deals with the relations of organisms to one another and to their physical surroundings), and "system," a set of things working together as parts of a mechanism or an interconnecting network. In the innovation, entrepreneurship, and impact context, an ecosystem includes all of the individuals and organizations (for-profit, nonprofit, government, and nongovernment), as well as the complex connections, interactions, and interrelationships among those elements. The interrelationships are crucial to the long-term health of the system as a whole, along with the system's individual components. In the context of considering impacts, the planet Earth can be viewed as one global ecosystem, with many nested sub-ecosystems (e.g., regional, industry, sector) that often overlap. Smaller ecosystems fit within larger ecosystems (like Russian nesting dolls). Adopting an ecosystems mindset means knowing that actions in one part of the entire system reverberate with consequences in other parts of the system, no matter how removed in geography, sector, or time—from the individual to the collective, from suppliers to consumers, and every intermediary in between. The changemakers in this section exemplify ecosystem roles, as well as relationship and process management among the elements.

CHAPTER 4

The Twenty-First Century Entrepreneurs

Entrepreneurs are the luminaries—the innovative visionaries with laser focus who transform new ideas into successful ventures. Their efforts create new realities for individuals, households, communities, industries, nations, and the world. They are typically the protagonists in any entrepreneurial narrative, propelling their ideas forward. They often face impossible odds, struggling to raise money and gain traction for the companies they build, making difficult choices, tested through crises and economic turmoil. They exemplify the most persuasive of sales voices, confront their own self-doubts, and solve issues of financing, production, marketing, and distribution. They subdue adversaries.

Many entrepreneurs have been known to mortgage their houses and neglect their families. In the end, fierce determination triumphs. The relentless hard work and sacrifices are rewarded. Their ideas take root in the marketplace. Their companies thrive, resulting in a triumphant IPO (initial public offering on the stock exchange). The result: untold riches for all.

BEYOND STEREOTYPES

Entrepreneurs are typically captivating, charismatic dynamos—yet formidable, exacting taskmasters. Some of the most celebrated icons are names recognized around the globe: Steve Jobs, Richard Branson, Michael Dell, Bill Gates, Jack Ma, Mark Zuckerberg (yes, most celebrated are still men). The entrepreneur stereotype arising from the touted successes of these men is an image of a white male college dropout who skyrockets to superstar and billionaire status with a revolutionary invention. This stereotype is the exception, not the norm. Story after story perpetuates a myth of heroes who started their ventures in a garage or a dorm room by designing some typically high-tech gadget or service that transformed lives, industries, economies. They reach into unknowable futures and with their revolutionary new products or processes disrupt staid, stale industries, often bringing about sweeping economic and social change. Their success is portrayed as the elixir of job creation, productivity, and economic growth. Yet the protagonists at the center of most entrepreneurial narratives are much more diverse than the legends suggest.

Entrepreneurs can be found in companies of all sizes and types, defying the stereotype. There is no shortage of bold, brave, and brilliant female entrepreneurs. India's Kiran Mazumdar-Shaw founded Biocon, now a global biotech pharmaceutical company (which she did start in her Bangalore garage). In global retail, while Jack Ma is most hailed around the world as the founder of Alibaba, others among Alibaba's eighteen co-founders, such as Lucy Peng Lei, were also integral to the phenomenal success of the e-commerce company. Historically, women entrepreneurs have tended to come from non-tech industries and are often more known for the talent that originally launched them to become widely known. Oprah Winfrey—known primarily as a television show host—led her Harpo Productions and OWN television network to superstar billionaire status and launched many successful spinoffs in the process: Dr. Phil, Dr. Oz, and Rachael Ray, to name a few. Similar entrepreneurial stories abound with Yang Lan (Sun Media

Group), Elle Macpherson (health and wellness), and Jessica Alba and Gisele Bündchen (beauty products). Other women entrepreneurs like Kendra Scott (jewelry); Diane von Furstenberg, Vivienne Westwood, or Donna Karan (designer clothing); or Maggie Beer (gourmet food empire) are often lauded more for their creative contributions than their entrepreneurial ones. Still others, like Thai Lee, CEO of information technology provider SHI International, are hardly known at all, despite being America's largest woman-owned business (with $8.5 billion in sales in 2017 alone).[1]

The hard sciences also abound with daring and gifted, but not widely recognized, female entrepreneurs. Dr. Sangeeta Bhatia—biotech engineer, medical doctor, professor, inventor, and serial entrepreneur—has attracted illustrious awards like the Lemelson-MIT Prize of $500,000 for her groundbreaking inventions and labels like "most innovative young scientist worldwide" or "one of the 100 most creative people in business." Bhatia's companies, Zymera, which has patented applications for in vivo imaging, biomarker discovery, and biosensing, and Hepregen, with its cell micro-patterning technology, have positively impacted the medical field across the planet.

In contrast to the stereotype of entrepreneurs as revolutionary change agents, many real-life entrepreneurs usher in incremental changes that ultimately have a cascading, multiplier effect, sometimes with paradigm-shifting ramifications. Take Joy Mangano—American serial inventor, entrepreneur, television shopping network guru. Mangano's business, Ingenious Designs (of which she is founder and CEO), is a multimillion-dollar company built from her own serial inventions—inventions characterized by incremental changes in design for products and industries, as well as monumental changes in quality of life for individuals, particularly women (like the miracle mop that revolutionized women's often back-breaking work). Just as Mangano's work had a positive impact for women's welfare, entrepreneurship with an environmental and social conscience is not new for many women entrepreneurs. Anita Roddick (The Body Shop) and Ulrike Klein

(Jurlique) were environmental and social impactors decades ahead of their time. They launched their lines of consciously harvested, natural, organic ingredient-based skin care products a generation before the word "organic" or "impact" became part of everyday conversation.

If the changemakers we consulted are prophetic in their visions of 2030, socially and environmentally conscious entrepreneurship for positive impact will be mainstream. No more silos. No more compartmentalizing where we make money and where we do good.[2] Entrepreneurship in the 2020s—fueled by new generational values, connective technologies, intergender and intergenerational transfers of wealth, along with a global surge in purpose—will be characterized by more and more people merging entrepreneurship with impact. As Fondation Demeter's Pascal Vinarnic cautioned: "[While the 2020s] may bring a world which is more dangerous . . . social enterprise, impact investment, whatever we call it, labels will be so out of fashion in the 2020s . . . everyone will be impacting—everything will be different."

WHO ARE THE TWENTY-FIRST CENTURY ENTREPRENEURS FOR IMPACT?

en·tre·pre·neur for im·pact (noun):

1) A person who sets up an organization or organizations, taking on financial risks in the hope of sustainability 2) Society's change agents; creators of innovations that disrupt the status quo and transform our world for the better.

The 2010s have witnessed a blossoming reverence for the entrepreneur who melds traditional entrepreneurship with a determination to contribute to the greater good. Changemakers we consulted see this convergence of entrepreneurship and impact cementing in the late

2020s as a new breed of entrepreneurs for impact become mainstream and prolific. Entrepreneurs for the twenty-first century—rather than being fiercely driven by financial gain above all other considerations—think and act to contribute to social and environmental gains against the world's pressing problems. Entrepreneurs for the twenty-first century:

- Prioritize positive social and environmental impact in all they think and do.

- Prioritize the greater good over individual and corporate financial gain (while not sacrificing organizational sustainability).

- Simultaneously think big picture and little picture—in both time and place.

  - Think in ecosystems—recognizing the local is nested in the regional and the global.

  - Think in terms of potential long-term impacts, as well as short-term.

  - Think in systems, circles, and loops, not straight lines with a beginning and an end. They know that what goes around comes around and goes around again.

- Focus on process as much as product, understanding that synergy hinges on the quality of relationships they build and nurture throughout the ecosystem.

- Collaborate with affected populations, and with others in their own and nested ecosystems, to develop products and services, rather than dictate solutions.

- Work consciously to do no harm, proactively assessing negative impacts as well as positive, and think and act in ways that minimize the negative.

Those of us with impact innovation and entrepreneurial intent can be more effective contributors to net positive impact for the entire planet when we hone the skills of thinking in terms of verbs, not just nouns; focus our efforts on processes, not just products and outputs; strategize with comprehension of our actions in the context of reverberating loops rather than linear sequences from beginning to end; and nurture relationships and dynamics, not just organizations or individuals.

Entrepreneur and Ecosystem Builder: Suzi Sosa

To be at the forefront of a global movement takes a special kind of confidence. **Suzi Sosa**, CEO of the for-profit social enterprise Verb (headquartered in Austin, Texas), exudes such confidence as she embraces the challenges of leading a budding entrepreneurial venture. Suzi has spent much of her professional life intent on growing entrepreneurial ecosystems. A self-professed "global citizen," she has long felt the pull of the world beyond the borders of the city or country in which she lives. Born in the United Kingdom and raised in the United States, Suzi is one of many leading social innovators around the world combining thought leadership with wide-ranging skills, business acumen, a results-focused drive, and ambition. They bring these traits, along with visionary action, innovation, and entrepreneurial sensibility, to contribute to the collective good. Suzi harbors a "big, hairy, audacious goal to create a movement, to create an entire generation of young people who see social innovation and impact as a path" to solving imploded economies, societies, and environments.

One of Suzi's first forays toward creating a movement included leading the Global Social Innovation Challenge at the University of Texas at Austin (UT). Designed to identify and support promising young social innovators dedicated to solving some of the world's most pressing problems, the competition was backed by Dell as a title sponsor in 2008, with the technology corporation providing an initial $300,000 grant (followed in 2011 by a $5 million donation). Dell employees volunteered to mentor. With this infusion, the annual challenge was able to provide tens of thousands of college student–impact entrepreneurs with world-class teaching and training, start-up capital, and access to a network of mentors and advisors. During its seven-year tenure at UT, with Suzi at the helm for most of those years, the challenge became the largest global student social entrepreneurship competition in the world. More than seven thousand teams from eighty countries participated during that time, along with more than three thousand Dell employees as mentors and judges.

Under Suzi's leadership, the challenge grew each successive year. Social innovators who made it to the final rounds rose above steep competition from thousands of other young entrepreneurs. Each year saw a short list of finalists flown to Austin for the final round of mentoring, culminating in a public pitch event. These young innovators constitute an impressive alumni list. Winning finalists include Manoj Sinha (2008), who launched Husk Power Systems to provide power in the form of biofuel made from discarded corn husks, benefiting hundreds of thousands in rural India in an affordable, scalable, and environmentally friendly manner; Daniel Paffenholz (2011) founded TakaTaka Solutions, whose affordable and environmentally responsible waste management services enabled cleaner and healthier communities for Nairobi, Kenya, residents; Diana Jue and Jackie Stenson (2012) initiated Essmart Global, a product distributor partnering with retail shops in developing countries, giving them access to innovative products that improve their customers' lives;[3] **Shital Somani** and **Vaibhav Tidke** won in 2013 for their solar conduction dryer, a cost-effective, solar-powered food dehydrator that enabled farmers to sell more of their crops by drying fruits and vegetables.[4]

In 2014 the Dell Global Social Innovation Challenge was spun out from UT to become the for-profit impact enterprise Verb. When Suzi co-founded Verb with her equally passionate co-founder, Tom Meredith (Austin-based philanthropist and Chief Financial Officer during Dell's early growth), they aimed "to unleash the power of entrepreneurship for global good." Their initial plan was to unleash such power by partnering with more organizations to design and implement social innovation competitions. Suzi's launching of Verb was the culmination of many other entrepreneurial adventures. By 2013 she had not only witnessed entrepreneurship up close from start-up to IPO with companies like Netspend and MPOWER, she had taught social entrepreneurship at UT and co-founded several nonprofits in Austin. Suzi vehemently believes that entrepreneurship is about creating things. In an *Austin Woman* magazine article, Suzi said, "I am passionate about entrepreneurship," especially innovation. "Not just for the sake of innovation, but as a direct response to a pain that somebody is feeling."[5]

During the first couple of years, Verb added some impressive names to its client list: Nike, MetLife Foundation, IBM, Dell Children's Medical Center, and the Everglades Foundation. These and other clients engaged Verb to curate social innovation competitions on a variety of pressing problems, such as access to basic health care (including eyeglasses); clean, safe water; empowering women, education and financial inclusion; and cures for cancer. These competitions helped grow impact entrepreneurial ecosystems in those countries and globally. By 2016 Verb was earmarked as one of the top "start-ups to watch" in Austin.[6]

More recently, the company has pivoted toward growing a movement of impact mindsets embedded into all corporations (large and small) via a purpose-driven learning and development platform for employees. Today, Verb is an unapologetic for-profit social enterprise that harnesses information technology, global networks, and knowledge. Their aim: to "develop the next generation of purpose-driven leaders," to cultivate impact thinking and doing through guided leadership training. Verb's intent is to unlock and cultivate human potential. Having started out focusing on nurturing small groups of social entrepreneurs, Verb has now expanded its reach to millions of potential positive impactors through organizations.

Suzi's attraction to entrepreneurship is matched with a fierce passion for positive impact—making the world a better, more inclusive place for all. Verb social innovation competitions (and the more recent employee learning and development platform) provide participants with opportunities to partner with experienced impact mentors. These mentors provide coaching on critical impact entrepreneurship skills—including business plan writing, networking, public speaking skills, and pitching ideas. Budding impact entrepreneurs are incentivized to be the "winner" with all of the resources (financial and otherwise) that winning brings. Verb social innovation competitions have attracted thousands of entrepreneurs and engaged tens of thousands of key stakeholders, including customers, employees, investors, and media. The competitions have contributed to the building of impact innovation ecosystems among entrepreneurs, recipients, and suppliers in the product/service chain, as well as corporate, foundation, and government stakeholders.

An example of the diversity of Verb's reach is the global challenge initiated by the Everglades Foundation, which partnered with Verb to find and foster "the world's sharpest, most innovative scientists, engineers, and researchers" to seek out creative solutions to the problem of phosphorus water pollution, not just in Florida's Everglades, but in similar water biosystems all over the planet.[7] This innovation challenge—the George Barley Water Prize, implemented over four years with $10 million in prize money—provides impact entrepreneurs with feedback from judges. As the best innovators progress through the screening stages, they are partnered with mentors to develop their ideas and capacity to market them, adding to the burgeoning impact innovation ecosystem across the planet.

Like many of the other visionary changemakers, Suzi believes companies can make attractive returns on investment (ROI) while doing good. Her indefatigable determination to guide Verb to contribute to a worldwide ecosystem of purpose-driven leaders in every organization is testament to her belief in the example she is setting for entrepreneurs everywhere. For the most recent phase of Verb's development, aware that 70 percent of Millennials seek purpose or meaning at work, Verb developed an innovative learning and development platform for employers to tap into and activate their Millennial employees' passion for purpose. Verb's virtual learning and development platform helps employees of organizations large and small to unlock their full potential through leadership training and a stronger connection to purpose. Their leadership training is tailored accordingly, potentially accelerating the positive impact of millions of people around the world. Engaged employees can be matched to customized learning tracks and volunteering opportunities, with access to Verb's global social venture network—the product of years of nurturing social entrepreneurs in more than fifty countries. Verb clients include multinational corporations to incubators and nonprofit, government and nongovernment organizations from a diverse array of sectors such as banking, retail, designer fashion, and organic food.

Ever intent on positive impact, Suzi laments, "How to make a big difference in a short life, that's what burdens me." She is one of the global trailblazers—an entrepreneur who has contributed to the growth of entire impact ecosystems (local and global) by nurturing impact entrepreneurs via social and environmental innovation challenges and encouraging purpose-driven leadership via an employee learning and development platform. She continues to foster impact thinkers and doers as entrepreneurs or intrapreneurs (innovators and entrepreneurs within large organizations), changing the world for the better—both within existing organizations and growing new ones.

NEXT GENERATION ENTREPRENEURS

The year 2020 heralds a changed generational landscape in business and geopolitics around the world. The beginning of the 2020s will see some superstar Millennials (who came of age around the turn of the millennium and now make up 33 percent of all adults and 20 percent of the Western workforce) catapult to top roles.[8] By 2030 both Millenials and Gen Z, or those born around the millennium (now numbering around two billion people), will constitute 75 percent of the global workforce.

As the dominant generation, their drive for net positive impact permeates boardrooms, cabinet rooms, and classrooms.

In survey after survey, Gen Zers express more concern and actions around social and environmental issues. They want to work for, buy from, invest in, and associate with organizations making a positive difference. They want to positively contribute to our planet and society more than past generations have managed to do. Young Millennial and Gen Z entrepreneurs in this global context reflect the values and priorities of their generations. We highlight four of these inspiring entrepreneurs in the remainder of this chapter. Because these young men and women have been nurtured and rewarded by innovation challenges like the Dell Global Social Innovation Challenge and Verb, they are literally the next generation in both a chronological and mentor-mentee sense.

The Serial Entrepreneurs: Vaibhav Tidke and Shital Somani

When **Vaibhav Tidke** and **Shital Somani** traveled from their homes in India to Austin, Texas, for the final round of the 2013 Dell Global Social Innovation Challenge, they were in good company.[9] More than 2,600 social innovation projects addressed issues impacting communities in more than 110 countries. The runner-up project, Foot Soldiers, transformed discarded rubber tires into affordable shoes for forty-eight million Bangladeshi people who could not afford proper footwear and were at risk of diseases associated with bare feet.

Vaibhav and Shital won, returning home to India with $60,000 for further development of their solar conduction dryer. The win in Austin came at a critical stage of development for their fledgling company, Science for Society (S4S). With most of their team still university students at the time, the prize money, as well as the connections they forged and the skills they developed, enabled the small team to take their product to the next level. They built a manufacturing facility, conducted pilots of three different technologies, and with U.S. Agency for International Development funding, explored the feasibility of the solar conduction dryer in Africa and other countries. The win also gave their initiative visibility and credibility at home and abroad.

Vaibhav, Shital, and their partners in entrepreneuring are at the leading edge of a wave of culture change around entrepreneurship and start-ups sweeping India. In a country where entrepreneurship was traditionally perceived as an inferior career choice behind professions like medicine and law, the status associated with starting a company is on the rise, a change that saw India recently ranked as the third-highest density for start-ups in the world.[10] Bangalore now ranks as the fifteenth fastest-growing venture capital and seed-funding ecosystem, right behind Austin.[11] This surge in entrepreneurial activity is being supported by the Indian government's "Start Up India, Stand Up India" initiative. Exponentially growing numbers of local and foreign accelerators, incubators, and venture capital are pouring into India's economy, including icons like Sequoia, Accel Partners, Nexus Ventures, Tiger Capital, Google Capital, and World Innovation Lab.

Vaibhav, Shital, and the S4S team are the new generation of entrepreneurs who do not compartmentalize impact. Diverse, collaborative, and community-focused, they are entrepreneurs looking to build robust global solutions to entrenched social and environmental problems with innovations in both technology and business models. They are at the vanguard of a burgeoning drive for social innovation in a country whose population is destined to be the world's largest by 2028. Other young Indian entrepreneurs starting up right after college, or as in Vaibhav's case, during college, include some of India's young entrepreneur living legends: Rahul Yadav, who founded Housing.com at age twenty-six; Harshvardhan Mandad, TinyOwl at twenty-five; Azhar Iqubal, News in Shorts at twenty-two; Prateek Shukla, Grabhouse at twenty-five; and Ritesh Agarwal, OYO Rooms at twenty-one.[12] According to one observer, India's youth are now more inclined toward launching a start-up instead of settling down with a high-paying job.[13] Young entrepreneurs like Vaibhav and Shital are motivated by the chasm between India's wealthy and the hundreds of millions of rural poor. Despite India's gains in reducing poverty, its 2016 Socioeconomic and Caste Census reveals a stark picture of widespread rural poverty and deprivation. Less than 10 percent of some three hundred million rural households have members with salaried jobs, and less than 5 percent earn enough to even pay taxes. Only 2.5 percent own a four-wheel vehicle. Less than 5 percent of school students graduate, leaving more than 35 percent of residents unable to read or write.[14]

While S4S is a deliberate and definitive team initiative, Vaibhav was the original visionary innovator, so the remainder of this section shines the light on him and his journey as a serial entrepreneur. Vaibhav was born in Ambajogai—a small town by Indian standards, with a population of around seventy thousand people. Ambajogai is widely considered the educational and cultural capital of the central-west region of India. According to Vaibhav, medicine and engineering dominate the career choices of those raised in the area.[15]

In a 2011 interview, Vaibhav described why he was drawn to chemical engineering: "Chemical engineering deals with basic science. And basic sciences can lead to actual creation and innovation."[16] While studying toward his bachelor's degree, Vaibhav found that his Ambajogai roots, his contemplation of the challenges facing his countrymen and women in rural India—food, health, clean water, power, and livelihoods—and his passion for the potential contribution of science to those challenges were what set him on a pioneering trajectory. He noticed that farmers selling their produce in his hometown did so with huge daily and weekly financial losses because of food spoilage: Fresh vegetables sold at the weekly Saturday market cost 20 cents per kilogram in the morning, by the evening, unsold vegetables were thrown out. The farmers had no way to store or preserve their crops.[17]

Investigating further, Vaibhav confirmed widespread prevalence of food wastage across rural India, not just in his hometown. He discovered that of the yearly harvested crops in India, farmers typically lose 20 percent to 30 percent of the 74 million tons of fruits and 143 million tons of vegetables produced, with dire ramifications. Missed opportunities for farmers to sell all of their foodstuffs and earn income often lead to subsistence levels of existence and poverty among farmers. Consequently, high rates of malnutrition can be found among India's rural children, as well as staggering rates of suicide among farmers (almost three hundred thousand farmers have taken their own lives in the last two decades).[18] Vaibhav calculated that the level of wastage, if distributed, was enough to give a kilogram of free food to every Indian household, every day. Vaibhav lamented that the wasted food could have been dried and preserved, raising market values of the products, yielding increased profits for farmers.

In 2008, while an undergraduate student, Vaibhav started incubating an idea for drying and preserving grains, fruits, and vegetables, and eliminating wastage of these perishables at a low cost using the sun. Other models on the market did not fit the daily realities of rural Indian farmers. They were either too expensive, too cumbersome, or required consistent, ongoing electricity (only sporadic supply is available in many rural areas of India). To fund the early development, Vaibhav started with just $6,000. Determined to make his vision a reality, Vaibhav applied his university stipend to product development, and when that was not sufficient, he taught Common Entrance Test students in nearby Aurangabad and Jalna to earn half of his start-up money. Even those funds fell short. Fortunately, in December 2009, Vaibhav was awarded a cash prize by the United Nations for his environmental work.

The struggle wasn't over. It took ten trial-and-error iterations to achieve success. In an interview Vaibhav admitted, "The first three years were the testing period. It was all about getting the first customer, entering the market, understanding the dynamics of the industry and requirements of the customers. Only from the last two to three years we have been generating profits."[19]

In December 2010, three years after he started, and by then in his second year of a master's degree at the Institute of Chemical Technology in Mumbai, Vaibhav was selected as one of two finalists from across India to travel to Germany to attend the Young Environmental Envoy Program sponsored by Bayer in partnership with the United Nations Environment Program. At the conclusion of the weeklong program, Vaibhav was presented with the Bayer Young Environmental Leaders' Award for the solar conduction dryer. Vaibhav returned from Germany a more globally aware citizen, heart-warmed by the level of international interest he witnessed regarding India. One of the most potent and impactful lessons Vaibhav took away was that being an entrepreneur could not be done alone, in isolation. Upon his return, Vaibhav looked to his own network of friends, family, and fellow students Shital Somani and Aditya Kulkarni, to join him in innovation for impact. Vaibhav, Shital, Aditya, and three others—with the inspiration, encouragement, and guidance of Vaibhav's professor and mentor Dr. Bhaskar Thorat—co-founded S4S to propel their innovation forward. Vaibhav and his collaborators had their own audacious goal: to bring together like-minded interdisciplinary students from across the country to work toward the development of sustainable technologies that solve many of rural India's problems. They wanted to tackle big challenges—food, health, water, power.

S4S started with India's endemic challenge of food security. They came together to use their different scientific backgrounds to further develop Vaibhav's solar-powered methodology to dry grains, fruits, vegetables, and seafood. Their innovation enabled farmers and fishermen to preserve and sell their produce at higher prices and with minimal waste. Vaibhav and his colleagues believed their solar conduction dryer solved several problems at once: "The technology reduces food spoilage, extends food shelf life, and allows nutritional value retention, helping the largely agriculture-dependent Indian population to earn more."[20]

Leap-frogging the usual technologies powered by electricity, Vaibhav and his colleagues developed solar-powered technology using the principle of conduction for heat transfer (assisted by convection and radiation). As Vaibhav explained, "This dryer will help in preserving the fruits, vegetables, and seeds with 80 percent moisture content or more. It is designed to dry grains after harvesting and before storing. Appropriate drying of the grains increases the shelf life of the grains as it makes it less prone to infections. This ultimately helps in reducing the post-harvest losses."[21] Their method was more hygienic, eliminated waste almost fully, reduced processing time by 40 percent, and cut costs by 50 percent, minimizing capital outlays, especially when compared to other solar and electric dryers.

When S4S was officially launched in 2010, it had incorporated as an NGO. Like other nimble entrepreneurs able to pivot as needed, S4S was re-incorporated in 2013 as a private for-profit company. The S4S team felt the for-profit business structure would better position them to commercialize the patented technological platforms. As S4S gained momentum, they partnered with companies like Bayer Material Science, development agencies like the U.S. Agency for International Development, academic institutions like their alma mater, the Institute of Chemical Technology, and private funding groups like the Gates Foundation. They have also won numerous international competitions like the Dell Social Innovation Challenge that was highlighted earlier. By late 2016, they added manufacturing. Their units now adorn thousands of buildings across India and in countries like Jamaica, Kenya, Cambodia, Sri Lanka, and Vietnam. Just 180 installations with farmers across India enabled a total processing of more than five hundred tons of vegetables and other produce per year—enough to provide two million meals.[22]

One of the key distinctions between Science for Society and other providers of agricultural produce dryers is that the S4S team is passionate, determined, and committed to enhancing the entire ecosystem. The solar dryer:

- Creates new business opportunities for smallholder farmers— men and women—in remote areas.

- Enhances nutrition and food security for participating farmers during the rainy seasons.

- Contributes to sustainable incomes for a large number of farming families.
- Creates self-employment opportunities in rural farming communities.

Committed to ongoing data-driven evaluation, the S4S team conducted pilot studies that revealed amplified positive impacts of the solar conductor dryers: reduced wastage, enhanced productivity, improved family and community incomes, and long-term sustainability in farming roles (with all the multiplier effects those bring in terms of health and education of other family members). An additional and striking positive flow-on impact of the dryer was improvement of average hemoglobin levels in local communities, the result of more nutrient-rich food available year-round.

Like other Millennial and Gen Z entrepreneurs focused on positive impact, the S4S team proved adept at improvisation and pivoting to optimize their impact. Parallel to developing technologies, the S4S team explored new models for dried food distribution, networking farmers and suppliers with S4S serving as the "aggregator" of dried produce from its own purpose-built warehouses. S4S has also applied science and its team's cumulative learning to other big issues facing rural India: health and water. S4S's first health initiative was triggered by personal connection and experience. After an S4S team member's sister suffered through two miscarriages, the S4S team tackled pre- and post-natal care for women in underserved communities. S4S team member Shantanu Pathak, a telecommunications engineer, was plagued by thoughts of the many women across India who had no access to even primary health care. According to a World Health Organization report, eight hundred women die every day in India from preventable causes related to pregnancy and childbirth. For thirty million pregnant women each year, 75 percent of whom live in urban slums or rural areas, proper medical attention and health care is inaccessible, contributing to the high mortality rate. Project mentor Medha Dhurandhar told *The Times of India*: "Every 10 minutes, a pregnant woman dies due to pregnancy-related complications . . . What is more disturbing is that 90 percent of these deaths can be avoided with regular access to health care."[23]

The team chose to confront one of the leading causes for maternal mortality: preeclampsia disorder, a pregnancy complication characterized by high blood pressure, anemia, and damage to organs—often the kidneys, resulting in excessive levels of protein in urine.[24] In collaboration with the United Nations, S4S embarked on the formidable objective to identify twenty-five thousand expectant mothers in the state for early diagnosis of high-risk pregnancies and early detection of disorders. To shepherd this project, S4S set up the CareMother initiative, with the mandate to develop a system that women across the country could easily access to receive appropriate medical care and diagnosis during their pregnancy. The team aspired to educate pregnant women; empower health workers, gynecologists, and government agencies with advanced tools to bring quality pre- and post-natal services to as many women as possible who would otherwise possibly die; and enable doctors to track all patients' records at one place.

The S4S team developed a portable, solar-powered CareMother kit, which consisted of sensors integrated with a mobile app for high-risk and regular pregnancy care. Weighing around three kilograms, the kit can be used by health and community workers for early and timely diagnosis of high-risk pregnancies—saving the lives of both the child and mother. S4S designed the kit so it could be integrated with public hospitals, government health-care databases, and Aadhaar, the Indian digital identification system (the world's largest national resident identification project—with each resident of India identified according to their biometric and demographic data, stored in a central database by the Indian government).[25] Vaibhav observed: "[The kit] allows basic, noninvasive medical testing at home with unique kit and mobile applications, enabling doctors to track and analyze patients with historical data, connecting doctors, patients, and families 24/7 by a mobile app, and early diagnosis of high-risk complications."[26] As part of their outreach, the CareMother team selected women from Mumbai slum communities and trained them as health-care workers. In rural villages, health-care workers use the kit to provide doorstep monitoring and real-time recording and tracking of health statistics of the patients. Doctors use the CareMother web application to oversee this work by remotely accessing patient details and even scheduling hospital visits. The kit has been successfully used by Doctors for You, a registered medical humanitarian organization, in the Govandi slum of Mumbai to detect high-risk pregnancies and a private hospital in Hyderabad, helping thousands of patients.[27]

Still only in his twenties, having been awarded his PhD, Vaibhav hopes to encourage more students to consider sustainable engineering as a career option: "We have a responsibility to deliver to the earth and environmental heritage for the benefit of coming generations."[28]

THE CO-DESIGNPRENEURS: HANNAH CHUNG AND AARON HOROWITZ

Hannah Chung and **Aaron Horowitz**—also exemplary of the new generation of entrepreneurs focused on doing good—represent an evolving movement whereby designers engage actively with end users for product and service development. That is, users and designers work in collaboration. They co-design solutions to problems. The interactive co-design ethos drives design from the earliest stages through as many iterations as it takes to complete the designs to ensure maximal benefit for end users.

Hannah and Aaron and their company, Sproutel, use this approach to create robots disguised as huggable toys. These high-tech medical machines masquerading as toys empower sick children and their families and friends with knowledge about how to manage their symptoms and stay healthy throughout their lives. The Sproutel team is at the leading edge of a seismic shift in both entrepreneurship and Western models of health care—a movement toward wellness and preventative education. A movement determined to enact positive impact on process as much as health outcomes.

As co-designpreneurs, like their fellow entrepreneurs in India, Hannah and Aaron started their careers intent on doing good. They were determined to apply the rigors of science, the knowledge of their engineering backgrounds, and their design thinking and skills to create products for ultimate positive impact. These targeted innovative products, and the process by which they are designed and produced, exemplify the new trendiness of user-based co-design.

Jerry—the cuddly, huggable teddy bear—took Hannah and Aaron to the lofty hallways of the White House, to President Barack Obama's inaugural White House Demo Day. Jerry's appearance is deceiving. He looks like a toy, feels like a toy . . . yet he is much more. Jerry is at the leading edge of a slew of purposefully designed high-tech tools that transform the way we think and act regarding health care. Jerry (and his siblings in the pipeline) is designed to help children and their families and friends understand and manage chronic childhood illnesses. In Jerry's case, his sole focus is for children diagnosed with type 1 diabetes. Other products in the works—at the intersection of design, consumer robotics, interactive education, gaming, and toys—are aimed at asthma, food allergies, obesity, and cancer, as well as the psychosocial accompaniments to these.

Hannah, Aaron, and Jerry's entrepreneurial path to the White House originated in personal experience and passion. Hannah recalls members of her father's family having type 2 diabetes, but she was not aware of just how serious the disease could be until her grandfather died of hypoglycemia. Aaron also brings personal history to Jerry's design. He lived with daily injections during his high school years, having been diagnosed with a growth hormone deficiency. He knows first-hand how stressful, scary, and potentially isolating these diseases and health-care regimens can be. Hannah and Aaron believe their personal experience, commitment, and passion bring special energy to their task.

Jerry the Bear started as a sketch on a Post-it Note when Hannah and Aaron were fellow engineering students at Northwestern University in Illinois. Jerry was conceived in response to the 2009 Diabetes Mine Design Challenge. Jerry became the first product of Design for America, a national network of student-led design studios intent on local and social impact through interdisciplinary design. Behind Jerry's cuddly facade is software for pediatric chronic disease education. Diabetic children across the United States care for Jerry by monitoring his blood glucose levels, giving him insulin, watching his carbohydrate intake, and feeding him a healthy diet through his food accessories. Jerry shares his feelings about all of these activities via a computer screen on his stomach. He comes with a free app for handheld devices and twenty-one animated storybooks about diabetes care. The app does not require a physical Jerry the Bear stuffed animal for people to engage in Jerry's world, thus widening his educational reach.

The design of the first robot toy was always a collaborative venture. As Aaron explains, "We wanted to take this thing that's really scary, diabetes, and make it a little bit fun and in doing so, giving something [children] want to engage with and want to take care of. If children start engaging in their own health care, it kind of helps set them up from a young age to build those foundational skills that they will need to practice for the rest of their lives."

For the Sproutel team, design started with extensive observation of children with diabetes. They set about visiting and talking with kids with type 1 diabetes, as well as their families and doctors. These interactions revealed what Aaron called an "uncanny pattern." The kids' own well-worn teddy bears—sometimes splitting at the seams, with body parts missing or very faded and worn pelts—were the recipients of children's pretend play efforts to inject their bears with insulin. Hannah and Aaron saw that kids were taking care of their stuffed animals in the same nurturing way their parents were taking care of them. Aaron recalls, "Some of these kids were even drawing up fake medical devices they would staple to the fur of their stuffed animal. We saw that behavior and thought, 'Wouldn't it be cool if that teddy could talk to them, educate them, and be their friend with type 1 diabetes?'"

Around the time Jerry was transitioning from prototype two to prototype three—when Hannah and Aaron were starting their senior year at college—they made the gutsy decision to move to Providence, Rhode Island. Hannah and Aaron formed their own company, naming it Sproutel ("to sprout"), and joined the Providence start-up accelerator Betaspring (finishing their final quarter at Northwestern by Skype). Today, with his combination of robotic, gaming, interactive, and educational software, Jerry can not only mimic daily real-world scenarios that diabetic children face, but he can also deliver medical-grade curriculum covering nutrition, exercise, sleep, and mindfulness for health and wellness education. Jerry is purposefully designed to develop a sense of empathy and understanding so that users can take an active role in their own diabetes care, and family and friends can understand and assist if appropriate. These days, thousands of children with type 1 diabetes and their families around the globe welcome Jerry to their health-care routine.

Like most entrepreneurs, the Sproutel team faced the relentless trials of raising money. Hannah and Aaron are as creative in sustaining their organization as they are in co-designing robots for health-care education. They've accessed traditional venture capital, grants, crowdfunding, Bitcoin, innovation competitions and awards, and strategic partnerships throughout the ecosystem (such as the nonprofit Beyond Type 1).[29] This openness to diverse, creative, and collaborative revenue streams is another hallmark of these twenty-first century entrepreneurs.

The Sproutel team's user-based, co-design approach to creating and refining Jerry yielded some helpful insights for designpreneurs embarking on similar journeys. Their tips include:

- Research, observe, question.
- Approach design with empathy.

- Involve users in the design process.

- Engage users meaningfully and authentically.

- Encourage users' stories.

- Treat users as equals or higher.

- Make the experience relevant.

- Co-facilitate user empowerment.

- Think beyond the initial use.[30]

Today, Hannah and Aaron enact these lessons in their development of new products for other diseases afflicting children. Aaron says that in the context of impact innovation, "the industry needs to look beyond existing tools and think about the 'idealized experience' and ask, 'What is the experience that we want our user, our consumer, to have in a future with no constraints?' The spinouts of that conversation might be shelved until a magic leap comes out . . . or they could be ideas that you might be able to build the correct technology building blocks."

Sproutel's co-founders describe their ultimate objectives as "incredibly audacious." They are aiming to put a bear in the hands of every U.S. child diagnosed with diabetes. By reaching children young—a "special time when they're still forming behaviors"—Hannah and Aaron hope Jerry and his future siblings will help children and their families learn effective health management habits, saving them from health crises later, while contributing to understanding and empathy in the child's own ecosystem. Hannah and Aaron see a special opportunity to make a positive change that will last throughout their users' lives. With Hannah's mechanical engineering and design training and orientation and Aaron's mechatronics education and experience in human-robot interactions, they envisage a med-tech toy industry of the future dominated by these technologies.

ENTREPRENEURSHIP FOR IMPACT INSIGHTS SUMMARY

Citizens all over the world are riding a wave of impact intentions and actions. The entrepreneurs described in this chapter are at the leading edge of this global movement. While they live at the epicenter of the entrepreneurial ecosystem, they are not typical of all entrepreneurs. They are leading the disintegration of old silos where business and doing good are segregated, sometimes at opposite ends of a spectrum. These twenty-first century entrepreneurs relentlessly apply their entrepreneurial passion and skills to contribute to the greater good. Like other entrepreneurs, they are intent on organizational sustainability and healthy returns on investment, and ensure sustainability through a multitude of revenue streams—including angel, venture capital, and impact investment; crowdfunding; traditional grants; low-interest loans; prizes from innovation awards; and sales from products and services. They are acutely aware of the most pressing societal challenges facing the people on our planet and apply their entrepreneurial skills to make a positive difference for those facing hardships posed by those challenges. These entrepreneurs, for whom impact is integral to their thoughts and actions, are acutely aware that one action can generate reactions throughout the entire ecosystem. They are leading the charge into the 2020s, merging business and positive impact missions. They are ushering in an era in which impact thinking and doing are fundamental threads of entire entrepreneurial and organizational ecosystems.

CHAPTER 5

The Designers

D esigners are some of the original creatives. Like artists, architects, and inventors throughout history, twenty-first century designers imagine what can be made and draw plans accordingly. They apply their imaginative and artistic talents to developing products and services for the greater good. Sometimes the quiet achievers humble, and gracious. Sometimes the enigmatic, intense recluses. Sometimes flamboyant, eccentric, and extroverted. Sometimes all of these rolled into one. Designers deploy unique combinations of playfulness and discipline, convergent and divergent thinking, whimsical daydreaming and reality testing, rebellious and staid problem-solving. Observant of both the minutiae of the moment and the big picture, they often conduct their work long before the outputs of their labor are celebrated. They are innovative visionaries who apply their lateral thinking and spatial envisioning talents to the designing of spaces, buildings, gadgets, tools, and processes that improve people's lives.

de·sign·er: (noun)

1) One who creates and often executes plans for a project or structure
2) One who creates and manufactures a new product style or design.

Designers of the twenty-first century deliberately enact diversity in service of innovation in design. They tackle social or environmental challenges as partners with locals, within the community system, as well as in the broader ecosystem. They bring co-design principles to problem-solving, with end users and other constituents up front and integral to the design process. Such co-designing collaborative initiatives—rather than design by outsiders from offices that may be miles away or even continents away—are the future.

These imaginative designers with a social conscience hail from many fields across the design spectrum—architecture, graphic design, photography, fine art, industrial design. Their work is not typically displayed in art galleries or museums, although impact designers may rapidly be becoming the next artistic frontier.

On 91st Street in New York City from October 2016 through February 2017, the Cooper Hewitt, Smithsonian Design Museum hosted a trend-setting exhibition to display design objects that contribute to the greater good: *By the People: Designing a Better America.* The exhibit was the result of curator Cynthia Smith's two-year search for projects that exemplified collaboration in developing creative design solutions for challenging problems, particularly in poor communities. Solutions that contributed to "more equitable, inclusive, and sustainable communities."[1] Sixty "innovative and impactful [sets of] actions" from across America were showcased. One such exhibit meandered through the neighborhoods on the south and west sides of Chicago. It consisted of vibrantly painted buses, retired from the Chicago Transit Authority, creatively redesigned as mobile single-aisle mini supermarkets. These colorful buses bring locally grown organic and sustainable foods to neighborhoods in underserved communities. Architecture for Humanity Chicago collaborated with local nonprofits—Food Desert Action and, later, Growing Power—to design the buses to enable some five hundred thousand Chicago residents living in neighborhoods classified as "food deserts" (lacking in fresh fruits and vegetables) to have the opportunity for affordable fresh food.

This example demonstrates our own commitment to showcasing thinking and doing, in this case designing, around processes, not just outputs, and services, not just products. The collaborative work of Architecture for Humanity Chicago, Food Desert Action, and Growing Power is an example of co-design processes to solve a community problem. The colorful buses may be beautiful artistic objects, but it is the joint designing of the social impact work, enabled by nurturing relationships and collaboration, being highlighted here.

Another innovative and impactful project spotlighted in *By the People* hailed from Chattanooga, Tennessee. There, local residents, volunteers, and architects formed the nonprofit Glass House Collective and worked together to transform a neighborhood marred by empty, abandoned buildings, vandalism, and crime. The collective created new sidewalks, bus shelters, and green spaces, and transformed a vacant lot on the main street by designing a central pop-up community space, complete with murals painted by everyone involved, a bulletin board, and a library. Not surprisingly, vandalism and crime rates in the area dropped dramatically, and as a result, the space continued to be used for this purpose well beyond a typical "pop-up" lifespan.[2]

By the People is not the first exhibit at the Cooper Hewitt to highlight products, services, and processes designed for positive impact in underserved communities around the world. Initiatives were designed to facilitate more inclusive and sustainable communities. In 2007 the museum showcased examples from across the globe of creative design solutions addressing systemic challenges for millions of people living in impoverished conditions. Also curated by Smith, *Design for the Other 90%* displayed an array of low-cost, often life-saving designs for individual applications. For example, a sixteen-gallon water container shaped like a tire or donut that could be rolled for long distances, even by children, enabled easier, more effective transport of precious water from the source to homes. Also showcased was another huge breakthrough, albeit in a smaller package—the "LifeStraw"—a drinking straw equipped with a purifying filter. This simple device—used in

Ghana, Nigeria, Pakistan, and Uganda—not only ensures clean drinking water, but also helps prevent the spread of waterborne diseases like typhoid, cholera, dysentery, and diarrhea.[3]

COLLABORATIVE DESIGN

These social innovations reflect an accumulating body of achievements at the intersection of design innovation and positive impact intentions. These impressive achievements have co-design by interdisciplinary teams at their core. The sparking of creativity to trigger groundbreaking outcomes when people from diverse backgrounds come together to tackle problems is not new in the mainstream entrepreneurial community. Accelerators and incubators—organizations designed to grow start-ups by providing a range of nurturing resources (especially mentoring) in one space—thrive on this cross-pollination. Serial entrepreneur Dr. Sangeeta Bhatia told *Entrepreneur* magazine:

> Innovation happens at the interfaces of different disciplines. . . . That idea that you can combine fields and really leapfrog in advances has been something we try to repeat over and over again by bringing in diverse teams with diverse perspectives and experiences.[4]

Such collaborative initiatives—where design meets innovation meets citizen engagement for the greater good—are forming a burgeoning wave across our planet.

THE DESIGNER EDUCATOR: MARIANA AMATULLO

At the leading edge of that wave is the ArtCenter College of Design. Nestled in the leafy hillside city of Pasadena, California, with commanding vistas overlooking the famous Rose Bowl, the college is situated in a wonderful juxtaposition of human presence and nature.

The conservatory-like educational approach of the ArtCenter

College of Design exemplifies innovative, entrepreneurial thinking with its mantra: "We prepare artists to share their creativity with the world." At Designmatters, the social innovation department of the college, students deliberately curate socially impactful innovation with interdisciplinary teamwork. They work across disciplines to advance positive change by applying design principles—for example, multidisciplinary teams working collaboratively with target populations—to design solutions to an array of socioeconomic and environmental problems affecting them. Designmatters (and the design methods deployed) has consistently been a first mover in the field, leading the United States and the world. As a cross-discipline design center and educational department, Designmatters cuts across the art and design disciplines in undergraduate and graduate programs offered at the college. Product designers, fine artists, illustrators, architects, environmental, industrial and graphic designers, and social innovators work in teams on the same societal challenge. Eighteen years after ArtCenter's founding, there are only a handful of educational institutions in the world offering these kinds of integrative social design programs.

As a research center, Designmatters curates leading-edge studies in design for social innovation. As a design consultancy, its multidisciplinary teams facilitate "real-world implementation of the projects with partner organizations." It also functions as a hub for facilitating external relationships that advocate design as a catalyst for social change.[5] Projects have included redesigning the patient experience for a pediatric burn center; the Safe Niños (safe children) and Safe Agua programs for slum dwellers in Chile, Colombia, and Peru; solar-powered, camel-carried medical refrigeration units in Kenya and Ethiopia; and "The Los Angeles Earthquake: Get Ready," a simulation and preparedness education program in California.

Dr. Mariana Amatullo, the co-founder and lead "architect" of Designmatters for the first sixteen years of its existence until summer 2017, and her colleagues have combined social entrepreneurship, public policy, sustainable development, and global health to form a unique hybrid design program. Mariana—design thinker, researcher, innovator, and educator—has been at the forefront of designing, facilitating, and training interdisciplinary and diverse design teams to enact socially impactful innovation for almost two decades. Mariana was thinking "design meets social innovation and impact" long before any terms like "social entrepreneurship" or "impact" entered the educational lexicon, let alone the public domain.

Mariana helped establish Designmatters in 2001 with a task force of faculty, staff, and alumni of the ArtCenter. They were so far ahead of the trend in combining impact and design that there was no field, let alone an "emergent trend."

Mariana believes the professional landscape for design in social innovation has reached a critical moment. Her quiet voice and gracious, unassuming manner belie the enormity of her ideas and actions:

> Designers are now acting as mediators, synthesizers, and key contributors of social and environmental challenges at a strategic level. Organizations are recognizing that designers bring a unique set of abilities and methods for developing human-centered artifacts, services, environments, and systems.[6]

Born in Buenos Aires to Argentinian diplomat parents, Mariana has long felt the inexorable pull of art, design, and impact work to facilitate less inequality in the world. Mariana was raised in cities around the globe, as dictated by her parents' diplomatic postings. While fellow Argentinians her own age were studying international nongovernmental organizations (NGOs) and United Nations (UN) agencies in textbooks and classrooms, Mariana was walking their corridors, meeting the strategists and front-line workers, and seeing up close what they were actually doing. She was at home in these unusual contexts, familiar with how such organizations worked, how they prospered or floundered.

Her familiarity with NGOs, international development issues, and the UN system would serve her well when she came to design and grow Designmatters. She was able to structure a number of creative partnerships with the UN to facilitate social design projects. Because of her initiative, the ArtCenter would become the first design institution to be formally affiliated as an NGO with the UN's Department of Public Information.

Having earned a *licence de lettres* from the Sorbonne University in Paris and a master of arts in art history and museum studies at the University of Southern California in Los Angeles, it was through working toward her doctorate—conducted while leading Designmatters—that Mariana combined her dual passions of design and social impact. Mariana's pioneering research at these intersecting fields sought to explore the value designers bring to this emergent field of impact design. Mariana considered design in a broad cultural context, "grounded in the richness of organizational practice." She included project case studies led by design teams at IDEO.org, frog, MindLab, and the former Helsinki Design Lab, as well as an ethnographic study of the Innovation Unit of UNICEF. In a field where efforts to quantify impact are in their infancy, Mariana measured how design abilities and capabilities—known as "design attitude"—are significant in advancing positive social innovation outcomes in projects. Her research established the first quantitative metrics demonstrating the statistical significance of design capabilities in the context of social innovation goals. Mariana was awarded her PhD from Case Western Reserve University, where she is a Scholar-in-Residence and a Design and Innovation Fellow.

Characteristics of Successful Social Innovators

- Skills to pursue problem discovery amid discontinuous change and organizational constraints;

- Courage to embrace mindful stewardship and responsibility for the greater good; and

- Ability to learn from the pluralism of perspectives that shape our evolving understanding of the world around us.[7]

Mariana and her team conceptualized and curated a portfolio of national and global educational design projects, research collaborations, and publications at the intersection of art, design, and social innovation. Under her leadership, core teams of the ArtCenter partnered with faculty, alumni, and students from the various design disciplines as well as experts outside design—for example, in international development, public health, and business. Partnerships are formed on a project-by-project basis.[8] Much of the cross-disciplinary collaborative work of Designmatters is aimed at developing "T-shaped" designers, or those designers who have strong, deep skills in their area of specialty (the vertical stroke of the T) as well as a social innovation mindset (the horizontal stroke of the T). Characterized by cross-discipline collaboration skills, lateral and critical thinking skills, empathy, and compassion, these designers join with others to tackle real-world challenges in communities around the globe. Designmatters graduates can go on to apply their skills as design social innovators in larger organizations as intrapreneurs, or in smaller design consultancies like IDEO and Design Continuum, which are equally devoted to positive impact. Edging toward their twentieth year, Designmatters and its cadre of trained social designers are having their own impact on the world's big social and environmental problems as they fan out across the world.

Today, the concepts and methodologies pioneered by Designmatters and the ArtCenter College of Design place Mariana, her colleagues, and her students at the forefront of international dialogue in design. While Mariana moved on to new adventures at New York's Parsons School of Design at The New School, she reflected: "The mission of Designmatters remains the same . . . as it did upon its founding: through research, advocacy, and action, Designmatters engages, empowers, and leads an ongoing exploration of art and design as a positive force in society. There are many compelling initiatives in our future."[9]

THE ENTREPRENEURIAL DESIGN COLLABORATIVE: UN TECHO PARA MI PAÍS

If Dr. Mariana Amatullo and her ArtCenter team led the edge of the wave of cultivating collaborative design thinking to solve social challenges, **Julián Ugarte Fuentes** and the team at Chilean social enterprise **Un Techo Para Mi País (Un Techo)** have led the wave in "doing."

In the late 1990s, massive numbers of people—from rural areas, cities, and nearby less wealthy countries—were lured to Chile's urban centers in search of opportunity. The result: sprawling ramshackle encampments at the periphery of Chile's major cities, particularly Santiago. Life in these *campamentos* reflected conditions in slums all over the world—no running water, electricity, or sewers, and limited opportunities to get ahead. Aspiring to higher education was typically a thwarted dream. Even when individual family members pursue higher education, the cost can potentially consume 40 percent of a typical campamento family's total annual household income.

Un Techo Para País ("A Roof for My Country")—which would grow to become one of the largest and most successful NGOs in Latin America—sprouted in 1997 when a group of college students and a Jesuit priest, Father Felipe Berríos, shared grave concerns about the unacceptable living conditions of more than two hundred million people living in abject poverty in the *favelas* (shantytowns) of Santiago and other Latin American cities and towns. Un Techo's cadre of volunteers—themselves earnest college students aware of their privilege—shared a perspective that the plight of each of us is the plight of all of us. They heeded the priest's invitation to act. With a decidedly non-handout, collaborative, holistic approach to pathways out of poverty, the young Chileans and the priest started collaborating with families living in poverty to co-design and build three hundred and fifty homes and a church in southern Chile's Bíobío region. With this purposeful, enterprising action, marked by working side by side with locals and end users, Un Techo Para Chile ("A Roof for Chile") was born. Their collaborative approach—no "us" and "them," only "us"—would become the hallmark of the organization as it expanded throughout Chile and beyond.

As Un Techo teams and their projects multiplied, they intentionally wove the people living in the slums into the co-creation of products and services that could improve their lives. Un Techo's collaborative, co-creating approach places the users, the people living in abject poverty, at the center of the solution design process—equal peers in a journey that enables the poor to author their own futures and those of their families and communities. Users are part of the process from the beginning, typically members of the teams who design products, services, and processes as equal collaborators, problem solvers, designers, and testers of solutions.

Father Felipe's public comments throughout the meteoric rise of Un Techo Para Chile reflect the Un Techo collective mindset that has pervaded all they do:

> Everything that is given to the poor makes them poorer. We never have to give. We can accompany the poor in their suffering, but not give them money. . . . You need to be able to say, "this is my home."[10]

Following their initial success in Curanilahue, the young Un Techo team embarked on a greater challenge: to co-construct two thousand new homes throughout Chile by the year 2000. Mobilizing a cadre of like-minded volunteers from universities and the wider community, they achieved their goal in 1999, ahead of schedule. In 2000 they set their sights to eradicate all slums in Chile by 2010. By early 2001, the volunteer movement aimed at poverty had taken root. Un Techo launched operational offices in other parts of Chile. By late 2001 they had opened their first offices in Peru and El Salvador. Un Techo Para Chile thus became Un Techo Para Mi País, which began expanding across the Americas. People living in impoverished conditions in Argentina, Bolivia, Brazil, Chile, Colombia, Costa Rica, Ecuador, Guatemala, Mexico, Nicaragua, Paraguay, the Dominican Republic, and Uruguay would benefit from Un Techo-facilitated collaborative programs, which have positively impacted more than eighty million people in nineteen countries. And counting . . .

In time, a series of long-term skills-development services were integrated into Un Techo's strategies, flattening social barriers and enabling individuals, families, and communities to design their own futures. Un Techo combined these programs with advocacy and lobbying to achieve legislative and other changes to enable social impact innovation and mobilize a countrywide movement of university student volunteers. The scope of Un Techo's impact across Latin America and the world no doubt far exceeds the wildest imaginings of Father Felipe and his young comrades when they first lamented the plight of the Chilean poor in 1997. Little could they have envisaged the positive multiplier impacts those first attempts at eradicating conditions of living in poverty would have. Nor could they have foretold how their countrywide infrastructure—built as they achieved their ambitious goal of eradicating slums by January 2010—would dramatically contribute to the nation's recovery efforts when an earthquake hit Chile's south-central seaboard in late February 2010. More than five hundred people were killed by the earthquake and its aftershocks; thousands more were injured or displaced as neighborhoods and communities were decimated. Un Techo's countrywide infrastructure, systems, and processes developed over the preceding decade proved instrumental in assisting the government work with poor communities decimated by the earthquake, not least of which were rebuilding efforts.

Un Techo's Centro de Innovación: Julián Ugarte Fuentes

In 2007, a decade after Un Techo's humble beginnings, the team (including Askan Straume, Andrés Iriondo, and Rafael Achondo) created the Centro de Innovación, or Techolab (Socialab). The brainchild of Julián Ugarte Fuentes, Socialab Chile was born to accelerate the positive social impacts started by Un Techo. As Julián said about the new program:

> If we continue to do the same things to overcome social problems—like poverty—we will spend too much time and many people will spend their lives in unacceptable conditions. We should innovate to find disruptive ways to overcome these problems. That's the reason why Un Techo created Socialab—a brand new platform to create new ways to overcome old challenges.[11]

Julián is originally from Chile's Viña del Mar—a seaside resort characterized by beautiful beaches and tranquil tree-lined streets. Viña del Mar is also home to one of the most important annual cultural events in the Americas, the Viña del Mar International Song Festival. The parallel dualities—tranquility and energy—endemic to his hometown combined to trigger innovation in Julián's work. Starting with Un Techo Para Chile's social programs when he was just twenty gave Julián unique opportunities to explore his own country while doing work that ignited his drive to *do*. He visited building sites and interviewed the people living in the campamentos who had limited access to clean running water, electricity, sanitation, and security. They left an indelible imprint on Julián. He became devoted to creating processes for initiating and nurturing social innovation projects, which he did for seven years from within Un Techo Para Chile. In 2012, with Un Techo's blessing and seed funding from the Multilateral Investment Fund of the Inter-American Development Bank and Movistar Chile, Julián spun off the Centro de Innovación and the independent Socialab. After ensuring a sustainable business model, Julián built a team dedicated to facilitating the design of solutions to functional problems in Un Techo housing projects related to water, sanitation, space optimization, and recreation.

In the first decade of its existence, Centro de Innovación has become one of Latin America's most successful NGOs. In a country whose socioeconomic divide is one of the worst in Latin America, the Centro de Innovación and Socialab Chile have created a countrywide and social innovation ecosystem predicated on activating the country's brightest young people in interdisciplinary and cross-boundary collaborations with people living in poverty, along with academics, entrepreneurs, thought leaders, and public sector representatives. Tens of thousands of students have collaborated and co-created with their fellow Chileans living in slums on impact innovation projects. These joint initiatives have positively touched the lives of millions living in extreme poverty, improving the quality of life for their respective communities and giving everyone "space to practice changemaking."[12]

Socialab

Julián, Askan, Andrés, Rafael, and the Socialab team were intent on revolutionizing how society responds to the unacceptable condition that is global poverty. They remain intent on revolution that results in maximum positive impact for resources expended. They believe that without revolution, too many people will continue to spend their lives in unacceptable, impoverished predicaments. Socialab is therefore designed to facilitate and implement disruptive ways to overcome previously intractable problems. Convinced that "you can build a better world *and* make money," they see people living in poverty as co-creators, co-innovators, and customers who are integral to their own pathways out of poverty.[13] Socialab teams intuitively know that although slum communities endure unimaginable hardships, they are also home to vibrant communities full of life, culture, and fun, communal support for their fellow humans. Socialab teams also intuitively know that collaboration with these communities affords opportunities for rich co-creation of solutions to the challenges they face.

Julián's compelling persuasive skills have made allies of some of the most powerful business and political leaders in Chile, many of whom served on Centro de Innovación advisory boards.[14] Socialab is dedicated to transforming high-potential creative solutions to social challenges into sustainable business plans—and ultimately into sustainable companies delivering disruptive change through their impact innovations. Socialab hosts frequent large-scale global competitions each year, inspiring the most innovative, scalable strategies for tackling social challenges. Winning submissions are showcased through festival-like events, which attract tens of thousands of people, contributing to the proliferation of widespread enthusiasm for social innovation. Winning social innovators are mentored throughout their remaining journey—with support and guidance from experts in the field, so they can grow viable, scalable, sustainable plans and processes for the implementation of the winning innovation. Winning social innovators are invited to join other social innovators at Social BB's coworking space in Santiago, designed specifically for co-creation of ideas through the formation of collaborative partnerships among members and stakeholders. Socialab's online platform creates a self-sufficient loop of social innovation, builds awareness and enthusiasm for positive social change, and helps mentor a whole generation of skilled innovation changemakers across Chile and beyond.[15]

Centro de Innovación and Socialab have forged synergistic relationships with government agencies (Socialab projects have the explicit support and endorsement of the Chilean Ministry of Foreign Affairs) and nongovernmental agencies, as well as corporations and academic institutions, including UNICEF, NASA, Microsoft, Masisa, Movistar, Unilever, Gerdau Aza, Sodimac, Coca-Cola, Singularity University in Silicon Valley, and the ArtCenter College of Design. Singularity University, like the ArtCenter, is an international leader at the intersection of design and social innovation, intent on educating, inspiring, and training the next generations of design leaders to address humanity's greatest challenges.

Safe Agua

One of Un Techo and Socialab's most powerful international partnerships—with Mariana Amatullo and the Designmatters team—began when the director of development at Un Techo, Rafael Achondo, visited Mariana at the ArtCenter College of Design campus in California in 2009. Rafael came to Pasadena to invite the Designmatters team to work with Un Techo, the Centro de Innovación and Socialab, and the residents of Campamento San José, one of the main slum communities on the outskirts of Santiago. The goal: to help improve conditions for the people living in that community.

This exemplary collaboration was named Safe Agua Chile and was later showcased as part of the Cooper Hewitt, Smithsonian Design Museum's *Design for the Other 90%* exhibit.[16] The Safe Agua collaboration was designed to tackle issues associated with the most precious resource on our planet: water. Most residents in developed cities around the world take clean, running water for granted, seemingly oblivious to experts' forecast for 2030—that withdrawal of water from aquifers and waterways could exceed natural renewal by 60 percent, with demand for water predicted to be 50 percent higher than in 2015. According to *National Geographic*, "underground water is being pumped so aggressively around the globe that land is sinking, civil wars are being waged, and agriculture is being transformed."[17] By 2030, the water lords and water warriors, currently confined to far-flung places like Yemen in the

Middle East or Northern Africa, will likely spread to the developed world. Particularly vulnerable are those regions prone to prolonged droughts (a phenomenon likely to be more prevalent as the volatility of our planet's climate becomes the new normal in the 2020s). With water scarcity comes other issues—poor health, economic hardship, and human effort focused on survival rather than achieving potential.

The residents of Campamento San José were already living with pervasive 2030-like water scarcity. Residents in these informal communities only accessed clean water when the municipal water truck delivered it (one to three times a week). The residents had to carry water from the trucks and store it in their huts, because viable infrastructure for running water was nonexistent. Daily tasks like bathing, cooking, and laundry required tremendous energy, effort, strength, and time in the campamentos. In many cases, the women of these communities carried water by hand for each of these daily tasks for their families. A glass of unclean water can make a child or an adult gravely ill. Most residents bathed "by parts," pouring a cup of water on separate areas of their bodies. Laundry could take a full day of physical labor. The time and energy required to deal with water scarcity-related problems is a major obstacle to earning a stable income and overcoming poverty.

Safe Agua Chile was predicated on the fundamental tenets of co-creation and collaboration and a belief in the potent power of cross-pollination of diverse areas of expertise to create new value. The project brought together residents of Campamento San José with Un Techo, Centro de Innovación, Socialab, and students and faculty from the ArtCenter College of Design. ArtCenter students and faculty hailed from environmental, product, graphic, and transportation design, and graduate broadcast cinema.

The Safe Agua Chile team co-created six solutions to Campamento San José's water scarcity-related problems, designed to improve the use, storage, and transportation of water. The Safe Agua solutions to acquiring, conserving, and efficiently dispensing this precious resource tackled different stages of the water delivery and consumption processes at a range of scales—from the community level to the individual household. For example, the Mila initiative resulted in a community laundry facility equipped with a gravity-fed water supply system and low-water-consumption washing machines. Once implemented throughout the campamento, these communal spaces not only have provided comfortable, hygienic places to launder clothes, but also serve as informal gathering places. They also have contributed to the campamento's economy by enabling some residents to earn extra money by doing laundry for other families.

In individual homes the Ducha Halo (halo shower) innovation yielded a low-cost portable shower made from easily obtainable and inexpensive parts (from any hardware store, for the equivalent of $17). The reLAVA initiative resulted in a multipurpose kitchen workstation enabling sanitary, efficient washing of dishes and cooking utensils within homes—previously an arduous, time-consuming task. Agua Segura produced a water purification kit for a five-gallon bucket; Gota a Gota ("drop by drop") is a gravity-fed system to simulate running water in individual households. Index de Innovación generated a communications strategy to encourage, celebrate, and publish innovations by and for people living in campamentos, so they could share their own inventions. When the 8.8-magnitude earthquake struck Chile in February 2010, some of these initiatives were accelerated into production so they could be deployed into the most decimated communities in the aftermath of the disaster.

Safe Agua Chile's co-design process, intentionally transparent to enable replication in other communities, started with designers living and working closely with community residents, followed by collaborative ideas generation, iterative prototyping of potential products, pilot testing, and ultimately, scaled implementation. In Cerro Verde, perched in the hills above Lima in Peru, Safe Agua Peru yielded its own innovations to improve quality of life. This too has been extended to other Latin American countries and parts of Africa. For example, the halo shower can now be found in the favelas of Buenos Aires.

Safe Agua has won awards and been recognized internationally. Besides being exhibited at the Cooper Hewitt, the program's achievements have been recognized and exhibited at the Royal College of Art and World Expo Shanghai United Nations Pavilion, the Spark Awards for Social Innovation in New York, and the Singularity University at NASA project. Even Nobel Prize winner Muhammad Yunus requested prototypes for display at fairs for social innovation and inclusive business.[18]

When Julián was interviewed about Safe Agua (and the collaborations that made it possible), he noted the power of community-based models of design when combined with social entrepreneurship. He said: "We don't believe in giving solutions to the people, but in creating solutions together."[19] And with the subsequent replication, production, and distribution of some of these innovations to other communities living in challenging predicaments, Julián's conviction that "you can build a better world *and* make money . . . a new paradigm of success" is becoming a reality.[20] And his reason for doing all of this? "Because we don't like poverty . . . so we have to move things quicker so there can be an end in sight."[21] And with those simple words, Julián underscores the contributions creative designers—armed with empathy, discipline, unwavering optimism, and a co-creation mindset—can make to enact disruptive social change against the world's most intractable problems.

ENTREPRENEURSHIP FOR IMPACT INSIGHTS SUMMARY

Creativity and innovation are far more likely when design or decision-making teams are diverse, whether in business, political, humanitarian, or other arenas. This isn't just because people with different backgrounds bring new information to the table. Study after study shows that simply interacting with individuals from different walks of life—different socioeconomic, geographic, racial, or religious backgrounds, and different professions—forces group members to prepare better, to anticipate alternative viewpoints, and to expect that reaching consensus will take effort.[22] Designers of the twenty-first century exemplify this multilayered perspective and collaborative, multidisciplinary approach to solving some of society's toughest challenges.

CHAPTER 6

The Ideas Facilitators, Mentors, and Launchers

T hey are the virtuosos of ideas generation and facilitation—often composer, conductor, concert pianist, and orchestra—all rolled into one. They bring extensive repertoires to provoke thought and catalyze action, imparting their skills and knowledge, nurturing minds beyond the ordinary, and fostering entrepreneurial start-ups toward the extraordinary. The ideas facilitators—the impact innovation educators, mentors, project and people nurturers, and launchers—aim to engage and challenge brains before they get pummeled into submission by a parade of formulaic, simple, rote answers to complex issues. Their words and actions fuel incessant curiosity.

Many ideas facilitators are coy about their achievements, yet their own innovations in thinking, processes, products, human connections, and networks (often occurring out of the direct entrepreneurial spotlight) have changed the world for the better. They tend to see themselves in the background, the periphery of the main action. In contrast to their own self-perceptions, many of the ideas facilitators we met are subtle dynamos, connectors of disparate elements of the innovation ecosystem, with a pivotal impact on individuals, organizations, and entire ecosystems.

THE IDEAS FACILITATOR EXTRAORDINAIRE: EDUCATOR, DR. PAMELA HARTIGAN

Educators are not people who simply parse out rules and facts. The good ones inspire awe at learning new concepts, new ways of thinking, and new ways of doing, and expand the landscapes of the brain. Educators foster the ability and capacity to think and reason, to question. Educators know they are there to support, encourage, guide, teach, inform, and inspire. They are guided by passion and principle, not reductionist tests and minimal standards. They can instill curiosity and awe as they shepherd the learner through the joys and frustrations of exploring new territories of the mind. Their impact, while initially on the individuals they tutor and challenge, is infinite.

> **ed·u·ca·tor** (noun):
>
> 1) The person who provides instruction 2) One skilled in teaching 3) One with a precious talent compounded from knowledge, experience, and a genuine desire and capacity to project that which one has learned to others.

Impact educators stand out for their commitment and capacity to spreading the passion, knowledge, and skills necessary to enable others to positively impact our world.

As a lifelong educator on how to make a positive difference without doing harm, **Dr. Pamela Hartigan** was no exception. Never hesitant about speaking her mind or challenging the establishment to think and act beyond their entrenched scripts, Pamela was a global citizen by birth and life experiences. Her big thinking has benefited some of the world's most iconic impact institutions: the World Health Organization and World Bank, the Schwab Foundation for Social Entrepreneurship, and the World Economic Forum. Her final days as a tireless educator were spent as director of the Skoll Centre for Social Entrepreneurship at

Oxford University, where she designed and taught innovative educational programs and research for aspiring impactors from all over the world.

Born in Guayaquil, Ecuador, the daughter of an Ecuadorian mother and American father, Pamela spent her formative years in Latin America. During that time Pamela—immersed in local culture because of the nature of her upbringing—developed profound and ingrained respect for people from all walks of life. In a 2012 interview, Pamela described growing up a child of parents in the upper echelons of diplomatic service as a mixed blessing. She recalled being essentially raised by household employees who came from less privileged circumstances. Rather than perceiving her surrogate family as less fortunate, or feeling paternalistic or maternalistic toward them, Pamela felt in awe of these resourceful people:

> They never treated me as if I was somehow different. That struck me massively, because they were the first of the "frugal innovators," making do with whatever they had and doing things that were really quite inventive and creative . . . I'm not romanticizing the way they lived, but the whole cult of charity—the cult of my mother's generation of "Oh, let's give away clothes to the poor"— never, ever, ever hit me. I was never part of that conversation.[1]

In the pioneering adventurer spirit that would characterize her life's journey, Pamela left Ecuador and traveled to the United States to study at the School of Foreign Service at Georgetown University at the young age of seventeen. She went on to earn two master's degrees from the Institut d'Études Européennes in Brussels, and then a PhD from the Catholic University of America. Her career and life were marked by a continual search for answers to some of the world's most intransigent problems.

Pamela started out working in grassroots organizations in Latino communities in Washington, D.C., curating inventive programs around adolescence, joblessness, and migrant issues. The success of these programs caught the attention of the World Health Organization, which asked Pamela to replicate these initiatives in Latin America. Once there, she was struck by the impotence of doctors and the medical curative model in the face of behavior-based social problems like smoking, obesity, diabetes, and HIV. Pamela saw a definitive clash between Western medical approaches to health problems and public health approaches. So she did what would be one of the hallmark characteristics of her career: She built bridges between the medical and the public health sectors. When looking back on this work, Pamela described her penchant for operating on the fringes of disciplines: "That's always been my forte, to be the bridge-builder between public health and medical approaches, whether it's corporate or grassroots-based approaches." Pamela strongly believed that "fringe people" or bridge-builders are critical in a world where different disciplines and approaches are siloed: "We've come to recognize that [good impact] is really about looking about the whole, not about compartmentalizing, analyzing, and forming a deductive process of how an intervention should be done."[2]

Pamela's big picture thinking, bridge-building, and innovative programing attracted the attention of a headhunter looking for an inaugural leader for the Schwab Foundation for Social Entrepreneurship, pioneered by Klaus and Hilde Schwab. Never shy in saying exactly what she was thinking, Pamela, in her initial reaction to the headhunter, insisted that she wouldn't work for Klaus Schwab if he were the last man on the face of the earth. Schwab, a German economist, engineer, and international mobilizer, had founded the World Economic Forum (WEF) in 1987. From her public health perspective, the young Pamela viewed the WEF as the "bastion of everything that was evil about the world." She saw the WEF's annual event in the Swiss Alps as an all-white male CEO talkfest in which they made decisions for the rest of the world.[3] Because Pamela was not afraid to scrutinize her thoughts or admit she was wrong, she relented after a few months and agreed to do a year of due diligence. In her new role at the Schwab Foundation for Social Entrepreneurship, Pamela traveled the world to meet people doing exceptional entrepreneurial ventures, including

Muhammad Yunus of Grameen Bank and Fazle Abed of BRAC in Bangladesh. She invited many of the people she consulted to joint deliberations at the Schwab Foundation headquarters in Geneva to share their stories with the board. The entrepreneurs persuaded the board to allocate $1 million for a prize awarded to the best of these pioneers for a different, more impactful purpose: to utilize the unique connection of the Schwab Foundation with the WEF to provide a platform for the social innovations being implemented. The entrepreneurs believed such exposure and involvement would bring legitimacy to the new models they had created, along with access to networks and capital. Pamela stayed as the foundation's founding director for eight years, until she assumed the role of director of the Skoll Centre for Social Entrepreneurship in the Saïd Business School at Oxford University. Pamela served the Skoll Centre enthusiastically until her death in 2016, just weeks after our last conversation.

A typical year in the life of Dr. Pamela Hartigan reflected her global citizenship and her bridge-building—whether traveling with Oxford's Skoll Centre championing impact entrepreneurs around the world, or putting her time and thought resources into building innovative scalable solutions to challenges affecting our future as a founding director of Volans, an organization designed to catalyze breakthrough change.[4] A self-labeled "pracademic" (a term she used to describe a person who has a PhD but practices their career outside academia), Pamela supported and influenced entrepreneurs and other actors in the impact entrepreneurial ecosystem as a director on their boards, delivering keynote addresses, and sharing other presentations all over the planet, through her teaching and mentoring at Oxford. Her contribution to international dialogue and action is undeniably vast. In one of her last interviews, Pamela observed: "We're on the cusp of building this massive ecosystem comprised of many different stakeholders around social change, and it involves all kinds of sectors, and bringing all those things together. I'm like a pig in mud. It's too good to be true."[5] The educators who follow in Pamela's footsteps have a powerful role model.

Pamela's thinking about social entrepreneurship was fraught with internal debate. Over the years she expressed polar opposite views, from "Social entrepreneurship is the way to change the world" to "I absolutely despise the term 'social entrepreneur.' What is an entrepreneur? It's someone who sees an opportunity, seizes that opportunity, [and] is highly resourceful in terms of how he or she leverages the resources needed to get that going."[6] For Pamela, a commercial entrepreneur and a social entrepreneur are two sides of the same coin—cut from the same cloth. This is contrary to how the commercial entrepreneur has been known to secure investors looking for robust financial returns, whereas for the social entrepreneur, money is a means to actually drive social change. "I dream of the world where every entrepreneur has to be a social entrepreneur, because we cannot continue the kind of path we're on unless that actually happens."[7]

In a provocative blog post she wrote for Oxfam in 2014, Pamela described her initial awe at the work of entrepreneurs focused on solving some of society's most intractable problems: "Twenty years ago I fell in love with 'social entrepreneurship,' its promise, and most of all, the stories of the champions that practiced this approach. They didn't take 'it can't be done' as a deterrent—[rather,] 'it's impossible' [was their] clarion call to action. . . . It was difficult not to become infected with the bug of 'social entrepreneurship.'"[8] According to Hartigan, the terms "social entrepreneurship" and "social enterprise" continue to dichotomize the commercial and the social spheres, when the reality is that "all commercial ventures have to be accountable for the social and environmental impacts they are having and all social ventures have to be financially sustainable in some way." Pamela was adamant that the entrepreneurial "mindset does not belong to any one sector" and can be found in the private and public sectors, the media, and academia.

Decrying the creation of false separation between "this is where we make money" and "this is where we do good," Pamela vehemently advocated for a world in 2030 where silos no longer exist. She saw a 2030 in which every organization enacts work reflecting awareness and proactivity to ensure net positive impact. Impact awareness and proactivity built into everyone's DNA. Educators following in her footsteps can serve their students of entrepreneurship effectively if they take a few pages from Pamela's teaching notes:

- Ensure all entrepreneurship encompasses positive impact and all impact work includes entrepreneurship. Encourage students to obliterate silos.

- Promote ecosystems thinking and doing.

- See those in less materially wealthy circumstances as wealthy in creativity, innovation, entrepreneurship, and resilience.

- Practice what you preach. Live a positively impactful life.

THE MENTORS

They are the polymaths blazing a trail that enables impact entrepreneurs to grow skills, build connections, and breathe life into ideas that evolve into companies. Often with extraordinary prescience, mentors see potential where others see constraints. They are the changemakers behind the scenes, nurturing, prodding, pushing, and challenging frontline changemakers to do better, be better. They are the mentors.

> **men·tor** (noun):
>
> 1) A trusted counselor or guide 2) A teacher or coach.

Mentors are intent on contributing to ultimate positive impact by nurturing the entrepreneurs, designers, investors, and others who make up the innovation and entrepreneurial ecosystem. They coach and counsel these changemakers on key knowledges and skills like honing ideas, translating ideas into sustainable and marketable action, building relationships, and growing networks.

Mentor, Co-founder of Changemakers and UnLtd: Michael Norton

In 1994, long before the word "changemaker" became imbued with the reverence and kudos it receives today, visionary serial entrepreneur **Michael Norton** co-founded the social enterprise prophetically named Changemakers in the United Kingdom. Changemakers' mission was to find new ways of engaging young people in social action. Two decades later, Changemakers "activates a global network of social entrepreneurs, innovators, business leaders, policymakers, and activists to build an Everyone a Changemaker world."[9]

Michael has been at the frontier of social entrepreneurship and impact in the UK and the world. Trained as a scientist and then working in merchant banking and publishing, Michael's penchant for changemaking has been evident since the early days of his career. Like so many of the changemakers we interviewed, the inexorable pull of social impact work has long held sway in his life. During the early days of his career, Michael established (on an entirely voluntary basis) the UK's first language teaching program for non-English-speaking immigrants in London. He managed to mobilize more than two hundred volunteer tutors for this program. Noticing a particular need in the Bangladeshi youth community in London, he mobilized a further fifty volunteers to teach a seven-day-a-week supplementary school program for young Bangladeshis.

Impact work became Michael Norton's life's work. His immersion in the social impact sector has been solidly sutured over years of dedication and commitment. Michael has helped found and mentor more than forty social enterprises. In the seventies he set up one of many global firsts: the Directory of Social Change, the leading provider of information and training to the nonprofit sector in the UK.

In the nineties, he set up the Centre for Innovation in Voluntary Action (CIVA) to develop, pilot, and fund new ideas for addressing social problems.[10] He also founded YouthBank UK to enable young people to act as grant-makers by supporting local projects run by other young people.

To amplify the impact of mentoring small cadres of social entrepreneurs, Michael co-founded UnLtd in 2002. The vision was to create a foundation for social entrepreneurs to promote and develop a much larger population of entrepreneurs for the greater good.[11] The founders hoped to "incubate"—through systematic nurturing and coaching—the next generation of entrepreneurs intent on positive social impact. As one of the world's first modern-age incubators for start-ups focused on social good, UnLtd was a groundbreaking development in the UK, signaling the permanent recognition and establishment of social entrepreneurship. Michael and his fellow founders wanted social entrepreneurship to become the norm.

Some of the UK's iconic social impact mentoring institutions and charities—Changemakers, Community Action Network, Social Enterprise Scotland, the School for Social Entrepreneurs, Comic Relief, Ashoka; Innovators for the Public, and the Scarman Trust—brought their hefty combined might to bear on that lofty vision. UnLtd launched with a £100 million endowment from the Millennium Commission as a permanent source of funding.

UnLtd's enduring legacy as a mentoring and launching incubator

Over the ensuing two decades, other mentoring trailblazers like **Cliff Prior** and **Katharine Danton** in the UK, Pooja Warier Hamilton in India, and **Zoe Schlag** in the United States have picked up the UnLtd baton, expanding its model in the UK, Asia, and the Americas. Along the way, these mentors tapped into the rising wave of scattered social entrepreneurial stirrings in their own countries and abroad. They are at the forefront, leading the convergence of those stirrings into a movement, elevating social entrepreneurship to the mainstream and, more recently, reverence.

Katharine Danton, who served UnLtd as director of Research and Policy and director of Strategy and Influence, is exemplary of UnLtd mentors combining vision and practicalities. In her roles, Katharine served as chief co-designer and architect of how mentoring is enacted at UnLtd. A psychologist by training, Katharine is evidence-driven. She has keenly watched the cumulative growth of social entrepreneurship in the UK and abroad. She says: "We are seeing a surge in the number of people stepping up with entrepreneurial solutions to social problems . . . It is critical that social entrepreneurs are supported not only to start up but to start well." To tap into the surge in support for social impact in the general population, UnLtd started its Going Mainstream initiative in 2016. Recognizing new intermediaries and innovative social impact business models, Going Mainstream aimed to contribute to the integration of social impact intent and activities into normal business. UnLtd embarked on a public education campaign, aiming to leverage its institutional knowledge and networks to work with others to break down the barriers faced by social entrepreneurs and thus maximize social impact.[12]

Under Katharine's leadership in research and policy, UnLtd demonstrated the benefits of organizations being skilled and open-minded in asking questions about themselves. UnLtd is adept at using research and bodies of evidence to inform its own ways forward. Katharine and former UnLtd CEO Cliff Prior embodied UnLtd's penchant for constantly looking for better ways to understand the programs UnLtd offers social entrepreneurs. The UnLtd team fervently believes that ongoing research data allows selection of the best methods to achieve their goals. UnLtd regularly conducts evaluations and follow-up research on the effectiveness of its programs, the entrepreneurs it launches, and their positive impacts.

Part of UnLtd's success is its capacity to innovate and expand into communities and age groups that reach entrepreneurs where they are.

Intent on growing the ecosystem beyond the small numbers it could reach with its mentoring, UnLtd started working with universities. Katharine recalled: "Back in 2010 we realized that we couldn't do everything that we wanted to achieve for social entrepreneurs alone. So we decided to set up this ecosystem of support." UnLtd's collaborations with educational institutions enabled it to amplify its own impacts. Its See Change initiative—a partnership with the Higher Education Funding Council for England—aims to embed a culture of social entrepreneurship inside the education system. As Katharine noted at a See Change conference: "It is important to promote understanding and acceptance of social entrepreneurship because kids need their parents to say 'yes, it's good for your career, go for it,' instead of asking them why they aren't just focused studying."[13] The program now includes ninety-plus universities and more than thirty colleges all over the UK to support social entrepreneurs within their institutions so they can get started and thrive. In 2014 UnLtd announced a partnership with the prestigious King's College London to provide opportunities for social enterprise development for students, recent graduates, and staff. At the launch of the King's College initiative, Cliff stated: "We're on the brink of a social entrepreneurship revolution. One in five new start-ups are now social entrepreneurs, and universities are leading the way with one in four start-ups by young people being social. It's time to get started and what better opportunity than King's College London's social entrepreneurship competition?"[14]

UnLtd is intent not only on mainstreaming social entrepreneurship in schools and universities, but also on harnessing the energy and impact intent of a burgeoning number of young people more aware than ever of the world's most pressing social and environmental challenges. Their Young UnLtd online network is the latest place to go for the UK's young social entrepreneurs and supporters. Young UnLtd facilitates opportunities for budding social entrepreneurs, including awards (cash and support), events, tools and resources, case studies, volunteer and training opportunities, as well as intern and partner opportunities.[15]

UnLtd is now a big organization that matches its big ideas. As the leading provider of flexible, personal support to social entrepreneurs in the UK and beyond, it offers a tailored mix of ongoing advice, networking, and practical support, as well as connections to funding. Since its beginnings, UnLtd and its spinoffs have mentored tens of thousands of entrepreneurs determined to change the world for the better, with more than fifteen thousand alumni in the UK alone. The entrepreneurs selected for UnLtd's in-person and online programs benefit from coaching on anything from writing a business plan to finessing a sales pitch deck, to fundraising for growth. As a result, UnLtd award winners are likely to be masters at juggling the demands of a start-up, fusing ideas and actions to grow successful "businesses," and modeling what can happen when some of the best entrepreneurial talent and skills are applied to solving some of the world's worst problems.

UnLtd deliberately focuses on growing the capacity of social entrepreneurs, not their particular scheme for tackling a social problem. **Cliff Prior** described his work with entrepreneurs at UnLtd as "a joy, partly because social entrepreneurs are absolutely full of optimism and ambition to improve the world, and partly because it's my background. . . . I've worked in a lot of different fields—mental health, social housing, community care, offender resettlement, learning disabilities, crisis intervention, counseling troubled young people—but all with the defining common theme of opening up opportunities for people."[16]

UnLtd's social entrepreneurs draw inspiration from teams of professionals and seasoned successful entrepreneurs who contribute to the creation of diverse positive impact start-ups that keep us wondering what will come next. These diversely skilled mentors remind us that growing successful entrepreneurs can have more to do with asking questions than giving answers. Mentors bring to the ecosystem the gift of frequently posing unexpected questions to draw out skills that may be slumbering inside of a budding entrepreneur or a potential investor. Mentors often perceive questions within different (sometimes broader) sets of problems, turning ideas and issues on their head by the mere posing of a "What if?" or a "So what?" query. UnLtd's social entrepreneurs can count on their mentors to raise these challenging questions, testing the limitations of their ideas by asking, "What is it like to be on the receiving end of your product or service?" The UnLtd mentors help social entrepreneurs build the scaffolding for their ventures, while connecting them with relevant professionals, veteran successful entrepreneurs, and other mentors—thus contributing to a stronger, more robust scaffolding for the entire ecosystem. An ecosystem with a shared regard for making the world a better place.

Not surprisingly in a time of global interconnectedness, mentors around the world have taken notice of UnLtd's successes and how it achieved them. UnLtd has been replicated in eleven countries, including India, Thailand, South Africa, China (Hong Kong), and the United States—with more UnLtds in process. These initiatives are exponentially amplifying the impact of UnLtd's mentoring and expanding its positive impact entrepreneurial ecosystem in the UK and across the globe. As a result, UnLtd is now the epicenter of a thriving hub of other mentoring organizations across the planet.

UnLtd USA and Techstars Founder and Mentor: Zoe Schlag

UnLtd USA founder **Zoe Schlag** started her impact career in South America. Feeling jaded by what she had witnessed in international development and aid programs, Zoe was disillusioned by the tremendous power disparities in communities. Because she felt inequities were exacerbated or even spurred on by international aid, Zoe headed to Mumbai to work with UnLtd India to participate in a different, more collaborative, local capabilities-based model. "My time working with UnLtd India challenged me to shift my understanding of tackling poverty—each day as I worked with our UnLtd India investees helping them develop their ventures, I watched a new narrative of entrepreneurship unfold. . . . This kept me wondering who their American equivalents were—the entrepreneurs based in the U.S. developing business models to tackle social problems."[17] Zoe was smitten by the "individuals with the ideas, passion, and entrepreneurial skills to create long-term solutions for some of the world's toughest social, environmental, and civic problems" and wanted to find and support them in her home country.[18] With a team of four fellow visionaries, she launched UnLtd USA in Austin, Texas, which was chosen for its existing vibrant innovation and entrepreneurial culture and ecosystem. UnLtd USA's mission: To find and back the most promising entrepreneurs tackling pressing social and environmental problems.

Only in her late twenties when we first consulted her, Zoe is an entrepreneur for impact entrepreneurs. Like its UK parent, UnLtd USA selected promising social entrepreneurs from around the United States for twelve months of customized support, from workshops to mentoring and networking.[19] UnLtd USA invested in the entrepreneurs' companies, $5,000 if in a seed stage, $10,000 in companies a year old or older. Rather than UnLtd USA taking equity, start-ups were asked to invest in another UnLtd company within three to five years. UnLtd USA's intent was to select the entrepreneurs with the most promise "to [launch] their potential as changemakers—accelerating their progress, developing them as leaders, and preparing their fledgling organizations for further investment and scale."[20]

UnLtd USA provided tangible, measurable support to help ventures not just get off the ground, but thrive. By offering hands-on coaching and training, minimal seed funding and high-level connections with other mentors, industry experts, media, and potential investors, UnLtd USA offered these impact start-ups access to all the capitals necessary to launch. Similar to venture philanthropist Pascal Vinarnic, Zoe and the UnLtd USA mentor team lived by a "give first," "pay it forward" philosophy. In Zoe's words: "We know from the tech world that entrepreneurial ecosystems thrive when they are led by entrepreneurs who reinvest their communities—in fact, Brad Feld and Techstars have pioneered a version of this with their Give

First principle. We believe that embedding this as a cultural norm is what will give this movement staying power, so we've designed pay-it-forward into everything from our seed funding to how we structure our program to how we work with our own partners."[21] UnLtd USA mentors and investors backed more than fifteen world-class impact entrepreneurial start-up teams, including:

- BlueHub Health, a digital platform for patients and health-care providers to collect, store, and share health-care information (acquired by Afoundria)
- Agua Dulce Farm, an organic aquaponic farm in Austin, Texas
- PelotonU, helping working adults earn a college degree debt-free and at five times the pace of community colleges

Thanks to high-quality, steady mentoring, the UnLtd network of entrepreneurs around the world have enacted some incredibly innovative projects, fusing ideas and action for social good, often cutting across cultures and entrepreneurial forms.

A controversial move: Removing silos

But successful mentoring is not without controversy. Seeing the trends before they happen is built into the very DNA of UnLtd. The organization made a conscious choice to embrace a future in which business and social entrepreneurs are not siloed, and in which social impact work in the UK and around the world will be done by all, regardless of the legal description of the organization or business form. This pivoting of UnLtd's strategic direction elicited so much consternation in two of its founding organizations that they seceded from UnLtd with a public protest. They cited "an erosion of the not-for-private-profit principles,"reflecting the conundrum that many social enterprises face: the tug-of-war between the need for sustainability (or profit) and the positive impact.

Despite this controversy, visiting any of the UnLtd offices around the world, especially when entrepreneurs are in residence with mentors, is endlessly inspirational. The UnLtd teams are deeply devoted to nurturing the capacity of entrepreneurs making positive social impact. They invest in gritty, vital, bold entrepreneurs intent on making at least their part of the world a little better. For twenty years, UnLtd's mentoring might has contributed to the growth of these entrepreneurs and positively impactful entrepreneurial ecosystems, placing them at the forefront of the wave of a worldwide impact movement, and challenging our ideas of what an entrepreneur can be. The gutsy projects cultivated and nourished by the global network of the UnLtd family will no doubt leave a permanent mark on the well-being of people—not only in local communities but across the planet.

Pivoting toward a preferred future: Techstars Impact

In October 2017, with prescient foresight of the diminishing silos demarcating entrepreneurship and impact, as well as the seismic shift toward impact being inherent in any entrepreneurial or business enterprise, Zoe Schlag pivoted UnLtd USA toward a new future. In a bold move, UnLtd USA joined forces with the global Techstars to launch Techstars Impact.

Techstars, originally started in 2006 for mainstream entrepreneurs, has evolved into an esteemed worldwide accelerator and network of high-potential start-ups. Its portfolio numbers more than one thousand companies (growing by more than three hundred per year), constituting some $10 billion in market capitalization. Techstars has raised close to $4 billion in capital, including from the Techstars venture capital arm. More than 90 percent of these companies are still active or have been acquired. By creating Techstars Impact Accelerator, Zoe is optimistic about taking the UnLtd USA mission—leveraging entrepreneurship as a tool to solve some of the world's greatest challenges—to a global scale. No stranger to impact enterprises, Techstars has already accelerated companies like Aunt Bertha, the United States' most comprehensive online directory of social service organizations, accessible to those in need; Fig Loans, a lender for low-income borrowers; Zipline, which builds drones to deliver medical supplies in Rwanda; and ConnXus, a business-focused software provider for sustainable sourcing. Folding in UnLtd USA to the Techstars network has enabled Techstars to grow its impact acceleration, gaining Zoe's network and experience in launching its global impact strategy. The accelerator fund is backed by notable Limited Partners that include Morgan Stanley Investment Management's AIP Private Markets team, the Impact America Fund, our own Tingari Foundation, and several high-profile individuals from Austin, including RetailMeNot CEO Cotter Cunningham. The first Techstars Impact Accelerator cohort of impact entrepreneurs from around the globe headed to Austin in 2018. Their entrepreneurial initiatives ranged from health care to affordable housing, security, and gender equity. The entrepreneurs received investment from Techstars Impact Accelerator and participated in an immersive, three-month accelerator program. This Techstars initiative reflects a growing trend, as entrepreneurs and accelerators apply their talents to a world increasingly being tested by population changes, escalating climate events, disappearing jobs, rising inequality, refugee integration, and shrinking civic space. Graduates in 2018 included stars like Pipeline Equity (a tech platform to eliminate gender bias in the workplace), Haven Connect (property management software aimed at streamlining the affordable housing application process), and MDaaS Global (low-cost diagnostic and primary health-care centers for Africa's "next billion").

THE LAUNCHERS

launch·er (noun):

One that launches: such as [a vehicle for launching an idea, an organization into the marketplace]. Nurturing them until they are sustainable.

in·cu·ba·tor (noun):

One that incubates: such as an organization or place that aids the development of new business ventures, especially by providing low-cost commercial space, management assistance, or shared services, until the venture is ready to launch as an independent organization.

ac·cel·er·a·tor (noun):

One that accelerates: such as [a vehicle] that speeds the performance of an action. In the entrepreneurial arena, speeds the transformation of ideas into marketable, positive products and services until the organization is ready to be launched as a sustainable entity.

They are often the epitome of the entrepreneurial spirit without being recognized as entrepreneurs. Yet their entrepreneurial efforts can profoundly contribute to the fabric of any innovation ecosystem. Incubators and accelerators—reflecting the escalating wave of cross-sector entrepreneurialism emerging in cities around the world—support start-ups with mentoring, office space, knowledge, and additional resources. They connect first-time entrepreneurs with serial entrepreneurs and potential investors. Often modeled after Techstars (Boulder, Colorado), Y Combinator (in Silicon Valley), and Capital Factory (Austin, Texas), accelerators' shared spaces are home to entrepreneurs representing tens of thousands of start-ups all over the planet. They have spawned many successful companies, such as Airbnb, Dropbox, Skype, element14, Criteo, Spotify, and Cambridge Silicon Radio. Funded by universities, governments, or corporations, accelerators and incubators create support systems of accountants, lawyers, organizational psychologists, and funders, and creatively curate connections among them.[22]

Incubators and accelerators are increasingly nurturing start-ups intent on positive impact. Europe's first accelerator specifically targeting technology-based social ventures, the UK's Bethnal Green Ventures, has invested some £1.5 million in more than eighty start-ups since 2012, serving more than 6.5 million customers.[23] Impact Hub, an initiative founded in London in 2005, has spawned locations from "Amsterdam to Johannesburg, Singapore to San Francisco." It boasts more than fifteen thousand members in ninety countries.[24] Other examples around the world include the Unreasonable Institute (U.S., now Uncharted); the China Australia Millennial Project (Australia); IMPAQTO (Ecuador); Agora Partnerships (Nicaragua, Mexico, Chile, U.S.); Koga Impact Lab (Paraguay); and Socialab (Chile). All nurture positive impact start-ups by providing tutoring, strategic consulting, and a holistic community and networks. Canada's Centre for Social Innovation builds on this rich heritage.

Centre for Social Innovation: From Canada to the United States

In its relatively short history, Canada's Centre for Social Innovation (CSI)—founded in 2004 by Tonya Surman of the Commons Group, Mary Rowe of Ideas That Matter, Pat Tobin of Canadian Heritage, Margaret Zeidler of Urbanspace, and Eric Meerkamper of RIWI Corp.—has garnered a solid reputation as a cutting-edge catalyst of social ventures. The seeds for CSI were sewn when this group of Canadian entrepreneurs lamented the more challenging contexts their fellow entrepreneurs seemed to face when trying to start and grow social enterprises. They noticed their social entrepreneur colleagues toiling away in costly workspaces, local coffee shops, or their home, often alone and with few resources. So, the group decided to do something. They applied their unrelenting drive, resourcefulness, and creativity to establish CSI. Since those early deliberations, the CSI team has been making a quiet but mighty splash in the shared workspace scene. Their community is home to more than one thousand social enterprises (nonprofits, charities, and social for-profit ventures), employing more than twenty-five hundred people, generating some Can$250 million in combined revenues, and spurring copycat spaces around the world.

The Centre for Social Innovation's forte is building coworking/mentoring spaces that nurture entrepreneurial talent to grow companies intent on positive impact. Each CSI location is essentially an impact entrepreneurial "launch pad." Their meticulously designed coworking spaces ooze cultures of informed creativity, bold thinking, risk-taking, and collaborative problem-solving for learning and growing ideas. The spaces are designed for spontaneous and planned meetings in fun, often funky contexts that exude repurposing, environmental consciousness, and positive impact. Mentors and coaches join the creative fray in both planned sessions and spontaneous gatherings in any of the many cool nooks and crannies.

CSI veteran team members see the creative, values-driven design of the coworking space as the key determinant for fostering entrepreneurial success. With four locations across Toronto, the CSI team enacted all they had learned in Canada in designing the space for their new digs in New York, which is where we visited with then-executive director **Eli Malinsky**.

Situated high above the thronging streets of New York City's Chelsea district, the sprawling 24,000-square-foot space buzzes with ideas. The building, an imposing converted warehouse, has been home to industrial innovation since the early 1930s. The CSI space on the thirty-second floor of the Starrett-Lehigh building on West 26th Street radiates a creative and innovative ambience from every aspect of the space's design. Eli asked, "Can you feel it?" not long into our conversation.

CSI intentionally designed a space that is at once "functional, whimsical, inviting, and energizing."[25] From delicate drawings to in-your-face wall hangings and light fixtures, CSI nourishes ideas with an edgy flavor. The diverse fonts and wording of the sign as you step off the elevator to enter the thirty-second floor is the first hint of "some of the most quirky, funky, office décor you'll find in Manhattan," according to *Convene* magazine.[26] CSI has designed in the answers to its founding questions: How do we tear down the silos that keep organizations apart? How can we best become a catalyst for social change?

CSI has described itself as a convergence space for innovators that aims to "catalyze, connect, and support new ideas that are changing the world."[27] It has developed an avant-garde model for leveraging cross-sector collaboration for social impact. Critical to their formula is the combination of a coworking space, community center, incubator, and hotbed of positive impact culture.

CSI's designers have mastered the art of being progressive without being pretentious, and the shared workspaces provide a context for ideas to spark, knowledge to develop, relationships to flourish, and collaborations to spawn—giving exposure to young social innovators, helping them develop into a cadre of savvy entrepreneurs for the greater good. A mix of cultures, disciplines, and sectors looms large in the intent behind the organization's careful crafting of the tenant population. With a determination to rewire ways of working, and drawing from local businesses and artisans, CSI New York has created any high-tech entrepreneur's fantasy office. The desired community culture is embedded in the design of the space—rows of shared desks, welcoming couches and alcoves for more intimate conversations, funky communal tables—all to encourage ideas testing and sharing, collaborative problem-solving, and network development. Everywhere you look blares "community"—the floor-to-ceiling chalk-drawn mural that details the faces of the hundred-and-fifty-plus social enterprise founders, inspirational quotes like "Be Bold" and "Embrace Chaos" painted on pillars throughout the space, and

Lily Tomlin's call to action on a massive blackboard that fills an entire wall: *"I said, 'Somebody should do something about that.' Then I realized I am somebody."* One massive pillar is painted as a vibrantly colorful floor-to-ceiling signpost that blasts "Meet, Learn, Work, Eat, Share" with arrows pointing in the directions where those actions might be found. The open plan workspace, with its alcoves, lounge areas, coffee spots, shared work tables, along with scheduled workshops or brainstorming sessions, promotes "forced collisions" to encourage conversation when ideas need bouncing, contemplation, and reflection. The repurposed furniture and fixtures emit evidence of other people's industry in times past, including meeting tables transformed from the building's original elevators.

Membership is rewarded by 24/7 access to the workspaces, lounges, meeting rooms, classrooms, Wi-Fi, equipment, programming, mentoring, and an "in" to a vibrant community of passionate changemakers. Tenants have included such diverse social enterprises as 100cameras, which teaches photography to marginalized children; Toilet Hackers, a start-up focused on providing sanitation around the world; SyStem, a "computer garden" for urban farming that grows food without soil or harmful chemicals (winner of the 2017 Zahn Innovation Competition)[28]; and the New York representatives of impact icons Ashoka and Echoing Green.

The CSI team views their role as "sparking instigation," not as the instigating force itself.[29] Their deliberately nurtured culture is part design, part alchemy. With a mix of communal spaces, the CSI space caters to a diverse spectrum and encourages "serendipitous collision" among all who walk the concrete floors. Consistent with Steven Johnson's concept of "the adjacent possible" (from *Where Good Ideas Come From*), CSI encourages a diversity of inhabitants in the space to facilitate peer conversations (ideas sharing, mentoring, challenging, affirming) and connections in ways that enable innovative ideas to transform into action. The CSI network is geared for cross-pollination. These interactions are stimulated and even engineered by CSI team members with job titles like community animator and exchange community animator. Eli told us:

> CSI's community animators are responsible for the social and psychological experience of the space. . . . They get to know community members—their needs, their interests, their frustrations—and connect them to internal and external resources that will help move them toward their goals.

With its un-siloed, dynamic workspaces, CSI—while steering clear of labels like incubator or accelerator, and instead choosing "launch pad"—provides much more than peer-to-peer conversations as budding impact entrepreneurs work together. CSI facilitates structured learning opportunities and access to impact investors or other potential funding sources. Its programs, events, and rituals are all geared toward fostering optimal social impact culture and action. The weekly "Salad Club," where CSI supplies the greens and everybody else brings an ingredient, offers a casual forum for everyone to chat and get to know each other and their work. The waffle breakfasts have a similar intent and effect, and the regular "Six Degrees of Social Innovation" gathering is part social event/part social experiment, choreographing a diverse mix of people to mingle, listen to presentations, or enjoy something entirely unexpected.

CSI Summits are designed to spur collaboration and shared learning opportunities.[30] CSI hosts a diverse array of workshops every month on topics that include community-based research, employment and labor law for entrepreneurs, revenue generation and business models for social enterprises, collaborative governance, networking social enterprises, and measuring impacts. And while the organization does not see itself as the architect of specific content details, it is an architect of knowledge and relationship building. As Eli mentioned in our conversation: "We don't develop curricula: We are really a platform, so what we try to do is be the connective tissue between people who have and people who need—whether that's knowledge or expertise or schooling or what have you."

The teams at CSI in New York and Toronto understand that the social innovation movement is gathering momentum in North America and around the world. Eli calls the wave of interest and action around social impact "a surge in the purpose-driven life," fueled by technology and Millennials, Gen Zers, and Baby Boomers who refuse to accept the increasing disparities of those at opposite ends of the socioeconomic spectrum. CSI is at the forefront of this movement.

ENTREPRENEURSHIP FOR IMPACT INSIGHTS SUMMARY

Educators like Saïd Business School's Pamela Hartigan; entrepreneur mentors like UnLtd's Cliff Prior, Katharine Danton, or Zoe Schlag; and start-up launchers like CSI's Tonya Surman and Eli Malinsky see and foster positive impact not as a separate discipline but as a problem-solving *approach*. Their contribution to the impact ecosystem shows how the fundamentals of entrepreneurship—combining innovation, opportunity, and resourcefulness to create enterprises—can and must be applied to improve people's lives by addressing market or government failures. Educators, mentors, and launchers are integral to the impact entrepreneurial ecosystem because their work enables others to realize and progress their ideas and initiatives toward a future where social entrepreneurship as a separate activity, discipline, or sector is redundant. They are working toward a planetary ecosystem in which every entrepreneur is positively impactful on social, environmental, and economic fronts, not just a conscious few.

CHAPTER 7

The Ecosystem Shapers

They are the big thinkers, the nuanced deliberators, the consequence detectors with a honed awareness of how one action or reaction impacts people, communities, and natural environments across all parts of a system. They are the ecosystem shapers.

It is increasingly recognized that entrepreneuring occurs in a complex interconnected set of systems. A broad interconnected, nested set of ever-changing ecosystems populated by diverse arrays of critical thinkers, makers, and doers. Ecosystems shapers pay attention to all aspects of the ecosystem—the individual elements and the dynamic processes that flow among the elements.

In this chapter, we introduce some of the inspiring innovators who shape ecosystems for the greater good, like Nick O'Donohoe, whose big picture, long-term thinking launched the massive trailblazing national social investment bank in the UK. We meet **Aria Finger,** the CEO of DoSomething.org who is passionate about mobilizing a whole generation of young people around the globe to contribute to a better world. We also share the story of "fierce" South African Colleen Magner, who exemplifies the multitalented complexity of many of the behind-the-scenes impact innovators. Subtle movers, shakers and ecosystems facilitators like Colleen and contributor to our book Moira Were are crucial components of any impact entrepreneurial ecosystem.

Each of these people and the roles they inhabit—industry maker, Millennial mobilizer, ecosystem facilitator—are critical parts of the intricate mosaic that constitutes the entire entrepreneurial ecosystem. The relationships among all the elements, and the processes that bind the elements—need to be nurtured for an entire system to thrive.

THE INDUSTRY MAKER: NICK O'DONOHOE AND BIG SOCIETY CAPITAL

Upon first encountering **Nick O'Donohoe**, you might not suspect this unassuming, deliberative, charismatic man with the lilting Irish accent was charged with creating an industry in the United Kingdom, if not the world. The UK has been at the forefront of impact thinking and doing, and Nick is one of the people leading the charge.

Starting his adult life studying mathematical economics and statistics, Nick initially put those number skills to work at two global financial powerhouses, Goldman Sachs and JP Morgan. Those financial principles seemed to continually lurk in his consciousness with social endeavors. At JP Morgan, Nick embraced early on the notion that entrepreneurs and investors could use market tools to solve some of the world's most pressing social and environmental challenges. He was a pioneer as senior sponsor of the Social Finance Unit. The next step for Nick was to put the learning from JP Morgan into practice on a national and global level.

The UK government has spearheaded many initiatives to build its social investment market. In 2000 the UK Department of Treasury established a Social Investment Task Force with a mandate to conduct an "urgent but considered assessment of the ways in which the UK could achieve a radical improvement in its capacity to create wealth, economic growth, employment, and an improved social fabric in its poorest communities." The task force proposed a number of measures, including tax relief, the development of community development financial institutions, the creation of dedicated social lenders, and the creation of a government-backed social investment wholesale institution. This bold innovation signaled the emerging importance of social enterprise for governments and led to the creation of Big Society Capital (BSC).

When BSC was announced in 2011 by then-Prime Minister David Cameron, along with founder Sir Ronald Cohen, Cohen stated:

> Today's launch of BSC marks the culmination of ten years of thought and effort by many individuals and organizations. BSC is the first of a new kind of organization devoted to providing finance in the interest of society. The depth and breadth of The Big Society Trust and Big Society Capital boards, and an anticipated £600 million in initial funding, will enable BSC to improve the flow of capital to social organizations from charitable foundations, institutional investors, companies, and private individuals. . . . Innovations such as the social impact bond and a burgeoning array of organizations operating across the social sector suggest that we are on the cusp of a revolution. The social sector now has the prospect of attracting the funding necessary to boost social entrepreneurs, much as venture capital and private equity started to do for business some three decades ago.[1]

With a simple mission to "transform social investments," BSC aims to facilitate investment in social sector organizations—charities, social enterprises, voluntary and community organizations—so they can access new sources of capital in order to grow. Rather than directly invest in social sector initiatives, BSC enables social investment intermediaries like banks, cooperatives, and impact investment funds. BSC's goal is to create a bridge between investors seeking both social and financial returns and frontline social organizations seeking capital. In short: to facilitate a British impact investment industry, to nurture and grow the impact ecosystem in the UK and beyond.

At the official launch in April 2012, Cameron asserted: "[BSC] is about applying business principles to tackle social problems on a sustainable basis—the institution's innovative funding structure carries no cost to the taxpayer and represents a new partnership between banks, government, and the social sector."[2] Britain's leading banks—Lloyds, HSBC, Barclays, and the Royal Bank of Scotland—joined the push to raise BSC's profile and propensity to fund social innovation in the UK. They jointly added another £200 million, raising the total capital pool to £600 million. When their commitment was announced, former Barclays Chief Executive Bob Diamond said: "We are delighted to support the government's efforts to transform the UK social finance market. . . . This is a ground-breaking initiative with the potential to be the catalyst for creating a sustainable social finance model in the UK."[3]

As a social investment wholesaler, BSC aims to increase investment in society by supporting organizations that directly invest in impact enterprises. These direct investors contribute in multiple ways: provide a bigger range of financial services to impact organizations, raise capital for onward investment, or help impact initiatives become more sustainable and resilient. BSC was also tasked with championing social investment with policymakers, investors, and stakeholders in the sector and the public at large. Since its inception, BSC has committed more than £525 million to more than two hundred and seventy organizations, many of these with co-investors. Organizations benefiting from BSC's disbursement of funds include Charity Bank, where savers can invest ethically and where impact enterprises and charities can secure loans they can't otherwise find; ClearlySo, an impact institution that works "exclusively with high-impact businesses, charities, and funds by supporting their capital raising activity through financial advisory work and introducing them to institutional and individual investors who share their objectives and values"[4]; and Real Lettings Property Fund, which funds real estate purchases for leasing to homeless families in London by St Mungo's charity.

BSC was one of a suite of initiatives instituted by the UK government to bring impact thinking and doing into the twenty-first century, including a creative suite of tax breaks and specific institutions that help build diversity and momentum in impact investment availability.

BSC has not been without its critics or controversy. Many of the people we interviewed, regardless of country or professional perspective, lamented that growing social enterprises, like growing any enterprise to scale, is not just about the money. They are about the innovation ecosystem, about developing management teams who can design and enact successful business plans, about building networks that enhance the organization's potential for success, about growing skills in scaling the venture for maximum impact, and about implementing sustainable business models exuding resilience through tough times. BSC's mandate was to ensure improvements in these indicators. But the task was not without challenges. Many impact investors feel angst about the hurdles faced in finding social enterprises ready and worthy of investment. The UK government's initial vision document acknowledged that ignoring all of the pieces in the social enterprise system might exacerbate these difficulties. However, the architects of the plan believed the sheer availability of very targeted investments in social impact intermediaries, especially those with mentoring capacity, would go a long way toward mitigating those difficulties.

One very vocal critic of BSC, former British Labour MP Leslie Huckfield, claimed that a social investment bank and other government social impact initiatives were merely a sign of the UK government's increasingly heavy reliance on more private investment to deliver public services.[5] This diminishing capacity of governments to fund social services was noted by several of the changemakers we interviewed in other parts of the world, reflecting a growing awareness that governments are increasingly strapped for cash and relinquishing provision of many social services. Hence the imperative for more resourceful approaches to encouraging the global movement toward all of society assuming awareness and responsibility for impact, and not just relying on governments.

The enormity of the challenge in creating an entire impact investment market was not lost on Nick O'Donohoe. He said, "While the UK has made very good progress to help make social investment a reality, it is still a small and rather fragile ecosystem."[6] Nick has conceded that even with the UK's global leadership in this arena, developing the social investment market could take decades.

Despite the critiques and controversies, BSC is an exemplar. With the almost daunting task of creating a movement, BSC's existence, alongside other initiatives, highlights the potentially instrumental and innovative role governments can play in how they encourage and facilitate the impact ecosystem and investments in it. The UK's suite of initiatives highlights the benefit for the greater good when there is bipartisan agreement on values and action around social entrepreneurship and impact, and the importance of a positive policy environment. With all of these ingredients to support the development of a social economy ecosystem, and with the existence of robust financial investment vehicles, the UK is leading the way. In the years since BSC's establishment, other governments, including Australia, Bangladesh, and Germany, have considered proposals to launch their own adaptations of the concept.

THE YOUTH MOBILIZER: ARIA FINGER WITH DOSOMETHING

In a company where being over twenty-six is the hallmark of "old," **Aria Finger** is anything but. In her mid-thirties and acknowledged "Chief Old Person" at DoSomething.org, Aria is a dynamo whose actions have matched her big ideas. Her lightning-speed combination of knowledge, skills, and passion has equipped her to be an integral part of the momentous scaling of DoSomething.org.

Founded in 1993 by actor Andrew Shue and his childhood friend,

Michael Sanchez, DoSomething.org is now one of the largest global organizations in the world for young people enacting social change. It pledges to "tackle any cause, anytime, anywhere." Aria's intense gaze conveys the radical focus that enables her and the DoSomething team to effectively mobilize millions of Millennials and Gen Zers to do good. Her zealousness and commitment exude from every aspect of her being. Aria's six-foot stature—along with her compassion and obvious drive—only adds to her aura as a doer and a changemaker. Like the wall-sized mural in the DoSomething offices that visually blasts "Because Apathy Sucks," Aria stands in the way of apathy in how she lives.

When interviewed by her alma mater, Washington University, Aria reflected on the key influences in her early life that impact her now.[7] Aria grew up in the Bronx and then Westchester County in New York as one of four children. She credits her parents with imbuing in her a sense of social justice and the importance of working to combat the unfairness of inequality of opportunity. Aria saw firsthand how early involvement in social justice advocacy and action can shape lifelong commitment.

Aria is a self-described "math nerd" and a "big athlete"—different, yet highly relevant skills that she puts into practice at DoSomething. Through sports, she learned the benefits of drive, determination, good coaching, practice, and teamwork to achieve an end goal. And with mathematics, Aria developed her capacity to immerse herself in the numbers, to see patterns, to ensure that business models are sustainable.

Aria strongly believes that anyone who wants to do social justice work needs to have a background in economics. She says, "It's a matter of understanding numbers to make sense of how the world works." She had an internship with a Washington, D.C., financial consulting firm that taught her how to use her economic, statistical mind in business, and after graduation, Aria worked with her father to start a social enterprise that helped high-achieving, low-income African American and Hispanic middle school students get into honors and advanced placement classes.

When she set about looking for a full-time job, Aria was drawn to social ventures. Intent on proving to her college classmates that working at a not-for-profit could be efficient, effective, and world-changing, Aria set out to do just that. By scouring Idealist.org, she came across DoSomething.org. She recalls, "I had never heard of [DoSomething]. It was a tiny organization with just six employees. They empower young people to take action on every issue under the sun. To me, that sounded so fabulous, in addition to their sort of cheeky, fun, exciting vibe."[8] Aria was attracted to the job description. Apparently the ideal person for the job was someone who was "equally comfortable watching *The Daily Show* and reading *The Economist*." Aria clinched the job and became an integral part of the meteoric growth of the organization. In the ensuing years, Aria relished doing a little bit of everything—coming up with new campaign ideas, writing content for the website, cold-calling sponsors, developing ways to engage more teens in for-purpose pursuits.

Within two years of starting with DoSomething, Aria was promoted to director of business development. Her finesse with numbers helped grow the organization's income streams. When successively promoted over the next few years to chief operating officer, Aria was thrilled at each step along the way. She says, "A lot of people are allergic to numbers, but by looking at an organization's expenses, you understand what its priorities are. I was excited to learn new things."[9] Don't mistake the youthful face and down-to-earth use of Millennial colloquialisms for any underestimation of Aria's capacity and drive. She is a savvy businesswoman.

After seven years with DoSomething and feeling perhaps that she had reached her "use-by date," Aria talked with then-CEO Nancy Lublin. In that meeting Aria told Nancy that as she'd been at DoSomething for so long, she should "probably get going." Nancy was not letting Aria go that easily. Instead, after much discussion, Aria was given the go-ahead to start TMI, a parallel business arm of DoSomething. The name was a tongue-in-cheek reference to "too much information." As Aria explains:

> TMI was an idea I had been bouncing around for a little while. Not only do we see a lot of young people want to participate in social change, we see a lot of brands that want to do it as well [but don't have the tools or experience to do it well]. So we use our expertise in marketing and motivating young people, and connect them to brands [like Keds, Microsoft, and Foot Locker]. All of the additional revenue of TMI goes back into DoSomething, allowing us to do more campaigns at even greater scale.[10]

TMI evolved into a successful in-house strategic consulting agency with a new name: DoSomething Strategic. DoSomething Strategic works with corporate brands and nonprofits on youth, social change, and technology. DoSomething Strategic effectively draws on the institutional knowledge and experience of DoSomething with youth around the world to help other companies and nonprofits gain insight into the youth culture and tap into the youth market for social good. Clients include the likes of Foot Locker, Microsoft, and Spotify. Shared space and other economies of scale keep overhead down for both organizations, and they pride themselves on running efficiently and cost-effectively. DoSomething Strategic revenue enables DoSomething to take risks it might not otherwise be able to fund, such as forays into new countries.

Thanks to Aria and the dedicated DoSomething teams, the organization sets the standard for mobilizing young people around causes that matter to them. In a 2016 blog post, Aria wrote: "If you don't think Millennials are paying attention, think again. After the Charleston massacre left nine dead last June, DoSomething.org reached out to its members—aged 13 to 25—for their responses to the shooting. Within days, we were bombarded with over 26,000 messages from young

Americans who described themselves as 'disgusted,' 'heartbroken,' and 'ashamed.'"[11] So Aria and her fellow "movers" did something. They set about amplifying young people's voices and gave them a tangible way to keep their schools safer from gun violence. The Guns Out campaign was born, a national initiative aimed at activating thousands of students to demand their college presidents take a public stand against guns on campuses across the country.

DoSomething's initiatives were made possible by Aria's bold "asks" of all and sundry to step up. She and her team proactively approached celebrity spokespersons, created canny public awards lists, and targeted powerful sponsors for specific initiatives who would also gain by their involvement. They ensured that campaigns and their quirky names appealed to the teens and young adults they were seeking to engage; artfully deployed the campaigns on their target audience's preferred social media platforms; forged strategic partnerships with school systems, sponsors, and patrons; and cleverly curated a culture of bold, out-of-the-box, collaborative decision-making processes.

Other DoSomething campaigns run the gamut of issues across the globe. Aria was instrumental in the Teens for Jeans campaign, which clothed half of all homeless New York City youth in just four weeks. Her work with DoSomething is full of other successes: The Give a Spit About Cancer campaign has been a large source of referrals (over 8,000) to the Be the Match registry for bone marrow transplants in the United States (resulting in more than fifty matches so far). Their Power to the Period campaign aims to provide period products for many of the 3.5 million Americans who experience homelessness each year, and Four-legged Finishers uses this generation's love for their pets to help educate others about the effects of cigarette smoke on pet health.

Create strategic partnerships

During Aria's tenure, and with full credit to former CEO Nancy Lublin, DoSomething has implemented strategic partnerships with celebrities around causes dear to their hearts. The organization was savvy in getting noticed by celebrities. In its annual "Celebs Gone Good" list, DoSomething has been able to amplify the impact it already achieves through existing celebrity partnerships by publishing annual "best at doing good" summaries.[12] Each year, DoSomething publishes the Top 20 celebrities who've "gone good" in any given year, and also selects five new "Celebs to Watch" in the coming year.

DoSomething's cheeky, fun, exciting vibe has not only held Aria captive for over a decade, but has also fueled her rise in the organization from campaign associate and one of six employees to the top job as the CEO of DoSomething Strategic's sixty employees. In that same time frame, DoSomething has gone from fewer than one hundred thousand members to more than five million members; from under $500,000 to over $6 million in corporate revenue; and from being mostly U.S.-based campaigns to working in more than a hundred and thirty countries. Lofty achievements, no doubt exceeding the wildest imaginings of the founders when they started the organization in 1993.[13]

Capitalize on social media and nontraditional platforms

Mobilizing five to six million teens across the planet around social and environmental causes is no easy feat. As evidenced by the success of these diverse and far-reaching campaigns, DoSomething has mastered the capacity to reach teens where they are, in their own language. DoSomething understands that teens are connected 24/7, not just to each other, but also to world events. DoSomething also understands that its target generation is more globally minded than any previous generation. Survey after survey reveals that more than 90 percent of teens who have internet access, particularly those in developed economies, go online daily. For the Gen Z generation, much of how they live their lives is tied to technology—they group chat, YouTube, Snapchat, and Instagram—with omnipresent connection to their peers.

DoSomething thus "[makes] it really easy and fun and sexy and entertaining and social to get involved." Aria and her DoSomething colleagues see this as a massive opportunity. "Young people are connecting and engaging with social media and technology more than ever. As a result, engaging them to a greater extent in activities [using] technology becomes easy and extremely effective."[14] To that end, DoSomething uses texting and an array of the newest social media platforms. It aims to cut through the barriers facing anyone desiring to make a positive impact—time, resources, funds, support networks, and so on. As the DoSomething website has stated, "We work to empower our members to change the world."[15]

Encourage diversity and collaboration

In the worldwide quest to mobilize young people, Aria leads a deliberately diverse young team, all passionate about making the world better. DoSomething's work culture fosters passion and innovation through fun but serious workplace rituals. Their "no-eating-at-your-desk" policy encourages breaks from the intense work for socializing and cross-fertilizing of ideas over a coffee. They convene weekly innovation meetings in which anyone—no matter their job level—can present ideas. The interdepartmental and campaign meetings ensure open communication so nothing gets lost. Twice a year, they implement a "Fail Fest" (an idea adopted from the Omidyar Network Executive Forum), in which a team member gives a PowerPoint presentation about a mistake they made and three lessons they learned—all while donning a pink feather boa. As the role model she is, Aria has presented at Fail Fest when her own failure held learning gems. In another attempt to trigger new connections, new ideas, and new relationships in their workplace, every six months the DoSomething team takes part in a "Reaping" process in which everyone changes desks or workstations.

DoSomething would not be where it is today if not for Aria and her predecessor's savvy business skills. When we asked the secret to her own success, Aria said: "Maintain radical focus: Do the most efficient, most effective delivery. Cut the inefficient, the ineffective." Pretty astute words for the then-thirty-two-year-old. Aria has shown how maintaining radical focus positively impacts all bottom lines. The DoSomething/DoSomething Strategic duo has effectively implemented a diverse stream of sustainable revenues that enable this organization not only to grow, but also to take risks. With DoSomething Strategic providing a steady stream of clients, DoSomething has also implemented a sustainable business model through strategic corporate partnerships. Aria has been instrumental in partnering with companies for campaigns and over the years has achieved sponsorship from powerhouses like H&M, American Express, Johnson & Johnson, Aéropostale, Sprint, and H&R Block. In describing her own success in building the business model and the corporate sponsorship that is a key part of their sustainability, Aria said, "I wasn't selling widgets, I was selling social change . . . And I knew that our campaigns would also truly benefit the corporate sponsor."

Not content to just do good by empowering and engaging young adults to "do" for a social or environmental challenge, Aria sees her role as facilitating an entire generation with the mindset, will, and skills to contribute to ameliorating those challenges. Aria loves her job, finds working with young people exciting, and marvels that they may be too idealistic, too fearless, and too fun. A familiar refrain of older generations observing younger! Not surprisingly, at the seasoned age of twenty-nine, Aria graced the cover for *Crain's New York Business* list of "40 Under Forty" in 2012. In 2016 she was a World Economic Forum Young Global Leader.

Aria intuitively understands what research on volunteering at all ages has long demonstrated: that people who volunteer when they are young are more likely to volunteer later in life, more likely to be engaged citizens and to vote. Volunteering for a cause has been proven to boost social skills and empathy, and to help people develop talents and find new strengths. A natural visionary, Aria also sees this wider contribution to society at large, beyond doing good in service of a particular cause promoted by DoSomething. She believes that empowering people to volunteer and serve contributes to society's happiness scale: "One of the top things that make people happy is doing things for others . . . [by engaging young people to do good] I think we can create a generation of happier [people]."[16] Volunteering gives young people a sense of place and connection. It also opens them to new experiences, people, and potential career paths.

THE ECOSYSTEM FACILITATOR, AN "INVISIBLE MIDDLE": COLLEEN MAGNER AND REOS PARTNERS

Behind **Colleen Magner's** beaming megawatt smile is a deep and abiding concern for South Africa's future. Colleen admits: "I am in a worried space." And she is not alone. While The World Bank described South Africa's peaceful political transition from apartheid to democracy as "one of the most remarkable political feats of the past century,"[17] as we turn toward the 2020s, South Africa remains vulnerable.

Reminders of South Africa's troubled and triumphant history and fragile present play out in the socioeconomic fabric of the nation. South Africa has a fragile dual economy outranking most other countries on indicators of disparity. In the two-plus decades since the new republic was created in 1994, some headway has been made in redressing socioeconomic and racial inequalities. But an ailing economy along with steadily increasing unemployment and pressure on power and water supplies has sustained inequalities. Exclusion prevalent in twentieth-century apartheid South Africa remains systemic in twenty-first century South Africa. More recently, the country has suffered in the wake of low commodity prices, slowing demand from China, and uncertainty about Brexit.

South Africa's political context has equally been afflicted with turmoil. The government has come under fire after a series of corruption scandals, struggles to contain labor demands and accompanying crippling strikes, and an inability to stop the outflow of capital. Efforts at land reform have fallen short of expectations. According to the World Economic Forum, in South Africa the richest 20 percent of the population accounts for more than 60 percent of total consumption, while the bottom 20 percent accounts for only 4 percent of the country's consumption.[18] With 60 percent of the country under age thirty, and almost 50 percent of those unemployed, it is no wonder Colleen is concerned. The 2015 and 2019 Afrobarometer public attitudes surveys reveal that a majority of South Africans share a deep sense of unease, believing that the country is headed in the wrong direction, having failed to advance the country on a range of socioeconomic indicators, including personal safety, economic circumstances, employment opportunities, racial relations, and disparities between rich and poor.[19] Colleen sees her country as suffering under the weight of conflicting narratives:

> The private sector naively thought: Let's just get on with the business of making money, keep the economy churning. Government got on with the business of providing services for the poor, sustaining the narrative of "We will provide" . . . hoping the provision would result in votes. They buried their heads in the sand in terms of understanding the scale of the problem. Both narratives have been disastrous. . . . The power brokers are seeing dichotomies . . . yet there is so much gray.

Colleen continued,

> As hard as we've tried to fix it, we haven't bridged the divide. This is not just a South African phenomenon. It's a global phenomenon. It is about proportional poverty, not absolute poverty. . . . In South Africa, most black people are very poor, unemployed, living on the poverty line. There is a small middle class, which is now mixed. Most white people live in that middle class. A bigger portion of the middle class is more black than it was, but they are

considered the elite. . . . So there's a populist backlash that is angry, that is disillusioned.

It is against this volatile backdrop that Colleen seems to vacillate between anguish and hope. Throughout our consultation, her ideas swung between almost polar opposite statements: "South Africa has lost its way," "We are a strong country," "We are a ticking time bomb," "We have enormous resilience," "It is a near-impossible task to deal with the social ills we currently face," "In any one day, I come across amazing individuals doing amazing things."

Despite her vacillation, Colleen acts in service of hope. A natural affinity for numbers and economics has given Colleen a strong foundation in rules, regulations, and numbers, reflected in her dual degree in law and economics. Her master's degree in organizational change and knowledge management conveys her capacity to bridge between the known and unknown, past and future, hope and despair. A natural systems thinker, Colleen envisages distant futures while simultaneously learning from the past.

The invisible middle

Colleen's capacity to bridge the ideal and the opposite, the macro and micro, the short and the long term, the past, present, and future, places her squarely in the category of changemakers that she calls the "invisible middle." These changemakers are the glue that makes change happen through a variety of means that are not as salient as the publicly bold actions of entrepreneurs or impact investors.

Management consultants, educators, creative administrators in government and nongovernmental institutions, all embody the invisible middle. These invisible middle ecosystem facilitators are critical to the health and evolution of the entrepreneurial ecosystem because they are masters of process, relationships, and mediation. As wizards of nuances, they are experts at orchestrating processes that fuel positive change. Having innate understandings of the dynamics among various parts and actors in the ecosystem, they see patterns well before others take notice. They are simultaneously adept at big picture thinking and local minute details. Invisible middles plant positive "ideas seeds" in diverse, multitudinous places throughout the ecosystem: by word of mouth, person to person, in workshops and other training opportunities, presentations at conferences and other speaking engagements, and through traditional media and digital social media.

These professionals are skilled at brokering connections and enhanced relationships among ecosystem participants to create connected networks. Invisible middles are often expert facilitators, adroitly but subtly choreographing individuals and groups getting together to spark ideas and information and skills exchanges. Invisible middles work their magic in quiet modesty, rarely seeking the spotlight.

Colleen embodies all of these attributes, enabling her and other invisible middles to bridge innovative ideas with action and impact. Throughout her career, Colleen has been a connector, networker, educator, researcher, writer, futures thinker, mentor, thought leader, innovator and entrepreneur in the facilitation space, as well as a challenger of the status quo. Colleen, in describing the "middles," uses fellow South African Alan Fowler's term "interlocutor." Another "pracademic," Fowler has been a Visiting Fellow at The World Bank, a founder of impact organizations, and an academic, consultant, researcher, and author. Colleen quotes Fowler's seminal work on the role of interlocutors as "assembling actors, guiding interaction, and embedding action in institutions. Interlocutors are not external to the outcome—they're not 'consultants' [in the traditional sense]. Quite the contrary—they hold deep commitment and attachment to the outcome."

Reos Partners

Colleen is passionately dedicated to enhanced positive outcomes for more people. With like-minded colleagues, she co-founded a different kind of consultancy, Reos Partners, to facilitate systemic change. Under Colleen's leadership, Reos Partners has developed a diverse and rigorous set of transformative methodologies for systemic change. The Reos team specializes in facilitating processes where people can work together to construct new realities, better futures.[20]

Reos Partners uses leading-edge processes to facilitate corporations, government, and nongovernment organizations (NGOs) in tackling their own challenges as well as intractable societal challenges. Reos Partners initiatives around process have been at the forefront of global thinking and doing regarding positive impact. These initiatives include the following:

- Sustainable Food Lab (global)

Launched in 2004, the Sustainable Food Lab was established to create living examples of mainstream, market-based sustainable fresh food supply chains from "farm to fork." Now a global collaborative initiative, the Sustainable Food Lab involves food system stakeholders around the world, including business, government, and civil society leaders from Europe, North America, and Latin America.

- Southern Africa Food Lab

In early 2009, Reos Partners joined with a group of diverse local collaborators to build an "innovation- and action-oriented Social Lab aimed at enhancing food security in southern Africa."[21] Stakeholders from corporate, grassroots, NGO, academic, and government sectors all work together to transform agriculture and food from farm to table, across the continent's south.

- Brazil Education Scenarios

Reos Partners brought together administrators, educators, counselors, students, and other key stakeholders in education. Using experiential futures scenario methodologies, the Reos team facilitated meaningful conversations and subsequent collaborative action across professions and sectors. This in turn stimulated national dialogue and action to combat the challenges in Brazilian education.

- Possible Futures for Health and Health Equity in the USA

In collaboration with the U.S.-based Robert Wood Johnson Foundation, Reos Partners convened a multi-stakeholder team of leaders from the U.S. health-care system. The objective was to catalyze open and reflective strategic thinking and conversation about the possible futures of health and health equity in the United States. Reos Partners facilitated conversations around what action was needed in the present to ensure the most equitable, cost-effective health care for the U.S. population by the late 2020s.

- Sustainable Oceans Lab (global)

The Sustainable Oceans Lab is a global initiative launched in 2015 that brings together diverse stakeholders from around the planet, including African biologists, European oil industry executives, Mexican fishermen, and traditional leaders from small island states to share ideas and knowledge on the challenges of cross-sectoral collaboration on a large scale. Their common goal: to facilitate sustainable oceans as the global population and its associated waste escalates through the 2020s.[22]

- Health Futures Australia

Obesity has been named one of the top three social challenges globally, with an estimated cost of $2 trillion. In Australia, 25 percent of children and 63 percent of adults are clinically overweight or obese, and those numbers are rising, along with associated health issues like type 2 diabetes, cardiovascular disease, musculoskeletal conditions, and some cancers. Reos Partners, in collaboration with Australian government agencies, designed this initiative as a multiyear, system-wide collaboration platform for making substantive positive impacts in the prevention of chronic disease in Australia.

In a move reflecting similar dedication and commitment to facilitating better futures for South Africa and its people, when asked how that might happen, Colleen responded with both thought and action. She documented her reflections about the conundrum both in her country and herself. In an article titled *The Invisible Middles* (later posted as a blog),[23] Colleen wrote:

> Today is South Africa's twenty-first Freedom Day, an appropriate day to reflect on the country's step into adulthood. I was recently asked the kind of question I'm used to asking, but I realized not used to being asked: "If you cast yourself forward to 2030 in South Africa, what would a good picture be and what are the steps that lead to this reality?" It was a disconcerting struggle for me to answer the question: "What could South Africa look like if the picture was better than it is now?" The obvious answers came to me first: There will be a reduced gap between rich and poor, more people will be in meaningful work, there will be better use of our scarce but still accessible shared resources, and so on. I think I even quoted some of the NDP's [South Africa's National Development Plan] targets. Then I ran out of what to say, and needed to pause: My answers didn't feel convincing or alive to me. . . .
>
> In imagining the future, I realized the importance of a number of "invisible middles" playing their critical, but not always obvious role. Invisible middles are the people, organizations, and groups who fly under the radar. They are not in the press, they are not the first line of public scrutiny, and they are not big or influential enough to effect change

independently. What makes them unique is that they have the purpose and ability to engage both the engine room and those steering the ship. They understand the trade-offs and conflicting interests between different sectors and yet know that there are also places of shared interest and concern. . . . In our work, I have come across many invisible middles working across sectors in South Africa, whether it be in organizations working with local government and traditional authorities on land reform, or people working within both corporate boardrooms and stokvels [invitation-only clubs of twelve or more people that function as rotating credit unions or saving schemes] on more inclusive financial products. These individuals and their organizations have the ability to "assemble actors": what we in Reos call "convening." The stepping up part will happen when there is more considered attention given to "guiding the interaction" as Fowler explains. . . .

So for me if the story begins in 2015 and ends in 2030, there will be multiple initiatives guided by the invisible middles to address unemployment, land reform, health care, energy, sustainable food supply, regional integration, social protection, infrastructure, and other burning issues. The invisible middles are critical connectors in South Africa, an environment that so often experiences intractable division. We won't necessarily all know about these invisible middles or hear about them in the press. But as we more actively seek them out and notice their role, we might experience a change in ourselves—how we make sense of our shared challenges, who to work with, and how we choose to act together.

Against the volatile landscape of her nation's challenges, Colleen Magner has a sustained worry: "In any one day, I come across amazing individuals doing amazing things—but not adding up to the kind of social change that will shift the trend—which is the massive divide. We are at a stalemate. Pushing hard—divide not budging . . . maybe the system needs to be more disrupted to change." Colleen Magner also has a dream: to see the multitude of small social innovation initiatives grow into a movement—move from small to systemic. The invisible little processes amalgamating with the larger flow of positives:

> There are enormous amounts of good will and resilience in this country from what we've been through. As much as there are forces of worry, there are thousands of small initiatives that keep things together. But the problem is they don't add up to a whole collective effort. Different parts of the whole are given voice . . . but they are all too small . . . [and] fall short. There is no South African story of our futures at the moment. It's fragmented . . . and in this mayhem, intent on facilitating meaningful tackling of the big issues facing South Africa—water, land, job creation, education, food security— is critical. . . . We need 4–5 initiatives, intentional efforts to bring together—to tip the scale about belief in what's possible.

Colleen's hope is not without caveats: "Change won't come without lots of disruption. Pressure and pain will increase. As a member of the comfortable middle class, I don't want that. Therefore we have to let go of [acrimony, corruption] . . . to achieve a delicate balance of managing disruption and staying connected to each other. We have the ability to do that." She sees South Africa's preferred future as one in which the currently divided national narratives transform into a language of oneness, a oneness in which no South African is excluded. Colleen says: "Our future needs to be in the sentiment, words, narratives of the people. At the moment, the sentiment, narrative, words have regressed. Not divisive or confrontational. For a better South Africa, new narratives are needed. We could say the same about many other countries, if not the world."

Invisible middles like Colleen Magner are critical to any ecosystem because they simultaneously pay attention to the big picture, the entire ecosystem, and the glue that binds elements of ecosystems together—the connections among the people and organizations that constitute the ecosystem. More than most others within an ecosystem, invisible middles think more deeply about interactions between couplings of people and organizations within and across ecosystems. They work tirelessly and strategically to create and nurture those couplings and groupings that will ultimately positively impact both the individual element and the ecosystem as a whole. Invisible middles are acutely sensitive to diverse ecosystem components and the ability to influence systems through conversations that connect (people to each other and to unifying narratives). Such conversations are often the ones out of the office, talking to all and sundry, brokering and cementing connections, subtly increasing the salience of central visions and shared values for positive impact and encouraging others to apply the visions to their own activities. Invisible middles are often found gently questioning and probing innovators and entrepreneurs in ways that extend understanding and skill, and facilitate richer relationships. They encourage experimentation and deviant thinking in processes and outcomes.

We should never underestimate the typically silent, potent power of invisible middles. We should reward them with credit for their attention to and skills around process. And we must learn from them by honing our own capacities to concurrently see big pictures, and to plant and grow seeds. They strengthen entire ecosystems by strengthening the relationships within—through gentle questioning, listening, encouraging, and connecting.

ENTREPRENEURSHIP FOR IMPACT INSIGHTS SUMMARY

These three impact changemakers—industry maker, Millennial mobilizer, and ecosystem facilitator—are vital for a robust ecosystem. They nurture processes and relationships that enable the transformation of innovative ideas into entrepreneurial initiatives, to sustainable provision of products and services that benefit all of society, particularly the underserved. At the macro level, institutions like the UK's Big Society

Capital—in funding an industry—ensure that high-potential impact initiatives receive the investment they need. Not just in direct product and service development, but also in growth phases so they can avoid the dreaded valley of death. Many potential innovations die for lack of resources needed to develop them to a stage where industry or investors can recognize and maximize their potential for marketplace success and delivery of positive social and environmental impacts. From a very different perspective, changemakers who mobilize their own or other generations to be involved in entrepreneurship for impact ecosystems add to a diverse, robust, and sustainable ecosystem. Finally, so much of what occurs in any ecosystem depends on often invisible changemakers who connect disparate ecosystem players and parts, who focus on processes, pull strings, broker and foster critical relationships, and plant ideas and action seeds everywhere they travel. Over time, we all benefit from the seeds blossoming into a vibrant garden.

CHAPTER 8

The Impact Influencers

The influencers are often the first movers in their field, the early thinkers, instigators, or adopters to whom others look for guidance. Influencers are thought leaders, highly knowledgeable about a specific subject or industry such as entrepreneurship, technology, or investing. They are the changemakers whose actions and opinions carry weight with their peers, colleagues, social and professional networks, and the public. They are role models who inspire emulation. They exude big ideas and bold thinking long before others have any inkling of what is to come. They are widely considered authorities, by their followers as well as the general population. They are sought by traditional media for their observations and opinions. Influencers can be journalists, academics, industry analysts, politicians, cause activists, professional advisors, bloggers, and more.

A DIFFERENT KIND OF INFLUENCER

The influencers we met are not particularly representative of the dramatic rise during the 2010s of "social influencers" found in online marketing. Online social influencers establish social media presences through multiple channels and attract massive followings on platforms like Instagram, Twitter, and Facebook. Many have built their own personal brands with followings that rival established global businesses. And they get paid by sponsors to influence.

In contrast, the *positive impact influencers* we met—while astutely utilizing online media and doing their share of blogging, vlogging, and newslettering with the best of the digital natives—also enact more traditional methods of influence. They model thought and action leadership through all forms of media: traditional news outlets, word-of-mouth, public speaking, networking, writing books, academic articles, blogs, and so on. They skillfully use social and traditional media for bottom-up, grassroots activism, as well as top-down policy change.

In this chapter, we'll meet several impact influencers and learn how they are helping guide others to expanded impact thinking and doing. People like Danny Almagor and his life partner in both work and play, Berry Liberman, who use a simple mantra ("Is it good for people? Is it good for the planet?") to direct their own thinking and doing in everything from real estate purchases to impact investments. Danny and Berry are not content to be role models to their own Gen Y and other generations on how to live and breathe positive impact. They use their positions in the spotlight to share what they have learned to inspire and influence more people to consider social and environmental impact in all they do.

The quietly spoken professor **Johanna Mair** wields a different kind of influence. As the academic editor of the *Stanford Social Innovation Review* in addition to her teaching duties at both Stanford University and the Hertie School of Governance in Germany, Johanna is in a unique position to dramatically shape knowledge and opinions around impact. She curates some of the most groundbreaking research on impact on the planet. In her journal articles and books, her theorizing and writing about key aspects of social entrepreneurship have significantly contributed to the evolution of our understanding of impact theory and practice.

Whether through public speaking, participating in or leading activism for a social or environmental cause, testifying at parliamentary inquiries, making submissions to government agencies seeking consultation on impact issues, or working directly for a governmental or lobbying agency, these influencers direct their knowledge and persuasive power toward changing policy to benefit the greater good.

Rosemary Addis has done all of the above in her impressive career. Advising prime ministers and government agencies, participating in the G8 Social Impact Investment Taskforce, and serving as the head of the Australian government's first Social Innovation Unit. Rosemary has been an influencer at the epicenter of social policy action. In the last part of this chapter, we share some of the insights she has gained from her rich international and Australian work influencing social impact policy.

THE GEN Y INFLUENCERS: DANNY ALMAGOR AND BARRY LIBERMAN

From an early age, it was clear that **Danny Almagor** saw and thought things outside the norm, and he was not afraid to speak up. In his final year at RMIT University in Melbourne, Australia, where he was studying toward a degree in aerospace engineering, Danny was assigned a project to design a bomber plane that could drop a hundred kilograms of explosives. Danny was furious. Why couldn't the project be to design a plane that could drop a hundred kilograms of rice to a community in need? After his vocal opposition, future assignments at RMIT became about designing projects to assist communities in need, not destroy them.[1] His questioning and subsequent action was one of Danny's first exercises in enacting lasting social impact. This small moment had a momentous impact on his trajectory. While sitting in one of those RMIT classrooms, Danny experienced an existential dilemma. He asked himself: "Why am I doing this?" His answer was epiphanous: "I wrote down all the things I was passionate about." Designing air force bombers was not on his list. Travel, the outdoors, adventure, buildings, the environment, and tackling poverty were.[2] During his studies, Danny embarked on a gap year of international travel. Intent on volunteering his engineering skills toward positive impact overseas, Danny secured a Churchill Fellowship to visit and learn from Engineers Without Borders in the U.S. and Canada, and traveled to other countries like Nepal and India to experience the work in action. In 2003, with seven university friends, Danny officially launched Engineers Without Borders Australian (EWB Australia). He served as CEO for almost a decade. Their projects included bringing clean drinking water, smokeless stoves, and electricity to communities in Cambodia, Vietnam, Sri Lanka, Nepal, and India. Danny won many awards for his role in these endeavors, including the Victoria Region Social Entrepreneur of the Year award and an Order of Australia Medal.

While running the nonprofit Engineers Without Borders Australia, Danny started a for-profit venture, Medivax, which specialized in immunizations in the corporate health sector. Catalyzing the Engineers Without Borders Australia and Medivax start-ups taught Danny how to build an organization on a shoestring budget. Although both provided valuable services to people, Danny noted: "For me, Medivax was about profit . . . Engineers Without Borders was about purpose." When he sold Medivax to a larger health-care provider, Danny was determined to combine profit and purpose going forward.

While Danny was exploring his dreams in Asia, fellow Melbournian **Berry Liberman** was lured by Hollywood Boulevard's bright lights and red carpet to follow her dreams in filmmaking. After graduating with a bachelor of creative arts degree from the Victorian College of the Arts, and armed with the feature film rights to iconic French-born Australian artist Mirka Mora's compelling story, Berry headed to the mecca of filmmaking, Los Angeles. To gain experience in the industry, she stayed there on and off for five years, screenwriting and directing short films.

Berry was weaned on talking work and business all through her childhood. Her grandfather, Jack Liberman, was a Polish refugee entrepreneur who had arrived in Australia in the early 1950s. When he discovered discarded damaged silk stockings in Melbourne's laneways behind stocking manufacturing factories, he asked if he could take them. Jack and his family repaired the stockings, and then he sold them on Melbourne's elite Collins Street as seconds. According to family legend, when the factories realized what Jack and his brother Chaim were doing, they began shredding the stockings. But young Jack had already saved enough money to buy the stocking manufacturing machines. It was the dawning of a family business empire that would grow at 30 percent per year for the next thirty-five years. By 2010, almost sixty years after arriving in Australia, the Liberman family empire was worth over A$2 billion.

Berry inherited the intense work ethic, dogged determination, and keen eye for opportunity that characterized her lineage. By her mid-twenties she had also developed an acute awareness of both the privileges and responsibilities of her heritage. When the adult Berry reflected on the effect that living and breathing business had on her family, she noted: "All meaning was centered around the business and I deeply understand the drive to succeed and to build 'bigger, better, best.' It was driven by a powerful survival drive following two world wars and a depression. This unrelenting drive had its consequences on me."

The death of her father when he was just forty-five and Berry a young child profoundly impacted her perspective on life. The adult Berry became dedicated to achieving a different balance: "It was clear to me that business should represent all stakeholders, not just shareholders. I am intensely aware of the privileges I have been blessed with, and that my role in life is to contribute to the world in a meaningful way, using our business as a tool for powerful change, to nourish my family and community and leave things a little better than when I arrived."[3] Toward the end of Berry's time in Hollywood, these sentiments were at the forefront of her consciousness.

One night after returning to Australia for a visit, Berry walked into a Melbourne pub and her own future. Danny, the twenty-six-year-old engineering graduate, and the twenty-five-year-old Berry recognized each other from school. They had both attended the same Melbourne college. Upon greeting Berry, Danny exclaimed, "Oh my God—we're adults now!" Meeting Danny triggered Berry's scrutiny of her own life:

> I really loved my time [in Los Angeles] and it was the foundation of my adult self. I was pushed really hard in the work that I did and I was exposed to a lot of amazing, pretty hardcore story-telling. . . . But then I turned twenty-five and I met my future husband [Danny]; I had this really striking awareness that if I stayed in LA, I'd get caught up in the vortex of working for [an Oscar] and I might miss out on the life I really wanted, which was to have a rich family and working life and be able to bring the two together.[4]

It was this synchronicity of values that also struck Danny. He later recalled, "We married one another because our values were so aligned. The environment, human rights, justice, art, business, creativity—we knew we wanted to live in the same world, and that we wanted to build that world for our kids."[5] Danny was not daunted by Berry's heritage, nor did either of them fall into a paralysis trap to which so many people who inherit wealth succumb. Instead they took a different approach, as Danny explains: "I think of inherited wealth, and the money that Berry and I now share, as a kind of relay race. The baton has been hard earned and passed on. We found ourselves in a position to truly change the world, and we were put there by the generations who came before us. There is nothing to prove—only more race to run! So we started thinking about how our values could be best put into action."[6]

Around that time, the couple read Bo Burlingham's *Small Giants*. Berry recalls that Burlingham "proved the paradigm shift that business could be great instead of big. We wanted to build businesses that are truly great from the inside out, driven by passion and integrity. The goal is to change the world and nurture the community, employees, customers, and the planet. It's not philanthropy. It is a sustainable, twenty-first century business model that looks at the benefits for all stakeholders rather than just shareholders."[7]

And so they created their real-life Small Giants to prove that "business can be great, instead of big." Building from Berry's early reflections on her family history and her own realization that growth at any cost was not a good model for Small Giants or for their lives, the couple's enduring mantra in considering any expenditure of Small Giants' resources became the trio of questions: Is it good for people? Is it good for the environment? Is it creating the world we want to live in? In an interview with *map magazine*, Berry recalled that when she and Danny set up Small Giants, "we wrote ourselves a bit of a manifesto and we really did ask what success was. For us, success looks a lot different to what we were brought up with. It's basically asking: Are we living a meaningful life? Are we engaging with meaningful ideas and amazing people globally and having enriching conversations? And is our family life happy and stable and nourishing for us?"[8]

Small Giants, which Berry and Danny have described as their business love child, was founded on the premise that business can be a powerful tool of change in the world.[9] It is an investment house that invests in businesses that Danny and Berry think will have great, positive impacts. Small Giants has created or invested in a diverse range of impactful businesses: The School of Life (emotional intelligence classes), The Sociable Weaver (environmentally sustainable building company), STREAT (homeless youth social enterprise)[10], Mossy Willow (regenerative farm and retreat center), and *Dumbo Feather* quarterly magazine. In 2012 they created the Impact Investment Group, committed to harnessing capital markets to drive change. The company promises "financial returns with deep social and environmental impact . . . to create the world we want to live in."[11] They also have a renewable energy arm with over $200 million in assets and a venture capital fund called Giant Leap.

Danny and Berry have heard the arguments against an entire asset portfolio being geared toward positive impact but strongly believe that purpose will lead to great long-term returns. Danny explains, "Many of the industries that are the main growth industries in the world today are deeply aligned with positive social or enviromental impact. Sustainable agriculture, renewables, sharing economy, electric vehicles, organics, aged care. I see plenty of places to make money and make a positive impact."[12]

While Danny and Berry support entrepreneurs enacting positive social and environmental change in the world, they lead the way by their own entrepreneurship. In 2012 Small Giants became the first Australian certified B Corporation. B Corporations are for-profit companies certified by the nonprofit B Lab to meet rigorous standards of social and environmental performance, accountability, and transparency.[13] There are now more than twenty-five hundred B Corporations in more than fifty countries around the world, representing over a hundred and fifty industries.[14] Since Small Giants' B Corporation certification, over two hundred other Australian businesses have followed its example. Danny and Berry were recognized internationally for their leadership and awarded a global B Corporation Champions Award.

While their values are clearly in sync, and the family business is truly the "Berry and Danny family," the couple is skilled at optimizing their complementary skill sets. Berry assumed the editorial leadership for *Dumbo Feather* in 2011 and sees it as a way to champion impact ideas. "We realized this publication could be the heart and soul of Small Giants—a litmus test for great ideas, people, and businesses around the world," she said.[15] For Berry, *Dumbo Feather* is a labor of love and obviously speaks to her passion for the creative arts—her Hollywood dream of combining the spoken word with beautiful images to tell positive stories of social change. As her partner in values and impact, Danny said: "How do we get people just to wake up and say 'What am I excited about? How can I be useful in the world?' and then pursue that journey, whatever that is?"[16]

When not investing in people and ideas that are committed to positive social and environmental impact, Berry and Danny are activist shareholders. Danny and Berry view *all* of their actions and activities through the impact lens. Unless they see positive answers to their core questions, they don't engage. But in circumstances where they must, they are pragmatists, using their financial power to influence positive change from within. For example, Berry and Danny use Bank Australia, a local Australian "ethical/green" bank, and when they need to finance transactions beyond the capacity of their local green bank, they work with the most impact-oriented of Australia's big banks. In their engagement with this corporate giant, Berry and Danny use their financial power as ultra-high-net-worth customers to nudge the bank's board and senior management to think about enacting more positive impact.

All of these impact business deals through Small Giants and the Impact Investment Group are additional to the couple's philanthropic contributions. They are keen supporters of charities related to the arts, community, education, and environment. Danny described his perspective on philanthropy versus impact investing: "Philanthropy is the venture capital of change: the bundle that we can risk to support new ideas and not expect anything in return other than impact. Impact investing is looking for financial returns as well as social and environmental impact. If Small Giants' investments don't do well, we have to cut our costs elsewhere."[17] Berry describes their journey as a work in progress: "Sure, we'll make mistakes. We're sailing into uncharted waters. Our attitude is that if you can make even a one-degree shift in the direction of your rudder, over time and distance, you continue turning and soon you will have arrived at a completely new destination to the one you were originally headed for."[18]

Berry and Danny embrace their journey as pioneers, as influencers, not only for their own generation, but also for all of us aspiring to a life of impact. In our first meeting with Danny, he did not hesitate to go into detail about how and why they do what they do, which was a mini tutorial in transforming any asset portfolio into a portfolio for positive change. Clearly, Danny's tutorial had a huge impact on our Tingari Group trajectory. As role models for positive impact thinking and doing, and with the high public profile ultra-wealth brings, both Berry and Danny speak at conferences, to journalists, and with others wishing to learn about impact. They even convene workshops and retreats on living and investing for positive impact. Berry and Danny's bottom lines are always: Is it good for people? Is it good for the environment? And is it creating the world we want to live in? As Berry said in one interview: "I live with my heart on my sleeve and values at the forefront of every decision." They are both moved by an intense sense of urgency about all that needs to be done in the world.[19]

THE POLICY INFLUENCER: ROSEMARY ADDIS

Professor Karl Weick, an eminent social psychologist, once wrote: "Careers consist of odd, whimsical, and deviant actions . . . because the predicates shape the person who in turn shapes the subsequent predicates."[20] Weick describes career predicates as "eccentric" because at the time such incidents (predicates) occur, they change career paths in ways that tend to be unexpected and become extraordinary as we make sense of them in retrospect. If there was ever a career trajectory blatantly exhibiting the consequential nature of "eccentric" predicates, it is the trajectory of **Rosemary Addis**.

Rosemary started her journey as a young lawyer, one of the last bastions of predictable, sequential, continuous, straight-line career path trajectories. The young Rosemary, armed with a First Class Honors law degree from Melbourne University, joined the eminent international law firm now known as Allens-Linklaters, and embraced the partnership track. Known for its work with many of the world's leading organizations (including fifty-five of the world's top 100 companies and more than seventy-five of Australia's top 100 companies), Allens prides itself on longevity, claiming some of the world's longest ongoing client relationships, with some lasting more than a hundred and fifty years. Rosemary clearly thrived in this arena. The first female lawyer sent overseas by the firm, she successfully sat the notoriously difficult New York bar exam and began advising Allens-Linklaters' global client base. Her hard work was rewarded within the firm with an equity partnership after eight years. In the legal profession Rosemary was recognized as one of the leading lawyers in her area of law by *Chambers Global*.

Rosemary was on the traditional linear trajectory toward the pinnacles of legal career success. On the cusp of partnership, as she assumed national leadership for the firm's new thinking and knowledge systems, Rosemary experienced an epiphany. She says, "Once I got the taste for systems thinking, leadership practice, and operating as a strategist, I wasn't happy going back to [legal] practice. I wondered if I could look myself in the mirror in twenty or thirty years' time if I didn't explore the ideas and strategies I'd been working with." Rosemary's peers and superiors must have been astonished when the young legal star jumped off the corporate law ladder. Her legal career became the backdrop for enacting her passion for positive impact, contributing to something bigger.

Rosemary started her own business to focus on different ways of thinking about strategic collaboration to build social and economic value. Her knack for seeing, being prepared to act on, and then seizing opportunities served her well as she transitioned sectors. A role with the Australian children's charity The Smith Family turned out to be prescient training in the social sector and the approach required for effective leadership and influence in social change. Rosemary recalls, "[The role] taught me more about policy, because even though I'd advised governments at senior levels and on large transactions, I realized I didn't know how to develop and usher through social policy." Rosemary also learned she was not a single-issue person. She explains, "The Smith Family focus on creating opportunity through education is something I really believe in. When I left there, I was asked to help start conversations about impact by The RE Ross Trust. This was the early stages of an ongoing reframing of the conversations *from* the act of giving *to* a focus on the impact being achieved and the resources organizations harnessed. We developed the first prospectus guide to help these organizations seek funding and finance."

Toward the end of the first decade of the new millennium, Rosemary's expertise had clearly been noticed. She was introduced to the head of the Department of Premier and Cabinet in Victoria, the second largest state government in Australia, and he offered her a job. Rosemary remembers, "It was a great learning experience. . . . By then I understood that you need to see how the sectors fit in the system, what it takes to work within them in different roles, to work out how you see where they intersect and where the gaps are."

This leap into public service would later reveal itself to be a seminal predicate in Rosemary's journey, catapulting her from state government to national, then international epicenters of policy and catalytic action for positive impact. As the Victorian government's representative, Rosemary led the shaping of the national reform agenda for the Council of Australian Governments across nine jurisdictions around the country. As assistant director of national reform with the Department of Premier and Cabinet, Rosemary drove thought leadership on policy for how the federal system could be improved and the processes to achieve them. A couple of years after commencing this work, a former colleague encouraged Rosemary to join him at the federal Department of Education, Employment, and Workplace Relations. There, Rosemary established and led the first Australian federal government social innovation function. Rosemary recalls the serendipitous, eccentric nature of these moves, saying, "I learned to reframe from thinking about how we create change in government to how we can create change *from* government. It is a privilege to work as a public servant. Creating better outcomes should be the essence of the job. Social Innovation provided a valuable opportunity to introduce an expanded toolbox for social policy." Rosemary and her colleagues designed all policy and programming from the question "To what end?," putting the focus on impact.

Their collective and diverse views enabled Rosemary and her colleagues to explore a broad range of approaches from traditional grant funding to new models for incubation and collaboration, from brokering connections with other sectors to adapting economic innovation policy for social issues. Understanding that the context in which social innovations are developing is global and influenced by long-term trends, the team learned quickly. Gleaning from the best policy and program initiatives in other parts of the world, they co-designed initiatives for the local context.

Rosemary became convinced that the future of impact depended on developing broader conceptions of the role of government beyond funder. She came to believe that "government has a distinctive role as policy and law maker—a clear contribution to setting priorities," going on to say that the "government often knows where the need is and has valuable data and evidence. But not all the answers. Working across traditional boundaries is central." These experiences drove home to Rosemary what she already understood innately, that "governance is the stealth weapon of social change."

Committed to breakthrough systems-level change for social innovation and investment, Rosemary immersed herself in the hard slog it takes to shape, design, and implement policy and programs for social innovation and impact on the national stage. Her timing was synchronicity in action. Corresponding with the tenure of Australia's first female prime minister, Julia Gillard, the priorities of the new administration—grounded in productivity and inclusion—enabled bold changemakers like Rosemary to thrive.

As Social Innovation strategist, Rosemary was determined to take the government beyond binary notions like social versus economic and private versus public to foster a more holistic ecosystems approach. She delivered new initiatives, including establishing Australia's first dedicated investment funds for social enterprise, and groundbreaking work on place-based impact investment in Australia. Rosemary also demonstrated different ways of working that included a collaborative "networked incubation" model of strategy and design for long-term change. Working with social entrepreneur Jane Vadiveloo and local Aboriginal communities, Rosemary and her team co-designed and incubated Children's Ground.

Children's Ground

In Australian Aboriginal communities, despite the infusion of gazillions of resources over the decades, there have essentially been no tangible improvements on key indicators of well-being. Children's Ground—vehemently not considered a "program" by its founders—takes a whole-of-community approach to tackling entrenched, often intergenerational social challenges facing these communities: Literacy, health and mortality, rates of incarceration, incidences of alcohol and drug abuse, and domestic violence. The evolution of Children's Ground exemplifies a unique collaborative model at the leading edge of place-based, community-driven impact initiatives.

Under the auspices of Rosemary's Social Innovation unit, the government provided financial, intellectual, and social capital to collaboratively pilot a new, independent delivery organization to take positive impact work forward in and with Aboriginal communities. A collective investment model—with ongoing funding from a range of sources, including the local indigenous community—ensures the sustainability of the venture while achieving local commitment to design and enact the programs.

Children's Ground's work is predicated on eight key principles: start early; stay for the long haul; work with enough families to achieve a critical mass, often year-round; deliver the whole, not the bits; innovate/use new ways; expect and deliver the best; assume and celebrate ability; and be led by child, family, and community. The evidence-based, collaborative community model (both in design and funding) was founded on local indigenous communities' quest for an education system that provided the skills to access the global world while enabling their children to understand their land, language, and culture—to be "strong both ways." Children's Ground puts these principles into practice through a suite of services for children and young people up to age twenty-four, their families, and their communities. These services focus on learning, well-being, and development, and many can be accessed in the multigenerational community center that sits at the core of the organization. Outreach programs and services to ensure accessibility for all are also included. According to Rosemary, Children's Ground is both long-term in its vision, with a minimum twenty-five-year time frame, and collaborative and culturally sensitive. Members of the local community are employed by Children's Ground as designers, researchers, and users. Many services are provided in the local languages.[21]

G8 Social Impact Task Force

In 2013 Rosemary's capacity for recognizing and seizing opportunities and for utilizing her strengths to successfully pivot to a new trajectory paid off, launching her onto the international impact stage. In June that year, then-British prime minister David Cameron—as president of the G8—announced the establishment of an international Social Impact Investment Taskforce. Australia's innovations in the impact arena were well known: a rich history of cooperatives, volunteering, social enterprises, and social impact investment initiatives, including the New South Wales government's early introduction of social impact bonds, one of the first state governments in the world to do so. Rosemary was invited to join the task force as Australia's representative.

The task force, chaired by Sir Ronald Cohen—a venture capitalist and a driving force behind impact investing in the UK—established working groups targeting specific areas of change. National advisory boards were set up in each member country to feed into the task force work and drive forward action in local contexts. Cohen observed at the time: "This is not about increasing or reducing public expenditure, but helping government to benefit from innovation and private sector capital in order to achieve more impact with the money it has."[22] Rosemary felt firsthand those pinched government budgets for social impact initiatives as she once again walked up a down escalator, a feeling of déjà vu from her early uphill forays into social innovation work. The Australian government was not ready to commit to social impact in 2013, so she had to fund her trip to the first task force meeting herself. But Rosemary recognized the opportunity for Australia, so she established and chaired the Australian Advisory Board on Impact Investment and co-founded Impact Investing Australia as a public good vehicle to drive strategy development and execution after her G8 task force participation.

After convening six global meetings in G8 member countries around the world, the task force delivered its final report, *Impact Investment: The Invisible Heart of Markets*. This seminal global impact agenda-setting document highlighted innovations from across the globe, trumpeting the potential of social investment—investments made into businesses and social sector organizations, directly or through funds, with the intention of generating social and environmental impacts alongside financial returns—to drive social progress. The report called for leadership from all sectors and pointed to the critical role of pension funds, philanthropists, community organizations, social enterprises, and critically, governments.

The role of government

Rosemary sees government support as critical to the growth of the impact market by adding channels that proactively build the market and increase resources directed toward impact-driven organizations. She sees government support and championship as instrumental in developing the impact investment ecosystem "with a variety of participants, [providing] incentives for more participation, and [helping] scale early stages of market development . . . [facilitating a market] that delivers measurable, improved outcomes for society, operating at scale, and demonstrating and promoting innovation and diversity in participants and products."

According to Rosemary, the state not only curates a thriving ecosystem but also encourages innovation for sustainable solutions to entrenched social problems: "Individuals, communities, and the economy benefit from impact investing through making more resources available for social purposes, new approaches to solving old problems, and greater accountability for the outcomes achieved." Such curating results in a flourishing impact investing ecosystem that mobilizes additional resources as well as inspires entrepreneurship and innovation for sustainable solutions to social and environmental issues.

In her cognitive map of the world, Rosemary smashes any silos segregating innovation, entrepreneurship, and impact:

> The more time I spend in [this arena], the clearer the interrelationship between social and economic progress becomes. The future is more agnostic as to sector and more focused on purpose and impact. . . . The toolkit for social innovation is the same: enterprise development, capability and talent, measurement, regulatory settings, and capital. The role for government is the same: as a market builder contributing to the market infrastructure and incentivizing participation; as a standard setter; and as a market participant using targeted funding to create a multiplier effect and direct capital to policy priorities. And if we can make the policy case for developing new industries and technology, why not for poverty alleviation and sustainability of our environmental and cultural heritage?

A Policy Influencer's Vision for the Role of Government in Innovation, Entrepreneurship, and Impact

As an exemplar of a local and global policy influencer, Rosemary Addis models diverse ways of thinking and doing around the role of government in social impact. Summarized below are the key government activities that full-time policy influencers like Rosemary shape.

- *Facilitate the entrepreneurship and impact ecosystem.*

Governments can signal interest in impact innovation, entrepreneurship, and investment; contribute to impact infrastructure from innovation to investment to scaling; inspire confidence for stakeholders to participate; reduce impact entrepreneurship and investment risks to encourage market development; incentivize impact innovation and efficacy; target government spending to foster impact initiatives; channel capital and other resources to foster impact innovation, entrepreneurship, and investment policy priorities; and incentivize the flow of investments into social objectives.

- *Mobilize, shepherd, and steward the impact market.*

Governments can play a critical role in creating and nurturing a dynamic market for impact investment that delivers measurable, improved outcomes for society, operating at scale and demonstrating and promoting innovation and diversity in participants and products. Market stewardship can remove barriers to investment and reduce the red tape that prevents greater participation by investors.

- *Be a role model.*

Governments can use some of their limited funding, including grant funding, to encourage the private sector to enter specific areas in terms of capital and talent. By participating in impact markets, governments can leverage and encourage private capital in priority policy areas and facilitate collaborations to develop greater outcomes.

- *Champion impact.*

When governments act as market champions, encourage more private investments, invest government resources, and mobilize additional resources, they spur the market for investing in innovation for impact.

- *Facilitate and fund impact evidence.*

Governments have an important role in funding research and evidence for impact innovation and entrepreneurship. Data collection, analysis, publication, and distribution often lack resources.

- *Recognize and reward impact changemakers.*

Governments can shine the light on fantastic practices with recognition such as awards and encouragement in specific areas. When governments introduce awards highlighting leading social enterprises, they are saying this area is important and these organizations and people are performing a great service.

Rosemary often cites international evidence and local examples demonstrating the potent power of government leadership in the impact arena. She fiercely believes that policy initiatives and relatively modest government spending can dramatically catalyze market activity aimed at positive impact. Like so many of her fellow impact influencers, Rosemary sees the imperative for bold action: "Without a focus on innovation for social benefit, we risk further entrenching disadvantage. Without a focus on developing capital flows to support enterprise, and encouraging talent and capital into the field, we are unlikely to reap the benefits of innovation in the Australia we want for our children that is fair and full of opportunity."[23]

Locally, Rosemary was lead author of the landmark Australian Advisory Board Report on Impact Investing strategy for Australia, *Delivering on Impact,* that fed into the international strategy. Globally, Rosemary has assumed a larger role, garnering international participation and engagement from global impact investment practitioners and organizations.

Global Steering Group for Impact Investment

In 2015 the G8 task force handed the baton to the Global Steering Group for Impact Investment (GSG) to take impact investment to a tipping point by 2020. The group expanded from the original G7 countries, Australia, and the EU to include seventeen member countries. Another eleven countries have national advisory boards or similar. The same cascading model as the G8 task force—the establishment of national advisory boards and strategies feeding into the global work—applies.

As a GSG member, Rosemary recognized and acted on the opportunity to contribute to local and global impact ecosystems. For Rosemary, the next important step in growing the Australian ecosystem for entrepreneurship and impact is to apply the lessons from other countries, indeed other fields of market-based activity, to get key impact infrastructure into the Australian market. Rosemary and her colleagues have forcefully advocated for the creation of an independent financial organization, Impact Capital Australia, building on the lessons from the UK's Big Society Capital, tailored for the Australian market. Like Big Society Capital, Impact Capital Australia would be predominantly wholesale, providing financing to intermediaries who would then invest directly in social enterprises (for-profit or not-for-profit) to grow their reach, encourage others to enter the market, and amplify ultimate positive impact. Also like Big Society Capital, Impact Capital Australia is designed to be a market champion, targeting barriers to growth and developing new, scalable opportunities for innovation and impact. "For us, seeing Impact Capital Australia actualized is a lynchpin because the combination of mission, mandate, and capital gives it the potential to really be a game-changer."

Rosemary's well-honed capacity to pivot between big picture and little picture, global and local, short-term and long-term, and her skills as a strategist and thought leader have positioned her for pioneering impact entrepreneurship roles in governments, corporations, investment houses, universities, and foundations locally and globally. It is not surprising that Rosemary was recognized for her contributions to impact innovation as one of Australia's "100 Women of Influence" in 2015, along with other well-deserved accolades.

THE RESEARCHER: JOHANNA MAIR

Graduating first in her class at the Vienna University of Economics and Business (Wirtschaftsuniversität) in Austria was probably not the first indicator of future achievements for young **Johanna Mair**. Other harbingers of her abilities quickly followed this feat, including a slew of frontier-shattering articles and books, three of which would land in the top twenty-five most quoted articles in academic journals in the first two decades of the twenty-first century. The first of these three articles (co-authored with fellow Vienna University graduate Dr. Christian Seelos), titled "Social Entrepreneurship: Creating New Business Models to Serve the Poor,"[24] contributed to a more theory-based, rigorously researched trajectory for the fledgling field of inquiry on social entrepreneurship. The second journal article, "Social Entrepreneurship Research: A Source of Explanation, Prediction, and Delight"[25] (co-written with Ignasi Marti), would become *the* most often cited and therefore most influential academic article in the decade following its publication. And it was Johanna's work with Ignasi Marti in Bangladesh, described in "Entrepreneurship in and Around Institutional Voids: A Case Study from Bangladesh," that paved the way for aspiring students of social entrepreneurship to conduct rigorous qualitative research that could contribute to the burgeoning field of study.[26] Indeed, Johanna's research and writings have helped frame the academic field of social entrepreneurship.

Following her studies at Vienna University in the early nineties, Johanna attended Johns Hopkins University in Bologna, Italy, earning a post-graduate diploma in international relations. Armed with such stellar qualifications, Johanna was drawn to the fast-paced world of international banking. Like numerous young star graduates recruited by the finance industry during that era, Johanna quickly became immersed in multiple aspects of the executive decision-making process. However, the call of more cerebral pursuits and the lure of academic inquiry proved too strong.

In 1996 Johanna moved to France to further her studies at the prestigious INSEAD (Institut Européen d'Administration des Affaires or European Institute of Business Administration). Consistently ranked by the *Financial Times* as one of the world's top business schools, INSEAD offered a global experience that no doubt suited Johanna's own orientation. Like so many of the changemakers we interviewed, Johanna is a global citizen, having lived a multi-continental life and speaking multiple languages. After graduating with a master's degree and then her doctorate, Johanna transitioned into mainstream academic roles, initially settling in Spain at the University of Navarra in

Barcelona, and later as a visiting scholar at Stanford University in Palo Alto, California. By 2010 she had assumed the academic editor's role for the prestigious *Stanford Social Innovation Review* (*SSIR*). Obviously talented at multitasking, Johanna also served stints as a visiting professor in social entrepreneurship at her alma mater, including their Asia (Singapore) campus, and at the Harvard Business School, where she is a regular visiting professor. Since 2012, concurrent with her roles at Stanford as a visiting scholar and academic editor, Johanna has been a professor at the Hertie School of Governance in Berlin, Germany.

Throughout her career, Johanna has been at the frontier of research in social entrepreneurship. Her pioneering research has greatly influenced the trajectory of the field and has contributed to its evolving breadth. Able to draw on her studies in management and strategy, as well as her work in the finance sector, Johanna has conducted and published groundbreaking research at the intersection of strategy, entrepreneurship, and impact.

Over the years, she has studied how institutions can both stifle and enable social and economic progress; the role of entrepreneurs in this process; market building and inclusive growth strategies in developing countries; and the emergence of venture philanthropy in Europe. Besides those highly influential early articles, Johanna and her colleagues have published a plethora of academic articles and books on topics related to social entrepreneurship, social innovation, and strategy.

Her rigorous academic work in collaboration with Seelos and Marti has been published in some of the most prestigious peer-reviewed journals in the world, and many have won awards. Johanna's recent collaboration with Seelos, the book *Innovation and Scaling for Impact: How Effective Social Enterprises Do It,* was nominated for the notable 2017 Thinkers50 Innovation Award.[27] Johanna's research acumen and teaching excellence have attracted awards in Italy (outstanding teaching), Spain (outstanding course design and teaching), and the United States (the Aspen Institute's Faculty Pioneer Award in Social Entrepreneurship Education).

Judging from Johanna's body of work, it would be natural to imagine a stereotypical professorial Dr. Mair: stern, quiet, bookish. In person, her piercing eyes, calm demeanor, and obvious comfort in silence—characteristics that bode well for a researcher—seem to reflect the rigorous thinking, careful deliberations, and consequent provocation of the field to move beyond the status quo. As one might expect from a fellow researcher, our consultation with Johanna was at once informative and provocative. Her challenging questions ensured that we too enacted the rigor of academic inquiry that has characterized her career. The academic study of social entrepreneurship is in its second decade, and the core canons of social entrepreneurship are still evolving. Johanna has been a key influencer since the field's beginnings.

Like Rosemary Addis, the keys to Johanna's success, besides her obvious powerhouse intellect, seem to lie in her capacity to simultaneously see the big picture and the small, the local and the global, the short view as well as the long. She says, "We have come a long way in terms of social innovation, the discourse, and also practice on social enterprise, but obviously we have many kinds of differences locally, geographically, issue-domain related, so it is still a relatively fragmented space, even if you look at the action that governments have taken—and this is also one of the interesting trends over the last four to five years that a number of governments across the world have embarked on social innovation, but the way they actually do, to use a more academic term, operationalize or contextualize social innovation very much differs now."

Given her own pivotal role in the evolution of the social entrepreneurship field and the impact ecosystem, another of Johanna's contributions is her capacity to be an observer of the ecosystem and share those insights to enhance the system and its component parts. "The focus is not so much anymore on the [individual] entrepreneurs, but very much on this ecosystem," she says, "but we are still very much operating on a global scale . . . designing solutions on our desk in Washington. . . . I think the opportunity for the whole field is that we take more seriously these bottom-up organizations and their learnings to inform our well-intended strategies."

Johanna's potent influence goes way beyond her obvious outstanding contribution to the social entrepreneurship field. Her core foundations of influence include shaping paradigms and refining definitions of social entrepreneurship; theorizing, researching, and teaching about best practice; and distilling and sharing exemplar thinking and practices. She has also done much to bridge the divide between academics and practitioners: supporting practitioners' efforts through research, case studies, and storytelling in the journals she has edited, and continually pushing toward more effective and rigorously tested research that ultimately benefits the communities in which social entrepreneurs operate.[28] Appreciation must go to Johanna and her fellow researchers, notably Christian Seelos and Ignasi Marti; they are at the forefront of an identifiable core of academic research in social entrepreneurship. Together, they have helped the academic field of social entrepreneurship, social enterprise, and impact find rhythm and build momentum.

ENTREPRENEURSHIP FOR IMPACT INSIGHTS SUMMARY

These impact influencers—Berry Liberman and Danny Almagor, whose work sets a positive example for their own and other generations; Rosemary Addis, not just pioneering policy and programming around impact at the national, regional, and global levels, but also facilitating more productive government roles in the entrepreneurship and impact arena; and Johanna Mair, thought leader, theorizing trailblazer, impact knowledge purveyor and distributor—all play vital roles in catalyzing positive impacts and contributing to the impact entrepreneurship ecosystem. They enable more and more people around the world to enact strategies that are good for people and good for the planet. In doing so, they bring about preferred futures for all.

CHAPTER 9

The Capital Providers:
Twenty-First Century
Philanthropists

F unders—the people or organizations that provide financing for entrepreneurial ventures—come in all shapes and sizes. Funders can be individuals, groups, or crowds. They can be traditional or contemporary. Some bring tightly controlled, expertly choreographed selection processes, while others are more laissez-faire, relying on gut and personal passions. Funders can hail from nonprofit or for-profit organizations, foundations, banks, corporations, government agencies, consortia, fully fledged venture capital funds, or niche impact investment firms. Funders may manage large or small sources of capital. Some spend their own money. Some spend the money of others. Funders can be angels or they can be demons: do-gooders who create negative impact with a pervasive sense of wealth and a white savior mentality, even emitting a smug obsession with their capacity to do good. Others bring genuine empathy, humility, and commitment to egalitarian collaboration, with any hints of elitism—financial, cultural, or otherwise—refreshingly absent. Instead, a feeling of gritty authenticity pervades their words and actions. Regardless of their individual defining characteristics, funders have an undeniable presence and purpose in the innovation ecosystem.

For impact entrepreneurs trying to navigate their way through this potential funding melee—aspiring to be the start-up gem unearthed by the savvy investor—the funding alternatives can be bewildering, even paralyzing. But as the third decade of the twenty-first century looms, impact entrepreneurs have more capital choices than ever. Independent research consistently reveals that, regardless of the source, only one-third of early stage funding typically comes from external sources in any given year.[1] Impact entrepreneurs can creatively and strategically choose among an array of options ranging from personal networks to crowds, corporations, grants, and awards. See the appendix at the end of this book for detailed descriptions of the many forms of capital. They can be as innovative in their funding alternatives as they are in their products and services.

Among all of the possible incarnations of funders with whom we consulted, we have chosen to spotlight three who stand out. First, **Dr. Lance Fors**. A renaissance man in the impact world, Lance's role depends on when you ask him, but he is a funder in many innovative and important ways, as an individual and as part of larger organizations. Second, we share more about **Pascal Vinarnic,** another renaissance funder. Pascal is exemplary because of his punctilious strategic and futures thinking about where and whom he funds. Finally, Australian businessman, venture investor, philanthropist, and boardroom philosopher **Sid Myer**. We place the spotlight on the very modest Sid because he exudes the courage to stand up against the blooming groundswell in favor of impact investing (and its accompanying calls for rigorous measurement), while affirming the important benefits of traditional philanthropy.

What is striking about these twenty-first century philanthropists is their humility as they quietly go about their work to contribute to the greater good. They don't see their work as "doing good," but merely and matter-of-factly "doing the right thing." Like so many of the leading impactors we consulted, standout twenty-first century philanthropists think small and big picture, whole-of-ecosystem, and very long-term. They want to amplify the positives and minimize the negatives, even if those negatives are not immediately obvious until the long term. They don't think in terms of reparation for their privilege, as writer Anand Giridharadas characterizes the impact work of rich global elites.[2] These twenty-first century philanthropists think and act with an awareness of "there, but for the grace of the universe, go I." They include an awareness of others in less materially fortunate predicaments as they quietly and modestly go about the work they do. They are innately committed to contributing to making the world better for all of us, not servicing their own needs above all else.

THE IMPACT FUNDER-MOBILIZER: LANCE FORS

Dr. Lance Fors is a multidimensional social impactor. It is impossible to imagine Lance operating at anything other than full throttle—and his "full throttle" breaks the sound barrier compared to most humans on the planet. At our first meeting, he did not appear to draw breath for the entire duration of our conversation. Everything about him was energized, from the excitement in his voice to the animated use of his hands to underscore a point. Lance speaks with relish, and any one question unleashes a bursting current of words. He is evangelical in his belief in the power of people to collaborate with each other to change the world for the better. Whether talking about his beloved tennis, his successful biotech company, or the networks of social impactors he leads, Lance has always been driven to enact his "highest and best use." Nothing else will do.

Tall and athletic, with a bearing that simultaneously exudes the abundant energy he seems to always carry with him, Lance also shows the humble confidence of someone who has so much to impart in too little time. There is a lot going on beneath his graying blond mop of hair. To the outsider, Lance has never been afraid of taking risks, making mistakes, and trying again. Interestingly, it was his foray into the world of professional tennis and his assessment of where such a career might lead that seemed to catapult him on the trajectory of innovation and impact that dominates his life.

After graduating from Hinsdale Central High School in Chicago, Illinois, Lance followed his dream of becoming a professional tennis player. Intent on becoming one of the ten best players in the United States, if not the world, by the time he was twenty, Lance enrolled and trained at the renowned Harry Hopman Tennis Academy in Florida. The Australian Hopman was one of the most successful coaches in tennis history, legendary for guiding Australian teams to a phenomenal fifteen Davis Cup championships. Hopman imparted to his protégés his unwavering insistence on being obsessive about fitness and clean living, rigorous in thought processes, dogged about work ethic, disciplined on and off the court, and treating officials, opponents, and the game of tennis with the utmost respect.

Lance spent two and a half years training at Hopman's camp. When Lance realized he was not going to be one of the top ten players, he reconsidered his life direction and headed to the University of California at Berkeley. After graduating with a BA, he went on to do a PhD at the California Institute of Technology. Both institutions are known for marshaling the brightest minds to address some of the world's toughest challenges.[3] He combined his mighty intellect and drive with the rigor, intensity, and discipline that was the hallmark of the Hopman camp to study molecular biology and biochemistry.

Lance's interest in science and the wonders of DNA were sparked in high school. Dr. Francis Crick and Dr. James Watson had not long before won the 1962 Nobel Prize for their description of the structure of genes and DNA within living cells. (It would take decades before the contribution of fellow DNA pioneer Dr. Rosalind Franklin was acknowledged by the world.) Lance recalled, "There are a few fundamental things you can point to which influence you in the course of your life. I was turned on to science, DNA, and the genetic code."[4] His interest and pursuit of knowledge in this field would later result in dozens of patents and an extraordinarily successful biotech company.

While most students might find the rigors of studying at Berkeley and Caltech to be all-consuming, Lance channeled his own intensity and discipline into buying, remodeling, and then selling houses in his spare time with his life and business partner, Shari Selover. Together, via their company Fors Investments (which Lance continues to own and manage), he and Shari renovated dozens of properties (doing much of the work themselves, which Lance labels "sweat equity"). Lance observed in 1990 that working for six years in their spare time made him and Shari millionaires.[5]

The successful renovation business also set in motion a lifelong tendency to share knowledge. Lance and Shari conducted workshops called "How to Profit from Buying Fixer Houses" across Southern California. In these workshops Lance shared lessons that are characteristic of his work: how to identify niche opportunities and how to engage in strategic long-term thinking and action. As he would later do in his impact investing, Lance looked for areas in transition and creatively used multiple forms of capital to transform something small into something much bigger. In sharing knowledge and skills learned along the way, he proved his dedication to sharing good fortune by giving time and resources to those with less opportunity.[6] During this time, Lance started and built a social enterprise to provide housing for individuals with special needs. This enterprise acquires, modifies, and rents out select properties long-term, enabling hundreds of individuals with special physical or mental needs to lead independent lives.

One of the fortuitous friendships Lance had forged at Caltech was with fellow scientist Lloyd Smith. Lance and Lloyd joined with University of Wisconsin biochemistry professor Jim Dahlberg to hatch a plan for a scientific adventure. They went from "just three guys with an idea" (about the potential of DNA enzymology for medical applications) to starting a company together. Third Wave Technologies was born and named in Lloyd's kitchen as the three contemplated Alvin Toffler's 1970 book *Future Shock*. In that seminal publication, Toffler described agriculture as the first wave of human economic progress, the industrial revolution as the second wave, and the information revolution as the third wave. The trio launched their technology company in 1993, aiming to be at the vanguard of the third wave of human economic progress.

The three founders provided some seed funding from their own savings, and Lance was creative in sourcing other funds. He was able to secure their first $4 million in funding from the U.S. government's Small Business Innovation Research grants.[7] Lance applied all of the lessons he'd learned in tennis and the remodeling business to grow Third Wave Technologies. In living his "highest and best use," Lance aimed for Third Wave's genetic analysis products to "grab and hold a major share of the market." The trio collaborated with major genetics research institutes, built a track record of success that would underlie stories for pitching to customers and investors alike, and generated excitement about what they were trying to do—and its importance. While Lance has described their joint venture as the "classic DNA garage experiment," the company became a major genomics force and a leading publicly traded biotechnology company. They developed and manufactured products that enabled the early detection and treatment of cervical, colorectal, liver, and other cancers.

At the time, Lance said: "We are in the information age for genetics. . . . We give the doctor the best information the doctor can get. In the clinical setting, it is life or death. It is the accuracy of the test that counts."[8] Prior to its IPO in 2001, Third Wave Technologies successfully raised $72 million in venture capital financing. When Third Wave went public, it was purported to be one of the largest biotech IPOs of that year. In 2008 the company was acquired by Hologic Inc. (a U.S. publicly traded company) for $580 million. That same year, Lance was awarded Ernst and Young Entrepreneur of the Year.

Silicon Valley Social Venture Fund

If Alvin Toffler had contemplated a "fourth wave," then social impact might well have been it. Lance Fors seems to be riding the fourth wave of his own life story. After selling Third Wave Technologies, Lance embarked on a new adventure. Having amassed significant capital, he decided to focus on entrepreneurship in the social sector, particularly systemic social change. He was interested in contributing to massive positive impact. As with all of his adventures, Lance started with research. He happened across a *Businessweek* article by Jessi Hempel titled "When Givers Get Together."[9] In the article, Hempel described a form of philanthropy that allowed donors to pool their funds to make a bigger impact while having a say in how their money would be used. Lance was intrigued.

His research led him to join the Silicon Valley Social Venture Fund (SV2) in 2005. Thanks to SV2's peer mentoring, Lance learned from other members how to assess nonprofits effectively, judge their needs, and recognize their potential to expand and make a bigger difference. He was hooked, not just by the potential scope of impact amplified by group investment, but also by the camaraderie created by the synergy of people working together on positive social change. His involvement in SV2 connected him to a number of social ventures that would capture his attention for over a decade. Two such initiatives were the New Teacher Center and Reading Partners. He invested in both of these, taking a seat on their boards and later serving as a vice chair and then chair. As with every opportunity he has embraced in his life, Lance ensured his "highest and best use" by giving these organizations his all.

Social Venture Partners International and Growth Philanthropy Network

Always looking to scale positive impact, Lance was drawn to the international social venture networks of Social Venture Partners International (SVPI). SVPI is a global network of venture philanthropy groups with member organizations in thirty-nine cities around the world and more than thirty-five hundred network partners. Members aim to maximize positive impact in their communities by supporting nonprofits with funding and leverage greater value with hands-on help and expertise. Again, Lance dove right in, taking a seat on the board. He served as chair for several years, applying and sharing the lessons he learned throughout his previous ventures: investment in solving problems, not "helping people"; understanding that people solve problems, rather than money solving problems; the need to focus on the solution and perpetuate what he calls "the language of positive action"; the importance of system-wide solutions; the duality of risk—the downside (possibility of failure) and the upside (the risk of missing opportunities); the critical role of long-term thinking; and the ever-present contribution of collaboration.[10]

Under the SVPI umbrella, Lance was able to scale his own impact, as well as those of his partners. For example, in China, he met Jaff Shen, the secretary general of China's Leping Social Entrepreneur Foundation, a Chinese grassroots nongovernmental organization (NGO) founded by a small group of renowned Chinese economists, scholars, and business leaders. Leping focuses on investing in leading social enterprises and advocating and facilitating investment in social ventures. Lance introduced the SVP model to Leping. The bold futures thinking that spawned Leping's pioneering impact work in China spurred their establishment of SVP China as part of the Leping Foundation, instantly connecting Leping to the international network, potentially amplifying its resources and impact. In summing up his belief in the potent power of collaboration, Lance observed: "Today, it's cooler to be a social entrepreneur than a 'tech' entrepreneur. But change is a team sport. It requires more players. A 'rock star' mentality doesn't help."[11]

Lance Fors models twenty-first century philanthropy in myriad ways. He practices humble, selfless giving in multiple arenas, including childhood advocacy, sweat equity in affordable housing, and curating and nurturing networks for synergistic positive impact. He understands the potent power of focusing on unique competencies and one's highest, best purpose. He is always thinking outside the box, looking for others who also think outside the box with systems-changing ideas that are actionable and capable of massive impact. Lance is convinced that amplified positive change is more likely to come from collaborations, partnerships, and networks.

THE VENTURE PHILANTHROPIST: PASCAL VINARNIC

Imagine running a marathon. Next, imagine running that race at −15°C to −20°C, often in strong, frigid winds. Imagine running this marathon at a latitude of 80° south, close to the South Pole, and at an altitude of twenty-two hundred feet above sea level, past penguin colonies, a glacier, and markers positioned in the snow and ice so the runners avoid treacherous crevasses. Sound impossible? Impossible is not part of **Pascal Vinarnic's** vocabulary. The French-born Pascal conquered not only that marathon in Antarctica but marathons on all of the other continents—Africa, Asia, Europe, North America and South America, and Australia/Oceania—earning him a place in the 7 Continents Marathon Club.

It may be this diverse and deep exposure to other cultures on every part of our planet that left Pascal—of all the changemakers we interviewed—most concerned about the plight of our planet and the future of impact in the 2020s and beyond. Pascal has achieved these marathon milestones while doing not one, but two parallel day jobs, one in private equity and mainstream investing, the other as a venture philanthropist, or impact investor.

Pascal has been involved in private equity for most of his career, focusing on portfolio management for distressed tech companies in the United States and Europe. He was recruited by Bain & Company in 1984 around the same time that Mitt Romney founded Bain Capital in Boston, Massachusetts. Under Romney's leadership, the firm skyrocketed to become one of the world's leading private multi-asset alternative investment firms. According to some sources, Romney's novel approach at the time—applying a mentor's philosophy to private equity, increasing efficiency, and finding new markets—worked spectacularly well.[12] As a partner with Bain, Pascal established Bain's Venture Capital operations in Paris and was Bain Capital's interface for its European business. He also headed the Bain Finance Services Group that specialized in support services to private equity clients in Europe and North America, providing advice on leveraged buyouts, mergers and acquisitions, and corporate finance. After Bain, Pascal went on to form his own firm, Ceres Finance, and worked as a turnaround specialist on behalf of investors.

While engaged in this heady whirlwind of turnarounds, leveraged buyouts, and mergers and acquisitions, Pascal was acutely aware of the gap between people with ample opportunities and those with limited opportunities. The genesis of Pascal's acute awareness of those enduring difficult life circumstances is hard to pinpoint. Perhaps training for and running marathons through some of the remote struggling neighborhoods on any of the six main continents left indelible images in his mind. Or being knowledgeable about the various causes for which those marathons raised awareness and funds, for example, the Antarctic marathon spotlights a nonprofit research group that measures the impact of tourism on the flora and fauna of Antarctica. Or perhaps it was there all along. He noted in our interview: "I come from a family where we were brought up with the idea that if you want to receive something, you need to give first. You need to help first, because if you help first, at some point, then [another] will help you."

Fondation Demeter

Pascal heeded his family's embedded values. A couple of years after leaving Bain Capital and establishing his own private equity practice, Pascal founded Fondation Demeter. Named after Demeter, the Greek goddess of agriculture, grain, and bread who sustained humankind with bounty from the earth, Pascal's foundation takes inspiration from Demeter's teaching humankind about sowing and harvesting. In Greek mythology, when Hades, king of the underworld, kidnaps Demeter's daughter, Persephone, to be his wife, Demeter goes searching for her and thus neglects the earth's crops. Zeus, king of the gods, realizes that a famine is threatening the mortals and ordains that Persephone spend the six arable months on earth with her mother and the remaining six months with her husband. This cycle of the seasons in Greek mythology yields lessons on the importance of reaping and sowing before any rewards can be achieved.

Fondation Demeter has practiced these principles in the twenty-five years since its founding in 1994, along with the principles that served Pascal so well in his private equity investing. In collaboration with the Fondation de France (Foundation of France), Fondation Demeter has focused on contributing to the professionalization of leaders of humanitarian actions so they can optimize and perpetuate available resources. As Pascal explains, the foundation assists others to become "more professional, more efficient, more effective [and] pay attention to the funds they get, to the result, to the impact . . . to be solutions bringers, not problem bringers." As a small family foundation, Pascal and his team believe the way to amplify their own impact is to be innovative risk-takers. So, Fondation Demeter only invests in pilot programs or entrepreneurial projects with massive potential for replication and exponential impact. At any one time, the foundation supports five to eight pilots anywhere in the world. Its ultimate big picture goals are to assist NGOs or their programs in achieving financial self-sufficiency and to enhance long-term societal impact and mindset shifts at the population level.[13]

Pascal invests much of himself into these ventures. Over the last two decades, Fondation Demeter has enacted cycles of focused investment, depending on where it sees the greatest need. For the first fifteen years, the foundation's resources were concentrated on microfinance in India, Africa, and Latin America. The reasons were simple. "If you did not involve the women in emerging markets twenty years ago, there was not going to be change because the men [as a movement] were not interested to lead the changes. Women enacted the grassroots change," Pascal recalled.

Fondation Demeter's second era has constituted more than twelve years of concentrated focus on at-risk youth. Pascal and his team believe in the capacity of at-risk youth to evolve so they can live and perform well in our world. Pascal believes passionately that youth are the vectors of change—for good or for bad. As Pascal says: "If we do not bring solutions to at-risk youth, they will become prey to all forms of extremisms: politics, religions, mafias—and the world will suffer even more from not having cared in time. . . . We need to show these at-risk kids there is a world for them and the world is welcoming."

The foundation only works where it has a local partner it can trust. Rather than traditional grants, it makes "returnable grants," or loans with no interest. Pascal describes the underlying approach and how it reflects his family philosophy: "I help you. When you repay your loan, you help me. But more importantly, you help me to help someone else. . . . We are recycling the money."

For example, in New York, Fondation Demeter collaborated with Defy Ventures, an organization focused on assisting ex-convicts. Pascal explained to us that Defy Ventures takes the approach that the drug dealer is already a businessperson (or, as the organization calls them, "Entrepreneurs in Transition"). Rather than focusing on what bad things these people may have done in the past, Defy Ventures and Fondation Demeter look at the potential and skills they have. Many ex-convicts have demonstrated that they know how to operate a business. Defy helps them channel those skills for good. The result of this capabilities-centered approach: close to nil recidivism during the first four years of the program.

Pascal Vinarnic is an inspiring role model for changemakers anywhere, a role model who gives the rest of us hope. And the principles by which Pascal operates—being solutions-oriented rather than problem-oriented; seeing capabilities, not deficiencies; thinking long-term global systems; enacting partnerships and entrepreneurial mentoring relationships, not donor-recipient power structures; treating people as human beings with unique but adaptable skill sets; taking risks to pilot new possibilities; and modeling professionalism, effectiveness, and efficiency with compassion—will all potentially contribute to more positive futures for us all.

THE NOT-SO-TRADITIONAL PHILANTHROPIST: SID MYER

While you would not know it from his very modest and humble demeanor, Sidney Hordern Myer, known as Sid, is a man of many substantive, often quiet achievements and great wealth. Sid's down-to-earth manner, the occasional glimpses of a wicked sense of humor, and the obvious capacity for empathy in so much that he says and does reveal a man content in his own skin. Sid's voice—often languorous—hints of his quiet, patient curiosity. This is a man not seduced by the short term. Prone to contemplation, Sid speaks from a place of penetrating consideration. This is a man who thinks big and far out.

Sid describes himself first and foremost as a businessman. But such a label is too limiting for the intertwined amalgam of roles he plays in his personal and professional life. By all accounts, Sid is equally at home in the boardroom—whether for-profit or nonprofit—as he is out on the land, atop a horse, honing his skills in the sport of cutting (he has placed in Australia's top national competitions); or with fellow Aussies with a keen interest in the future of agriculture. Like his grandfather and father before him, Sid exhibits a remarkable capacity for integrating his business, philanthropic, and community interests.

Sidney Hordern Myer is the eldest of the third generation of the Australian Myer family. His generation is affectionately known as "G3" to family insiders, although Sid is not a fan of being labeled as a member of any generation. It cannot have been easy growing up with the name Sidney Myer. So many iconic Australian buildings, organizations, and awards have the Myer name emblazoned on their facade or letterhead. In Melbourne alone, one can find the fabled Myer Department

Store towering over Bourke Street Mall; the Sidney Myer Asia Centre at the University of Melbourne; the Sidney Myer Music Bowl in Melbourne's entertainment district; the Sidney Myer Foundation; the Myer Family Company; and the Sidney Myer Performing Arts Awards, to name just a few.

Sid's grandfather, the first Sidney Myer, was at the vanguard of human-centered employment practices in Australia and the world, providing a hospital and dental clinic on the Myer Emporium store premises. Myer's philanthropic gestures were pioneering and impactful in times of great need. His immense public gifting started in 1926 when he donated 25,000 Myer Emporium shares (purported to be worth £50,000 at the time) to the University of Melbourne to boost education during a time of increasing poverty. This gift paralleled the substantive donations he made to major hospitals suffering shortages in the aftermath of World War I.

Myer was just as generous in the arts. A violinist himself, in 1929 he initiated a series of free outdoor concerts in Melbourne's botanical gardens featuring the Melbourne Symphony Orchestra. These gatherings morphed into annual concerts that continue to this day, one hundred years on. These concerts were so successful that they resulted in Myer's ultimate long-term gift to the city of Melbourne and its people (through the subsequently established Sidney Myer Fund)—the Sidney Myer Music Bowl.

From the wellspring of Sidney Myer's hard work and values, successive generations have carried the family contributions to both business and society to even greater heights. According to recent estimates, since the Sidney Myer Charitable Trust (now the Sidney Myer Fund) made its first grants in 1938, the fund has disbursed more than a billion dollars in today's currency values.

The Myer family's capacity to sustain the core values of bold entrepreneurship combined with positive impact through the generations is a paragon for other families aspiring to intergenerational values transfer. The endurance of these values is no accident. In a similar spirit to

Australia's indigenous peoples' transference of knowledge in songlines, the Myer family holds intergenerational retreats, referred to as "corroborees." These gatherings of the extended family at family rural or city properties facilitate informed dialogue across the generations. To inject the latest ideas into the family mix, business and community groups are also invited to participate in workshops to "define a just and good society." The family philanthropy is often a subject of robust debate.

In their philanthropic pursuits, as in business, Myer family members (especially Sid) have a knack for sensing emergent or future trends long before they are on the public radar. Christine Edwards, former chief executive of the Myer Foundation, noted that the family has a history of looking for "bigger ideas" in its philanthropic activities. They have been first movers for many critical initiatives affecting Australia as a nation and its place in the world. Myer family members across the generations have been supporters of indigenous rights, dialogue for enhanced mutual understanding between mainstream and Muslim minority populations, Australia's relationship to the world, the critical importance of the arts to the fabric of society, and the impacts of climate change on the land. Edwards observed, "[The Myers'] engagement is just phenomenal. . . . They don't stop. They are people driven by values."[14]

MFCo and corporate leadership

Sid Myer, now in his early sixties, is one of many carriers of the family flame. Sid asserts: "No one of us holds the key to the family's name. . . . It's a collective effort and sustained over time, consistently applied. I just happen to be in one of the many family leadership places at the moment." Sid's siblings, Rupert and Samantha, as well as numerous cousins, have all played roles in building on the family legacy of enterprise and impact. In the last five years, G2, G3, and G4 of the Myer family, exemplifying the bold, entrepreneurial spirit from which they have sprung, have been involved in a major transformation of the

Myer Family Company. By 2014 the firm was managing close to A$3 billion for more than one hundred and twenty wealthy family client groups, having doubled these statistics over the preceding five years. Always futures-oriented, the firm was reorganized in 2014 and changed the name of the company to MFCo. It appointed an external CEO and board chair and added two external board members who served alongside Sid and his cousin, Martyn Myer, then chair of Myer Family Investments (MFI), a client of the larger MFCo.[15] This transformation set an example of good governance with both diversity and externality. The changes clearly leveraged the firm's strengths. MFCo won Euromoney's award for Best Family Office Services in 2013–2014 and its award for the Best Ultra High Net Worth and Best Succession Planning and Trust firm in 2015–2016.[16]

In June 2017, alert to opportunity and masterfully capitalizing again on MFCo's winning formula, the Myer family merged MFCo operations with Mutual Trust, established by the Baillieu family (another of Australia's richest families), to create a multibillion-dollar wealth management and intergenerational advisory powerhouse. Commenting on the benefits of the merger, Sid, as the new chair of MFI, noted in his characteristic, understated manner, "Both [companies] have a strong heritage, are culturally aligned, and together they offer the prospect of a unique and compelling offer to clients."[17] The philanthropic positive impact thread of the Myer family's work is clearly one of the attractions for investors. As with money management firms around the world, MFCo, now Mutual Trust, is seeing and acting on the trend of investors seeking investments that target positive impact while minimizing negative impacts.

Sid Myer still holds leadership positions across the Myer Group's portfolio. Sid serves as a director of the newly formed financial and wealth management conglomerate Mutual Trust. He chairs the MFI board and the Estate of Sidney Myer, is a trustee of the Sidney Myer Fund and the Yulgilbar Foundation, and is a director of the boutique investment fund manager consultancy Copia Investment Partners.

Sid's journey up the ladder of the Myer Group of companies is classic family succession planning that other wealthy families might do well to emulate. Among his many roles, Sid spent twenty years as CEO of the Yulgilbar Group of companies, reflecting his lifelong involvement with its farming activities, not least of which is his cutting horse prowess. The Yulgilbar Group encompasses a portfolio of local and international investments including agricultural, property, and business interests in Australia and offshore. Yulgilbar derives from Sid's mother's (Sarah) side of the family, being a rural property initially purchased by Sid's maternal grandfather, Sam Hordern, in 1949. Yulgilbar's thirty-five thousand acres—with the mighty Clarence River meandering through—are located in northern New South Wales. The name Yulgilbar was the word used by local indigenous people for "a place of little fishes" to be found in the river. Since the early 1950s, Yulgilbar Station has been a cattle and horse stud, pioneering breeders of Santa Gertrudis cattle and quarter horses originally imported to Australia from King Ranch in Texas.

Foundation for Rural and Regional Renewal

Intertwined with his business engagements, Sid has been an active influencer in Australia. He is a modest and understated yet compelling thought leader and power broker, both in business in general and in the financial and agricultural industries specifically. He is also a key influencer of Australia's links with Asia, and with impact investing and philanthropy. In a manifestation of his longtime love of and involvement with the land, Sid was founding director of the Foundation for Rural & Regional Renewal. The foundation came about through a joint initiative led by Sid's father, Baillieu Myer, and former Australian deputy prime minister John Anderson, along with the Sidney Myer Fund and the Australian government. Arising from concerns about economic and social decline in many of Australia's rural areas in the late 1990s, the foundation is a unique collaboration between government, business, and philanthropy. It seeks and disburses funds aimed at programs facilitating improvement in the lives of those living in rural, regional, and remote Australia. The foundation's long-range intention: to promote "vibrant, sustainable, and adaptable communities" in these areas. It funds place-based, locally driven programs, predicated on the belief that "community members are best-placed to understand community needs, wants, and aspirations."[18] The foundation is a strong advocate for community-based solutions for community issues.

Asialink

Another of Sid's long-held personal passions is furthering Australia's links with Asia, which he helped facilitate during his tenure as chair of Asialink at the University of Melbourne. In the late 1990s, Sid and his wife, Fiona, and their young family moved to Kuala Lumpur to oversee the family's business interests in the Asia-Pacific region. This period of immersion in Asian life fueled Sid's belief in the imperative for close and well-developed ties between Asia and Australia. Sid served as chair of Asialink from 2004 to 2017 and as chair of Asialink Business from 2013 to 2017. During the years of Sid's chairmanship, Asialink—with astute foresight regarding Asia's burgeoning growth as a global center of economic power—advocated for investment in developing Australia's workforce to be "Asia ready and capable"; identified the individual and organizational capabilities most critical to business success in and with Asia; defined effective strategies that businesses could implement to improve Asia capabilities within their organization; and made recommendations about the role for governments and educational institutions. Asialink's work led to the establishment of a National Centre for Asia Capability (now Asialink Business), to help position Australia for the demographic changes sweeping the globe in the next decade and beyond, when Asia will likely be the new epicenter of power.

While Sid describes himself as a businessman first and philan-thropist second, his contributions to the impact arena can hardly be separated or underestimated. As with his grandfather and father before him, Sid's business activities are deeply intermingled with his contributions to the wider society. He is very clear about what enables the philanthropic work of the family and is modest about his own contribution: "I'm engaged in the philanthropy of my grandfather in that I'm a trustee of the Sidney Myer Fund and I have been a direc-tor of the Myer Foundation. It is important to note, however, that in those roles of being a trustee or a director, we are custodians of some-one else's philanthropy. It's not my money that we are administering or granting or giving away."[19] In a family that has devoted at least 10 percent of its wealth to charitable causes for one hundred years, Sid gives dollars and time, personally and through the Sid and Fiona Myer Family Foundation. He has served on the board of Zoos Victo-ria Foundation, chaired the board of the National Asian Languages and Studies in Schools Ministerial Reference Group, and headed the Beyond Australia Task Force, funding Australian programs in Asia and the Pacific.

Although he would shy away from the description, Sid Myer is emblematic of the Myer family story, a story of lifelong achievement through dedication to bold entrepreneurship, a strong work ethic, peo-ple-centered values, and futures thinking in business and in impact. The trajectory of the Myer group of companies is a story of strident expansion, not just of conservation of wealth but of enviable growth. A trajectory made possible by bold creativity, innovation, resilience, family sticking together, education, values, and ideas exchanges across the generations—along with unprecedented and exemplary support for those in less fortunate predicaments. Sid is also emblematic of twenty-first century philanthropists whose positive impact work is enmeshed in business work.

While Sid publicly asserts that the family "business" is the main show, he and his family members' contributions to the wider community, to a better Australia, are just as integral to who he is and what he does. His modest acknowledgment of this is quintessential Sid: "Sure. . . . You can't forget the family legacy and a family history of engagement with the community. . . . My prime drivers are to be supportive and interested around the things I believe in."[20]

Given the family name and rich philanthropic legacy, one might be justified in expecting Sid to be a traditional philanthropist, gifting resources only to those causes close to his heart or pivotal in perpetuating the family business interests. To give in the short term to causes that are trendy or have public relations value. But what makes Sid not-so-traditional is his willingness to speak out (even if his views rail against the establishment). He supports ideas and actions whose positive impacts might not be known for decades and desires to invest both time and other resources to educational and policy initiatives that, while benefiting individuals in the short term, ultimately benefit the country and the world in the long term. He works to orchestrate gatherings of diverse peoples with shared values and overarching interests—to chat, debate, question, challenge, grow, learn.

ENTREPRENEURSHIP FOR IMPACT INSIGHTS SUMMARY

Paradigm-challenging author Anand Giridharadas accuses traditional elites and rich philanthropists of engaging in "philanthropic side-hustles doubling as vanity projects while doing harm in their day jobs." He charges philanthropists with hawking self-aggrandizing solutions to some of the world's most difficult socioeconomic and geopolitical challenges, without understanding the complexity of these problems.[21] While conceding that today's elites may be among the most socially concerned in history, Giridharadas chafes at the notion that financially successful entrepreneurs and business moguls are uniquely suited to solving the world's toughest social predicaments with their philanthropic gestures. Twenty-first century philanthropists Lance Fors, Pascal Vinarnic, and Sid Myer hold no such illusions. Each is integrally involved in the collaborations and partnerships that characterize their giving of resources, and each is simultaneously focused on the local and the global, the short and the long term, intent on minimizing harm by sustained commitment to doing the right thing for their communities, their nations, and the world, not just serving their own interests.

CHAPTER 10

The Twenty-First Century Venture Capitalists

Venture capital (VC) plays a pivotal role in fostering innovation ecosystems by training cadres of start-up teams who contribute to the ecosystem in perpetuity. Venture capitalists are known as intrepid risk-takers, big bold financiers, entrepreneurial enablers, and start-up whisperers. Their capital is often revered for its reputation as the money of invention, facilitator of innovation, creator of jobs, bringer of innovative cutting-edge products to markets, and engine of economic growth. As Distinguished Professor Andrew Corbett (Babson College Entrepreneurship Division) told the *Financial Times*: "There is money and then there is smart money. . . . funding that comes with insight, counsel, and networks . . . can be as valuable as the money itself."[1]

Success stories like the early investments of venture capitalists in Apple, Dell, Intel, Airbnb, Genentech, and Dropbox fuel their stellar reputation. The *National Venture Capital Association Yearbook* asserted, "Venture capital has enabled the United States to support its entrepreneurial talent and appetite by turning ideas and basic science into products and services that are the envy of the world."[2]

In this chapter, we focus on venture capitalists who are at the vanguard of evolved, nontoxic, positively impactful VC practices. Before introducing these twenty-first century venture capitalists, we share further detail about aspects of the VC industry that must transform toward more positive net impact.

TROUBLED PASTS

As we approach the third decade of the twenty-first century, the VC industry—particularly at its historical epicenter in the United States—is struggling under penetrating scrutiny enabled by the very technologies the industry nurtured into life. Connective technologies have enabled unprecedented analyses and exposés of venture funds and industry performance as a whole, particularly in relation to exorbitant fees. Lack of diversity in the industry—in terms of both the investors and the entrepreneurs they back—and widespread abuses of their positions of financial power have brought exposure and derision. Damning revelations of former high-tech darlings like Facebook and Google (with Facebook even called a "digital gangster" in British Parliament for its blatant exploitation of users' personal information) have triggered increased scrutiny about unethical practices that range from the grossly blatant to the more subtle. Actions to counter the deep unethical technological undertow have so far fallen woefully short. Optimal twenty-first century futures must include a cadre of VC firms committed to funding technologies that positively impact humankind, not do harm the way many organizations currently do.

Calls for transparency

Despite the reverence the venture capital industry has traditionally attracted, actual performance is not as glowing as VCs imply. VC industry performance measures are not uniform and typically rely on self-reporting, often relying on venture capitalists' internal evaluations of portfolio companies. Independent audits virtually never happen.

Performance comparisons with public indices or benchmarks like public market equivalents (e.g., S&P 500; Russell 2000, 2500, or 3000 indices, MSCI World Index; MSCI ACWI Index, MSCI EAFE Index) are rare, though on the rise.

Inclusion and treatment of minorities

As we edge into the 2020s, the male-dominated VC industry is under intense scrutiny for its exclusive men-only culture. The statistics are telling. In 2017 a paltry 8 percent of partners in the top 100 VC firms globally were women (less than 1 percent, black women), and only 1 percent in critical investment decision-making roles. Seventy-two percent of VC firms had never even hired a woman on their investment teams. Entrepreneur statistics are equally bleak. Women receive only 2 percent of all venture funding annually, despite owning 38 percent of the businesses.[3] Angel investors (95 percent of whom have traditionally been men) show similar dismal levels of investment in women entrepreneurs.[4] Interestingly, democratized crowds are not so biased: 35 percent of Kickstarter investments have women CEOs.[5]

The mid-2010s also witnessed accumulating exposés of cover-ups of damaging behaviors in male-dominated VC cultures within and beyond the firms. As in other industries, bad boy behaviors were hushed and protected by a conspiracy of silence and covert systems of settlement. For the miniscule number of women who do work in VC firms, connective global transparency-facilitating technologies have empowered more and more of them to speak up and step out of their own dark experiences.

Profits despite impacts

Some analysts see these exposés of poor performance and exclusive men-only cultures as reflecting a deliberate avoidance by those in tech and VC of the negative impacts of what they do. As the rise of populism reveals, narratives about new technology being good for us don't play so well outside the enclaves of wealthy elites. Some argue that Silicon Valley has a definitive lack of empathy for those whose lives are disturbed by the Valley's technological wizardry.

New Yorker writer Om Malik urges giant data-driven oligarchies like Facebook, Google, Amazon, and Uber to be aware, accountable, and responsible for the impact their algorithms have on shaping popular opinions in our society. Malik warns, "People become numbers, algorithms become the rules, and reality becomes what the data say. Facebook as a company makes these bubble blunders again and again. . . . It is time for our industry to pause and take a moment to think: As technology finds its way into our daily existence in new and previously unimagined ways, we need to learn about those who are threatened by it."[6] Add the accumulating body of compelling research revealing algorithmic biases around gender, ethnicity, socioeconomic, or health status, and it is clear that the time for critical examination of the damaging consequences wreaked by these technologies is now.

TWENTY-FIRST CENTURY VENTURE CAPITALISTS

Despite these dark stories, there is light. Many twenty-first century venture capitalists defy the clubby, "vulture capital" stereotype. Many VC firms have invested in positive impact start-ups along with an array of other biotech, education, and sustainable energy companies. Many VC firms foster community; contribute to the ecosystem by their involvement in incubators, universities, government bodies, and public speaking engagements; and work with their portfolio companies to ensure net positive impacts. Growing pressure for positive impact amplifies these "pay it forward" possibilities.

Women venture capitalists are spearheading the transformation away from the dark side toward a more positively impactful VC industry. Against the backdrop of gender biases in entrepreneurship and capital provision, the global surge in purpose, and the biggest intergenerational transfer of wealth in the world's history, women are poised to be majority controllers (70 percent) over the world's capital by 2030. And because women tend toward more responsible, for-purpose investments, the power of women as investors is bound to make a formidable difference.[7]

In this chapter, we meet three inspiring women (continents apart) who are the faces of transformed twenty-first century VC. They are egalitarian, inclusive, compassionate, and gracious. Their cutting-edge entrepreneurial experiences and stellar educations, combined with their deliberate thoughtful considerations of minimizing negative impacts while maximizing the positive, show the potential for VC to contribute to the greater good, not just the economic.

THE DRAGON HUNTER: MICHELLE DEAKER

It cannot have been easy to be the only woman left in the boardroom of one of Australia's largest media conglomerates, Seven West Media. Especially when the corporation was under fire for its handling of executives' abuses of power, particularly over treatment of women. However, if being the only woman was a challenge in that context or in any other of the many business meetings in which she finds herself surrounded by men, **Dr. Michelle Deaker** is not telling. Her belief that real change only happens from within an organization drives Michelle to be a participant of and activist for change, not an onlooker or commentator.

Behind Michelle's piercing gaze and gracious smile is a steely intelligence—both bookish and (Wall) street smart. With bachelor's and master's degrees in science and a PhD in applied science, Michelle could easily have pursued an academic career, but the entrepreneurial compulsion was embedded in her DNA. Michelle's grandmother, Ann (McDonald) Butt, started her own dance school as a way to advance her performing arts career, and her mother, a dance teacher, founded The McDonald College, a school specializing in the performing arts.[8]

Upon leaving university, initially to support her mother with a grant to invest technology into the performing arts, Michelle established an IT consultancy specializing in computer hardware and software. Coinciding with the late 1990s dot-com boom, Michelle set out to create something unique.[9] She founded E Com Industries. A hugely successful prepaid card and e-voucher business, E Com grew to service more than a hundred major retail brands, including giants Coles Myer and Woolworths, with operations in Australia, the United Kingdom, South Africa, and New Zealand, and eventually managed A$700 million in retail funds. In December 2005 Michelle sold E Com Industries for A$30 million to the UK's Retail Decisions. Michelle stayed with the new company to oversee expansion into Europe and the United States.

OneVentures

By 2007, lamenting the Australian entrepreneurial talent drain to the United States, Michelle harbored a vision to support Australian innovative ideas from conception through to commercialization. Ever the entrepreneur, she founded her own VC firm, OneVentures. She was intent to practice what she had learned from the ups and downs of her own entrepreneurial journey to mentor entrepreneurs in her future investment portfolios. Because E Com had grown swiftly through the boom, and then collided with the dot-com crash, Michelle had lived the challenges of streamlining a business in difficult times, and she had experience with making difficult work environments better with progressive ideas.[10] Michelle works hard to create positive working environments with flat management structures, nurturing active contributions from the entire team, proactively fostering shared vision and commitment, and ensuring team-friendly policies and processes like job flexibility and solutions for working mothers.[11] Michelle works hard to create positive working

OneVentures aims far higher than global or national averages for women in top venture and entrepreneurial roles: At last count, 30 percent of its investees are women entrepreneurs, almost three times the global average. Within the firm, two of the three General Partners are women and 50 percent of the firm's investment team is women, resulting in a culture far removed from the misogyny of twentieth century VC.

The OneVentures approach is very hands-on, reflecting the team's core strengths, including their experience as entrepreneurs who've grown their own companies. "We've run our own companies and been through our own exits. I took E Com through the tech wreck and then raised money for OneVentures at the height of the [Global Financial Crisis]," Michelle says. "So I think I've learnt some resilience about finding paths to market when others can't." The OneVentures team is very dedicated to mentoring their founder-entrepreneurs. They are often seen leading group or one-on-one coaching sessions on topics ranging from how to deliver the best marketing pitch to the psychology of VC decision-making. Such coaching helps ensure that mentees develop and retain critical skills. Michelle asserts, "We don't just give them a big wad of money. We help them structure what they'll do with our money and we support them through identifying the key performance indicators for the businesses so we know they're on track . . . Most of the time it'll go to driving the business forward, such as product development staff or sales and marketing staff because our companies often have great products but no sales and marketing expertise."[12]

The OneVentures team likes to invest substantively, aiming to buy 20 percent to 30 percent of a company. They are committed to help grow businesses with their own intellectual and network capital alongside financial capital. With over A$320 million under management, OneVentures represents the next iteration after VC 2.0 (firms raising small funds and focusing on greater returns rather than large fees—evolving from research showing that the larger the fund, the lower the returns).

They look for innovations with potential for monumental positive impact. As Michelle described: "We ask if the business is going to be disruptive, if it's going to be a game-changer."[13]

Smart Sparrow

Several of the companies in the OneVentures portfolio are indeed potentially paradigm-shifting game changers. At least two have attracted Bill & Melinda Gates Foundation attention and funding, despite Bill Gates's voiced disgust at VC's "pathetic" financial returns. Smart Sparrow, a disrupter in education around the world, provides an educational courseware platform that enables instructors and supporting staff to design online courses completely from scratch, including interactive content (such as the ability to manipulate objects and modules on the screen), along with quizzes, virtual labs, and other multimedia features. Spun out from the University of New South Wales in Sydney, the company is a product of the doctoral research of founder Dr. Dror Ben-Naim. Smart Sparrow's platform has resulted in more than eight thousand educators creating twenty thousand online courses.

Now based in San Francisco, Smart Sparrow counts more than one hundred and fifty universities and another fifty companies and organizations as clients. A leader in the digital education space, Smart Sparrow has been acknowledged nationally and internationally: LearnX Impact Awards (Best eLearning Design, Best eLearning Model, and Best Learning Services), the U.S. Department of Education's educational virtual reality challenge (EdSim), and the United States' *The Chronicle of Higher Education* (one of nine top tech innovators), to name a few.

Vaxxas

Another of OneVentures' paradigm-shifting portfolio companies is the biotech firm Vaxxas. With technology originally developed at the University of Queensland, Vaxxas reflects OneVentures' capacity to identify game-changing innovations when they are in their embryonic stages, and then provide the financial, intellectual, and network capital to nurture the company through commercialization and sustainable business. Vaxxas scientists developed Nanopatch™ technology that delivers lifesaving vaccines through a small patch applied to the skin (looks like a small Band-Aid). The Nanopatch releases vaccine material directly to the large numbers of key immune cells immediately below the skin surface, providing an effective, less scary alternative to needles. The device has already attracted attention from the World Health Organization and pharmaceutical giants like Merck. If successful, Vaxxas' Nanopatch has the potential to revolutionize vaccine delivery, impacting global mortality rates from infectious diseases, while contributing to the eradication of others, like polio.[14]

A model for VC 3.0

Michelle and her colleagues—with their deliberate catalytic role in the entrepreneurial ecosystem of nurturing companies with the potential to contribute to a better world—are VC 3.0. They model many qualities that the coming generation of the VC industry would do well to replicate.

Focus on Local Development

Michelle and her team actively discuss the potential impacts of the companies they back, as well as how OneVentures is positively influencing the wider Australian and global ecosystems. Michelle is a humble and modest, yet fierce and relentless activist for enhancing Australia's entrepreneurial and innovation sectors. In addition to the contribution she makes as an engaged investor and board member of fledgling and established companies, Michelle and her OneVentures colleagues are active in their contribution to Australia's innovation economy. For a small country, with a population slightly smaller than the population of Texas (and a land mass the size of the United States), Australia ranks near the top internationally on research excellence, inventiveness, discovery of new ideas, quality of universities, and medical research institutes. Yet it ranks very low in turning those ideas into successful businesses in the marketplace.[15] Michelle and the OneVentures team have been dedicated to changing these ratios and ensuring that Australian innovators and entrepreneurs don't get lost in a funding "valley of death" as they try to grow.

The OneVentures team actively advocates for changes in government policy to foster innovation and commercialization, pointing out that limited growth funding often forces companies into premature share-market listings or pursuit of other markets, taking the economic value of Australian ideas offshore. Reminiscent of her dream to stop the brain drain when she founded OneVentures in 2007, Michelle argues: "The government has a role in filling a structural gap. . . . A lot of these companies . . . are not really getting the [funding] oomph that will turn them into great companies."[16]

Look for Dragons Instead of Unicorns

Unlike many of her fellow venture capitalists around the globe, rather than aspiring to find the next unicorn (private companies with valuations greater than $1 billion), Michelle is far more interested in populating the ecosystem with lots of "dragons" (companies yielding returns equal to the amount of the VC fund).[17] Michelle urges fellow investors to back companies that can have a highly successful business and great human impact. "[Financial] success stories such as Uber and Facebook are exceptions. . . . We focus on hunting 'dragons,' companies that ideally return the whole of a fund to investors."[18] These companies—while not yielding gargantuan profits—positively change the lives of their customers, employees, or end users with reasonable, healthy returns for investors. An ecosystem predominantly populated by dragons can avoid the pitfalls of unicorns.

THE DOWNSIDE OF UNICORNS

- Stratospheric valuations of unicorns can drive up valuations of attractive lower-tier start-ups, resulting in rushed due diligence processes to quickly clinch deals.

- Concentration of capital in a small number of companies may trade off capital for thousands of very sturdy, hardworking, and long-lasting smaller companies (dragons).

- Cashed-up companies may scale up before they are ready, resulting in high burn rates and setting their companies up for down rounds.

- Overvaluation means less opportunity for exit.

Time journalist Kevin Kelleher's scathing criticism of unicorns echoes these concerns about negative impacts: "Ride-sharing giant Uber, lodging disruptor Airbnb, [and other unicorns] have intimate connections to consumers and would be broke without them. All couldn't care less, it seems, when it comes to sharing their success with those consumers."[19]

Commitment to finding and nurturing dragons is a prescient aspiration as we approach the 2020s, a decade in which Asia's power will rise. In many Asian cultures, dragons are revered. Seen as primal forces of nature, religion, and the universe, dragons typically embody the positive collective history of ancestors and are often associated with wisdom and longevity. Michelle's role as a dragon hunter reflects her dedication to positively contribute to the wider ecosystem, to the greater good. She says: "I find you do better when doing something larger than [the] self . . . can be a real driver for me."[20] Doing better by nurturing financially successful, positively impactful companies; curating rich, deeply connected relationships among elements of the innovation ecosystem; modeling twenty-first century transparency in both financial and impact indicators.

It is not surprising that *Mulan*, one of the few movies featuring a female warrior who befriends a dragon, also rejects gender stereotypes while showing how commitment to things larger than ourselves can lead to amazing feats. According to a review in *The New York Times*, the film also "presents most of its male characters as buffoons."[21] In VC 3.0, buffoons will hopefully be extinct and warrior dragon hunters with empathy and commitment to positive impact will have become the norm.

THE CONSCIOUS CAPITALIST: SARA BRAND

Dr. Sara Brand knew precisely what she wanted from her life in eighth grade. According to an interview in *Austin Woman* magazine, Sara believed she was going to become a mechanical engineer and give speeches about how fighter planes worked.[22] Two decades later, Sara may not be giving those fighter plane speeches, but as one of the few female mechanical engineers on the planet with a PhD, she does give speeches imploring women to embrace their power in STEM (science, technology, engineering, and math) careers, as well as in entrepreneurship and finance, especially venture capital investing.

Growing up, Sara was blessed with parents who infused her with an unquestioned knowledge that she could do anything she wanted. In middle and high school in the late 1980s, Sara was attracted to math and science. Her passion led her to Austin, Texas, where she studied engineering at the University of Texas, gaining her bachelor of science in mechanical engineering. She subsequently earned her master of science (mechanical engineering), PhD in green design and manufacturing (public health and energy), and a management of technology certification at the University of California, Berkeley.

Sara decided to stay in California after she earned her PhD, initially working in semiconductor research. Venture capital and management consulting followed, then the C-suites of large tech companies including Intel, Applied Material, and later, Advanced Micro Devices

(AMD), where she led business units of up to $100 million. While Sara's initial roles in the semiconductor industry were more technical, it was at Fremont Ventures in San Francisco where she first tasted the role that would beckon her in the years to come. A private $150 million venture fund, Fremont Ventures, was named one of the top 10 venture capital firms for adding value to portfolio companies. Sara recalls: "I loved it because it was the perfect blend of using my technical background [and] helping companies with whatever they need business strategy-wise. I knew I really wanted to do that long-term."

Sara's tenure with AMD would also prove critical in pivoting her back to venture capital, but with a difference. During her ten years at AMD, where she progressed up the corporate ladder, Sara led the integration of the company's $5.4 billion acquisition of Canadian company ATI Technologies. Serendipitously, Sara's work at AMD landed her back in Austin at the company's local campus. In the first years back in Austin, Sara and her husband, Kevin, embarked on their own entrepreneurial adventure (Sara contributing before and after her AMD workday). Disappointed in local beer choices, they decided to start a boutique microbrewery, (512) Brewing Company, in 2008. By 2015 the brewery was producing eleven thousand barrels annually.

Mentoring women globally: removing the blinders

In her role at AMD, Sara was one of the few women in engineering and tech. As such, she was invited to become the executive sponsor of the Global Women's Leadership Forum.[23] The role was an eye-popping catalyst for Sara, bringing her out of a state of gender-blindness into consciousness about the realities women faced in male-dominated workplaces, particularly those she so loved. She remembers being virtually blind to the fact that she was the only woman in these work contexts for years because she was just used to it: "It was [preparing for the forum role] that I realized I was the only vice president who was a woman with any technical or operational background. I was very surprised."[24]

Sara's epiphany led to other realizations about her own experiences:

> As I got more senior and actually very senior, I was often in the
> background doing a lot of the work and not getting the credit. I
> worked for three Fortune 500 CEOs and I remember not speaking
> up very much, and sitting at the C-suite table not taking a lot of
> comments personally. But now I hear stories of how a woman will
> bring up a point at a meeting and then some guy brings up the
> same point a few minutes later and people say, "Great point, Jim,"
> and give him the credit. Well, that stuff happened to me all the
> time. But I did not take it personally. . . . Now when I look back,
> I think, "I can't believe this was happening the whole time and I
> didn't realize it."[25]

Sara's research on gender diversity revealed that while women constitute the majority of college graduates over the last thirty years, the
number of women in corporate leadership roles remains abysmal: Less
than 5 percent of Fortune 500 companies are run by a woman, and
only 17 percent of Fortune 500 board seats are held by women. Sara
laments that these numbers have not shifted in thirty years but sees
huge potential to contribute to changing these inequities.

Sara knows where she sits amid the statistics. Women comprise[26]:

- 60 percent of bachelor's degrees earned
- 50 percent of science and engineering degrees earned
- 30 percent of mechanical engineering bachelor's degrees earned
- 15 percent of engineering employees
- 7 percent of mechanical engineering employees
- 6 percent of venture capital professionals
- 1 percent of venture capital general partners

Rather than finding these statistics daunting, Sara sees opportunity. She knows other percentages:

- 85 percent of consumer decisions are made by women.

- 10 percent improvement in VC fund performance for VC firms having at least one woman partner.

- 30 percent more successful start-ups either went public or sold for more than their total capital investment when VC firms have female partners.

- 63 percent better financial performance when enterprises have all-women founder teams.

- 35 percent higher returns on investment (ROI) and 12 percent higher revenue growth for venture-backed companies run by a woman (compared to those run by men), using one-third less committed capital.

- 30 percent higher returns on assets (ROAs) in high-tech companies, when additional women are added to the board.

- 35 percent higher return on equity (ROE) of Fortune 500 companies and 34 percent higher ROA if women are in leadership roles.

- 53 percent higher ROE for Fortune 1000 companies in the top quartile for executive-board diversity than those in the bottom quartile.

- 200 percent more female executives in successful venture-backed companies than in unsuccessful ones.

- 6 percent more in profits for businesses with 30 percent or more female executives.

- Heightened collective intelligence of groups when women are part of the group, such that teams with more women outperform teams with more men.

Sara came to an uncompromising conclusion about herself: "[When] my eyes opened . . . I realized I wasn't being much of a role model for other women."[27] Sara's journey to consciousness gave her the impetus to enact dramatic change to her trajectory. She remembers thinking: "I don't want other women to go through what I did. That's not the model I want for a successful woman in corporate America to look like."[28]

True Wealth Ventures

Sara wanted to get back into venture capital, with two key differences: a substantively smaller fund (Fremont Ventures was $150 million) and a gender focus—investing in women-led businesses that have been notoriously undercapitalized.

Austin, Texas, seemed ripe for the systems-transforming initiatives Sara envisaged. While ranked No. 1 globally for tech-enabled environments for women entrepreneurs (with Texas second in the United States for fastest growth in the number of women-owned businesses), Austin ranked a poor sixteenth for capital invested in women-led businesses and fifteenth for attracting and supporting women entrepreneurs.[29] Seeing Austin's women entrepreneurs missing out on capital, Sara recognized a huge potential. Her "aha" moment came when she learned the correlation between enhanced company financial performance and women in leadership roles. She realized that nobody else in the southern United States was focused on investing VC dollars in women-led businesses.[30] In pondering a leap into VC, Sara was stunned to realize she had never met a woman venture capitalist in all her years of working in the San Francisco Bay Area and Austin. While Sara knew women-led VC firms were not new across the United States—with pioneers like the Women's Growth Capital Fund, founded by Patty Abramson in Washington, D.C., in the late 1990s—a female-led VC firm specifically investing in female entrepreneurs was new in Texas.

In 2015 Sara resigned from AMD and joined forces with fellow trailblazer Kerry Rupp to found True Wealth Ventures. Their mission: invest in women-led start-ups focused on growth markets in consumer health and sustainable products. The pair makes a formidable team, bringing complementary educations, skills, and networks to their new venture. Sara, the science and engineering PhD; Kerry, the Harvard MBA. Sara's entrepreneurial experience—integrating start-ups into larger companies, managing corporate mergers and acquisitions, co-founding a microbrewery—complements Kerry's experience growing companies from the earliest stages. Together, the two women bring a comprehensive, rigorous approach to due diligence and funding.

In 2016 they set out to raise their first fund. Intentionally small in comparison to average VC firms (heeding data showing that smaller VC funds outperform larger funds), Sara and Kerry believe their size enables them to invest where other VC firms cannot: in a company's seed stage of growth. As Sara said: "There are so many outstanding opportunities to make investments that have simply been overlooked. . . . We expect to get higher financial returns just by the diversity of the portfolio." In an echo of Michelle Deaker's call to populate the ecosystem with dragons rather than unicorns, Kerry adds, "In a small fund like ours, we can have a great multiple on the fund without having to have a Google or an Airbnb."[31]

Sara and Kerry are also excited about the potential of their fund to have multiplying positive impacts on the wider community. In September 2017, True Wealth was granted impact fund status from the Global Impact Investing Network, a first for a VC company with a gender lens. Their specific investment thesis—to get more women to the leadership table, particularly in the sustainable consumer and health sectors—sets them apart. Earlier in 2017, True Wealth won a $250,000 grant from the U.S. Economic Development Administration, an award targeting initiatives focused on regional economic development in underfunded areas. In a feat of creativity, Sara and Kerry submitted the application with the argument that, as primary consumers, *women* are an underfunded region.

Besides their commitment to fund this vast underfunded "region," True Wealth focuses on gender-diverse companies as a sound investment strategy because gender-diverse companies yield equal, if not superior, returns on investment. Given that women make most consumer decisions, Sara and Kerry believe that companies designing products and services for female consumers will be poised for even greater success, especially products that address issues directly impacting women: maternal mortality, clean water, and safety.[32]

Sara and Kerry see the potential for multiple positive impacts. Investing in companies that significantly improve the lives of women and girls accelerates social change and drives returns. Goldman Sachs documented this "gender dividend." Women tend to reinvest 80 percent of their increased wealth back into their families, health, education, and nutrition, lifting everyone. Only 40 percent of men do so.[33] Besides the financial returns and positive impacts, research on contributors to entrepreneurial success affirms True Wealth's gender strategy. Sara asserted: "The primary criterion when making an investment is the financial return. . . . There is also a feel-good component. . . . Our fund focuses on people who care about social issues such as gender, health, and sustainability. It makes them feel good that they can make money and do good things at the same time."[34]

True Wealth conducts due diligence on hundreds of companies and invests in less than 5 percent of them. Sara and Kerry's initial investments reflect their entrepreneurship + positive impact = success ethos as well as the rigor of their approach. Their very first investment, Unali-Wear, founded by serial innovator Jean Anne Booth, won the Woman's Way Women-led Business of the Year award in 2016. Booth's Kanega smartwatch is a life-alert and medications reminder device empowering senior citizens and those with limited mobility. Booth praised True Wealth: "True Wealth has been a fantastic partner, providing back-channel support that helps us close additional money to build the business. Because [they] understand women entrepreneurs, it allows you to more quickly focus on the business—without first having to overcome unconscious [or conscious] bias."[35]

True Wealth's second investment was in BrainCheck, a Houston-based start-up headed by CEO Yael Katz. BrainCheck is a mobile brain function measurement platform that resulted from twenty years of research at Baylor College of Medicine and was later spun out of the Texas Medical Center's TMCx Innovation accelerator. Experts see BrainCheck's technology democratizing sophisticated psychological neuro-testing in a way that can help an aging world population identify and treat dementia earlier than ever before. The platform is also the basis for a BrainCheck app that enables people at home to identify signs of concussion.[36]

In a similar approach to OneVentures, once inducted into the True Wealth portfolio, entrepreneurs are immediately ushered into a unique community. Twice a year, True Wealth convenes events to bring together investors (80 percent of whom are women) and leaders from their portfolio companies to facilitate beneficial connections and additional mentoring opportunities.[37]

Because of her own journey to consciousness, Sara feels responsibility from those years of blindness to be a catalyst enabling others (men *and* women) to uncover and counter their own unconscious gender biases. True Wealth does this through role modeling, coaching, and mentoring budding entrepreneurs and venture capitalists, as well as raising awareness and educating women to become investors. For aspiring young female venture capitalists, the company mentors interns from the University of Texas Venture Fellows Program. These MBA students assist in organizing and navigating the True Wealth landscape, gaining vital VC experience. Given that VC is such an exclusive industry, difficult to infiltrate, such experience can be momentous.

Sara and Kerry are at the leading edge of the wave of women embracing their financial power, a wave that will grow and crest during the 2020s as women become the majority owners of the world's financial capital. Like other VCs before them, the True Wealth duo found that high-net-worth women, especially, while generous in philanthropy, have not focused much on investing. Sara noted: "Women haven't been investing very much in venture capital or even as angel investors. Increasing those numbers is really exciting on making sure we're sustaining the innovation economy in this country." True Wealth regularly holds awareness-raising sessions across Texas for potential women investors, sharing the compelling statistics about the benefits of women entrepreneurs, venture capitalists, and investors in unleashing the power of the female wallet. To complement these initiatives, Sara is also a founding investor in Portfolia's Rising Tide Fund. An initiative of the Kauffman Foundation, Rising Tide is a learn-by-investing fund and an angel-investing network for women that includes more than a hundred Limited Partners from twenty-two states and five countries. Most of the Limited Partners—with diverse backgrounds from entrepreneurial ventures, C-suites, family offices, and corporate boardrooms—have never invested in a venture fund or an entrepreneurial company before. Like True Wealth, the Rising Tide Fund considers women-led companies an untapped lucrative market for investors.

Through these strategies, True Wealth ultimately enhances the entire ecosystem by boosting the diversity of both doers and investors. Sara knows how women can hold themselves back from achieving and strongly believes that getting more women into leadership roles will naturally attract more gender-diverse leadership teams. "More women will see it, so they can be it."[38] While she is her own harshest critic about her past blindness to gender diversity, Sara knows her early experiences of coping and thriving in male-dominated worlds inform her passion to diversify the ecosystem going forward. She reflects: "Looking back, I think I should have worked more gently or subtly on changing things as an insider versus just accepting the situation. But if I'd been more attuned to what was happening, I might not have put up with it and then I wouldn't be where I am today."[39] Today, Sara leads the charge for the diversity sea change that is coming.

THE IMPACT PURIST VENTURE CAPITALIST: JENNY ABRAMSON

Dressing as Wonder Woman at a Halloween celebration a few years ago was no masquerade for **Jenny Abramson**. Parallels between Jenny and the superhero icon are hard to miss: embracing and building on rich female heritage, strength and resilience in a male-dominated world, commitment to doing good, and purveying hope. Wonder Woman—first conjured by William Marston in 1941—is the embodiment of feminine strength and capability, courage, unerring compassion, inclusivity, and commitment to making the world a better place. It is fitting that Jenny Abramson donned her costume.

Jenny describes her own journey into the thick of tech and venture capital as less than traditional, and her trajectory provided many predicates that would serve her well in combining impact and finance. After graduating from Washington, D.C.'s, first racially integrated school (Georgetown Day School), Jenny flew to the opposite side of the country to Stanford University. It is not easy to stand out in such a lofty environment, but Jenny did, graduating with a bachelor's and a master's degree in four years. After Stanford, Jenny channeled her values and Stanford training into health-care equality as a Fulbright Scholar at the London School of Economics, focusing on the ethical, political, and legal implications of the Human Genome Project. It was through her studies at Stanford and the London School, her subsequent time in business at the Boston Consulting Group, and her work on program strategy and development at Teach for America that Jenny came to understand the significant role business can play in solving the world's greatest inequities and challenges in health care, education, and beyond. She thus headed to the hallowed halls of Harvard University to earn an MBA. Again distinguishing herself amid the highest of high achievers, Jenny graduated with honors and a rare Dean's Award.

After Harvard, the lure of her hometown, Washington, D.C., was strong. Jenny embarked on a nearly eight-year career with The Washington Post Co. The words of former CEO Katharine Graham—"Do well in order to do good"—resonated with Jenny. She recalls, "I didn't have a specific career path I was seeking. I have been lucky to have interesting opportunities arise with a commonality among them related to doing something that makes an impact on society."[40] During her tenure with The Washington Post Co., Jenny led a range of businesses from turnarounds to start-ups and played a leadership role in broader company innovation efforts. As general manager of *The Washington Post Magazine*, Jenny helped lead the magazine's redesign. The Post kept adding to her impressive spectrum of responsibilities: publisher of *FW* (*Fashion Washington*) and general manager of *Washington Post Live*. During her time at The Washington Post Co., Jenny witnessed and participated in massive organizational transition as the company moved from print to digital and beyond.[41] Such experiences transforming organizations facilitated her thinking about how organizations can and must evolve while retaining their best attributes. Committed to giving back, Jenny took a leave of absence to manage the Transformation Management Office at DC Public Schools, work she looks back on as a thrilling and invigorating experience that enhanced her understanding of how organizational change is achieved.

Personal and LiveSafe

After The Washington Post Co., Jenny made a conscious decision to help create change and to work with organizations enacting positive impacts on communities. She was drawn into the world of tech, first with Personal (a private personal network and data vault for individuals to manage and control access to their digital information), and then with LiveSafe (the Arlington, Virginia-based maker of safety and alert technology for universities and businesses). The tech industry appealed to Jenny for its potential to produce quick results at scale, as well as constant innovations.[42] She was drawn into a leadership role at LiveSafe, an opportunity that gave her firsthand experience as a tech CEO before she launched into venture capital. "I was blown away by what [LiveSafe] had built and the impact it could have. . . . The idea of empowering people with the phones they use every day to make themselves and their communities safer [was] a really powerful one."[43] The app design team, which included a Virginia Tech shooting survivor, made it possible for students to send texts with video and photos to convey unfolding events live, thus aiding the management, prevention, and solving of crimes. When Jenny left LiveSafe, the app had been customized for universities and institutions across more than twenty U.S. states, with many more in the pipeline.[44]

Jenny's time at LiveSafe had a profound effect on her trajectory. As CEO of a tech company in the impact space, she experienced that when "you do good for the world you can accelerate financial returns."[45] LiveSafe showed Jenny the compounded value of impact businesses; however, the dearth of capital going to companies with gender-diverse leadership teams and impact-oriented for-profit businesses was blatantly salient.

Rethink Impact

Jenny put her values into practice, joined an investment firm, and founded Rethink Impact. Listed as one of B Lab's Best for the World Funds, Rethink Impact specifically invests in businesses using technology that can solve global challenges while finding untapped market opportunities. Jenny described the Rethink Impact approach: "We focus on companies that touch on the UN Sustainable Development Goals . . . education, health care, financial inequality, environmental sustainability. . . . We think it takes both the public sector . . . and the private sector to tackle these issues."[46]

Given her experiences as one of few women among other executives in the tech space, along with her strong entrepreneurial lineage, Jenny was determined to fund women entrepreneurs. "I was surprised, given the number of impressive women who had graduated with me from Harvard Business School and the fact that women start businesses at twice the rate of men, that female CEOs get only 2.19 percent of venture capital dollars. . . . The data clearly show there is a market opportunity here," she said.[47] Rather than lambast men in the industry for their shortcomings in not investing in women, Jenny is again informed by data: "Venture is a pattern recognition business. . . . With [less than] 6 percent of venture capitalists who make decisions being women, it's no wonder that less money goes to women entrepreneurs. . . . That's where some of the opportunity and some of the unconscious bias lies."[48] Knowing the data shows gender equality creates sustainable growth and improves a company's bottom line, Rethink Impact works to tap into that opportunity.

Rethink Impact has invested in a variety of impact companies, including Change.org (the for-profit petition platform) and EVERFI (a digital education company). In 2017 Rethink Impact led the Series A financing of Ellevest, a financial tech start-up on a mission to end the gender gap in investing and personal finance via a digital investing platform. The platform aligns women's investments with their financial goals and risk tolerance. Predicated on women's financial experiences rather than men's—longer lifespans, different salary arcs, different risk tolerances, and the possibility of extended time off from work—the Ellevest platform has a distinct competitive edge over competitors for female customers because it is based on data about women.[49]

Women's Growth Capital Fund

Jenny was raised to believe that success is defined by what you give back to your community as much as it is by status or monetary returns. Like Wonder Woman, Jenny had strong female role models, particularly her glass ceiling-shattering mother, Patty Abramson. In the late 1970s, as one of three female partners of a promising new marketing and communications business, Patty tried to secure credit for the fledgling firm. Banker after banker agreed to loan Patty and her partners the money *only* if their husbands would co-sign. Patty eventually found a banker without such demeaning terms and her firm flourished, but she did not forget.[50] Twenty years later, Patty and two colleagues founded the Women's Growth Capital Fund. Based in Washington, D.C., with a mission to invest specifically in enterprises run by women in the Mid-Atlantic region, the fund became the largest women-run source of VC in the United States at the time. The firm raised $25 million from sixty-five investors, 70 percent of whom were women, and eventually raised $50 million, including a Small Business Administration matching award. Patty said: "It's about getting our foot in the door. It's about having a place at the table."[51] To counter systemic barriers to women not getting more than 2 percent of dispensed venture capital, the Women's Growth Capital Fund helped women entrepreneurs develop the networks that would provide capital and access to larger financial markets. Patty also founded WomenAngels.net, the first female angel investment club in the United States to invest in the early "seed" stage of women-led start-ups. With a $75,000 membership fee, these female angels showed that women clearly had the mettle for risky business.

Like Wonder Woman—and her mother—forging new frontiers, Jenny's efforts in impact innovation and investment have been publicly recognized. She has been featured in *Forbes' 2018 Investment Guide* and named one of Washington's 100 Top Tech Leaders in 2017, one of Washington's Tech 25 in 2017, and Top 40 Under 40 in 2015.

It may have taken almost eight decades, but the Wonder Woman of the twenty-first century has grown into a potent force, amassing respect from millions of fans around the world, including boys of all ages. The incarnation of Wonder Woman in the 2017 film directed by Patty Jenkins was seen by many as the culmination of the icon's history. The film smashed box-office records around the globe: highest-grossing film directed by a woman, highest domestic opening for a film directed by a woman, highest-grossing superhero origin film, largest U.S. opening for a female-led comic book film, fifth-highest-grossing superhero film in the United States, twentieth-highest-grossing film in the United States, and seventh-highest-grossing film of 2017.[52] Some question why it has taken over seven decades to give the longest-running and most well-known female superhero her own film while her male peers have headlined features, animated series, and major comic-book events for eons. Others celebrate the dawning of a new era of egalitarianism and female achievement without misogyny, a point in women's history when the attributes that make Wonder Woman so radical—her unabashed femaleness, unerring compassion, worldly wisdom, and courage to act as a catalyst for the greater good— are built on rather than derided.[53] As one comics analyst noted: "She is, in short, the living seed of change."[54] So too are Michelle Deaker, Sara Brand, and Jenny Abramson.

ENTREPRENEURSHIP FOR IMPACT INSIGHTS SUMMARY

In the globally connected 2020s landscape, exclusive, negatively impactful entrepreneurial endeavors pursuing profit regardless of collateral damage will increasingly have nowhere to hide.

The rising twenty-first century venture capitalists are forging new, more positive futures in the entrepreneurship and investment arenas, standing out in this new landscape as they lead by example. They understand the negative financial, social, and environmental impacts of male-dominated bastions of entrepreneurship and capital. They are conscious of the positive performance statistics that overwhelmingly show the multiple and diverse positive impacts for including women and minorities in key executive roles. They consciously curate inclusive, positively impactful entrepreneurial ecosystems. They nurture companies that seek to avoid exploiting people or the planet for profit. They invest in more positive futures for all, not just with their dollars, but with their attention to the processes of collaboration, brokering and nurturing relationships, partnerships, and networks; and with their passion and commitment to a better world for all of us through more positively impactful innovation and entrepreneurship.

PART THREE

Toward 2030: Which Future?

We now shift our focus toward the horizon, to events beyond the present time, and toward the infinitely possible number of alternative futures that await us. As we turn to face those futures, more and more of the world's citizens are aware of the implacable avalanche of converging forces—climate, geopolitical, socioeconomic, technological, psychosocial—that will affect how our individual and collective futures will unfurl. We steer toward what lies ahead with curiosity and informed imagination. We start by conjuring what our world might be like on the other side of the 2020s. What issues will become most urgent? How might the very definitions of value and success be transformed? And, practically speaking, how might innovators, entrepreneurs, and investors identify and take advantage of opportunities for their organizations and stakeholders while contributing to the greater good and not doing harm throughout the ecosystem? If we were bestowed the opportunity to choose which futures become our individual and collective realities, which futures would those be?

In this final section, we provide more detail about what we learned from the inspiring innovators, entrepreneurs, and investors we consulted—the thinking and doing we all might adopt to enact positive impacts that contribute to more positive futures for all. We relate how twenty-first century changemakers live and breathe impact—not as an outcome but as a process, and not as an add-on to doing business, but as an innate way of thinking and doing every day in work, play, and life. We share insights on measuring impacts (positive and negative) throughout our own and other ecosystems. We do so with awareness that what works in one place might not work in another, that tailored, nuanced approaches capture nuanced complex impacts. In concluding, we consider our own connection to all of the inhabitants of planet earth for all millennia—past, present, and future. How small actions by anyone, anywhere, anytime can combine to have disproportionately large impacts on someone or something, somewhere, sometime. Utilizing these knowledges—to daily think and do so that more people experience net positive impact—is our imperative.

CHAPTER 11

Likely Geopolitical and Socioeconomic Futures in 2030

"Tomorrow, and tomorrow, and tomorrow, Creeps in this petty pace from day to day, To the last syllable of recorded time; And all our yesterdays have lighted fools The way to dusty death."
—*Macbeth*, William Shakespeare, 1606

E ven William Shakespeare lamented how quickly the future is upon us. Perhaps in this twenty-first century, future-telling will no longer be the realm of science fiction or mystics. Technology will facilitate accurate peering into coming times, a keyhole for the curious into the outcomes of alternative pathways. While we cannot predict the future at this point in our history, the capacity to construct evidence-based scenarios of multiple possible futures is abundant, with futurists and forward-thinking impact changemakers leading the charge. Futurists have acutely sensitive antennae for discerning impending change and often detect emerging patterns long before they are salient to casual observers. They build realistic future scenarios predicated on evidence from the past and juxtaposed with extrapolations into the future—a fusion of history, analytics, and imagination, of past and multiple possible things to come.

A deeper understanding of the patterns of change—and potential disruptions—is enabled by futures studies and strategic foresight. The purpose of futures studies, foresight, and longer-term thinking is to invite people and organizations to make more informed and imaginative decisions in the present in the face of new challenges and complex dilemmas, and ultimately, to facilitate better futures for all. With our co-researchers at the Institute For The Future, we systematically and exhaustively scoured credible forecasts for various possible futures for the planet. We synthesized these analyses with insights from our consultations with impact innovators.

This chapter shares the results of comprehensive research and analysis of future realities for our planet, along with apparent forces and emergent trends, which will shape the way we will live and work over the next decade or two. We hope to provide individuals and organizations with context to help navigate the territory ahead.

DOMINANT GLOBAL TRENDS TOWARD 2030

Between now and 2030, four dominant global trends will shape the environments in which all people, communities, and organizations (large or small) operate. These four fundamental "givens"—if we follow trend lines rather than headlines—are highly probable. Individuals, communities, organizations, and national and global governance institutions face an imperative to enhance their capacity to navigate these global realities. Because these realities are by their very nature characterized by volatility and potential for extreme impact, the capacity of individuals and organizations to pivot from their current trajectory to preferred futures as they traverse the territory ahead will be critical. In the next section, we look more closely at four of the most consequential contextual trends that will affect our capacity to maximize impact in the coming ten to fifteen years—changing global populations, escalating environmental jolts, intensifying socioeconomic divides, and escalating tensions between extremists and mainstreamists.

Changing global populations

Babies born on the eve of the twenty-first millennium will celebrate their thirtieth birthdays in 2030. As young adults, they will live in a world in which the most populous country on the planet will be India, closely followed by China. In 2030 the global population is estimated to be almost 8.5 billion people (up from 7.3 billion in 2015). Almost two-thirds of them (61 percent of the world's population) will live in Asia.[1] The United Nations (UN) predicts that, between 2010 and 2030, India, China, Indonesia, Pakistan, and Nigeria will account for almost a billion births. The number and proportion of children living in the world's poorest regions and countries will continue to grow rapidly.[2] In some countries, the population of school-age children will double during the 2020s.

With our global population growing most significantly in especially vulnerable spots on our planet, the burdens of childhood diseases, health care, and water and nutrition resources will grow dramatically. These population changes will intensify pressure on natural resources, especially water, food, and energy. According to the UN's Food and Agriculture Organization, every single day on our planet welcomes two hundred thousand more mouths to feed, literally. As global population soars, we will need to produce the same amount of food in the next forty years as we did in the past eight thousand years.[3] Add these statistics to UN warnings that excessive use of antibiotics in meat and poultry supply chains is severely compromising the availability of clean food and water, with a rippling effect of frightening health and financial consequences (estimates suggest 10 million deaths and $100 trillion in costs), and we see a picture of life on our planet in the next two decades buckling under the strain. In late 2012 UNICEF declared population growth to be the biggest threat to poverty reduction in most African countries.[4]

Jolt (noun):

1) An abrupt, sharp, jerky blow or movement 2) A sudden feeling of shock, surprise, or disappointment 3) An event or development causing such a feeling 4) A serious setback or reverse.

(verb): 1) To disturb the composure of: shock 2) To interfere with roughly, abruptly, and disconcertingly 3) To give a knock or blow to.

Escalating environmental jolts

From the beautiful mountainsides of Haiti or Puerto Rico to the coastal areas of Japan or Chile, the increasing frequency and severity of weather events triggering massive loss of life and property is the stark new normal. Between 1980 and 2010, annual global loss events more than tripled—from two hundred and fifty to more than eight hundred and fifty annually.[5] These loss events, or environmental jolts, include extreme temperatures; prolonged drought; catastrophic bushfires; ferocious winds; hurricanes, cyclones, typhoons, and floods; as well as landslides and earthquakes. Extrapolating these worldwide loss events during the last three decades through the next decade, to 2030, reveals the world is experiencing a mushrooming of ever-more-devastating natural and human-made disasters. This pattern, reflected in graphs and maps from multiple sources, is unequivocal. By 2030 such loss events around the world are projected to quadruple from when records began in 1980.

These environmental jolts amplify the vulnerability of people and organizations all over the world to further poverty and hardship, disease, instability, and conflict. And in our globally connected world, as we have seen with bird flu, swine flu, and Ebola, the vulnerability of poorer populations to spreading pandemics is just a plane ride away from massive urban populations in developed countries.

Environmental jolts often have insidious rippling effects. Climate events, when juxtaposed against other phenomena, like rising prices of arable land and quality food that only foreigners can afford to pay, exert incredible pressure on communities and can fuel conflicts. These troubling realities will only worsen as we progress through the 2020s. For example, in Australia—a country whose inhabitants long ago adapted to the scarcity of water—the city of Melbourne was recently put on notice: The city will likely run out of water by 2028.[6] Against this dire warning, ecological dystopian novels, such as Paolo Bacigalupi's *The Water Knife*, are not too fantastical. Set in the American Southwest, the characters of this story fight for usable water for their increasing populations using illegal "cutting" (extracting) of water, which throws the entire United States into civil war. Novelists, like artists, filmmakers, and impact entrepreneurs, often grant the rest of us an evocative glimpse of what is to come. Other dystopian novels, like Emily St. John Mandel's *Station Eleven*, or Peter Heller's *The Dog Stars*, illustrate imminent futures in which pandemics spread so rapidly around the planet by unsuspecting intercontinental travelers that 95 percent of the world's people are wiped out.

Researchers from around the globe confirm the bleak realities depicted in novelists' futuristic conjurings. Scientists have no doubt that water will be an increasingly scarce resource. In most countries, electricity is the primary consumer of water because power plants need cooling cycles to function. If energy and power sources do not diversify before 2040 (developing and using more energy systems that do not require cooling cycles such as wind and solar), the competition between drinking water and energy demand will only intensify.[7]

Increasingly frequent and intense natural and human-made disasters will leave hundreds of thousands dead or injured and millions more displaced. The predicted loss of property and profits is astronomical. The anticipated rise in these loss events over the coming decades and the consequent danger—to lives, property, livelihoods, and our environment—are unprecedented. The UN Office for Disaster Risk Reduction warns that if these risks of major disasters are "not reduced, expected future losses will become a critical opportunity cost for development, diverting valuable resources away from capital and social expenditures."[8] With environmental jolts quickly becoming the norm, the capacity to endure these "new normal" events and pivot toward alternative positive futures will be an essential capacity.

Intensifying socioeconomic divides

Decimating disasters, waves of refugees fleeing geopolitical conflict and malnutrition, financial woes, and the rise of terrorizing extremists might indicate widespread doom and gloom. However, many analysts remind us that an abundance of countries around the world enjoy robust financial health. For most on our planet, such relative financial prosperity will likely continue as we journey through the 2020s. Many analysts see the financial health of some regions and countries shifting the financial axes of the world, moving from the West to the East.[9] The Asian Development Bank (ADB) projects that the combined national wealth of India, China, and the Association of Southeast Asian Nations (ASEAN—a grouping of ten nations including Thailand, Indonesia, and Vietnam) will exceed the combined wealth of the United States and Europe by 2030. Former ADB president Haruhiko Kuroda stated: "These three regions (India, China, and ASEAN) are on a path to significantly improve the quality of life of their citizens—in aggregate approaching half of the world's population by 2030."[10] This includes their business sectors. The World Bank reported that developing economies are becoming major investors in the world economy, and that by 2030 they will account for more than sixty cents of every dollar invested.[11]

World investors are following this trend from the West to the East, increasingly investing in Asia. In the global venture capital industry,

Asian investments during 2015 eclipsed the European market in terms of the number of deals and amounts of funding, making Asia the second biggest private equity market behind the United States. Venture funding to China-based firms in 2015 was up 315 percent compared to 2005, not because more deals were made, but because larger rounds of financing were invested in each deal. This trend is likely to continue through the 2020s. Add these statistics regarding Eastern (particularly Chinese) investment in the West, the countries along the Silk Road and other parts of the world—especially into emerging economies desperate for infusion of resources to build much needed infrastructure—and we see the rise of Asian financial dominance creeping across the globe.

The rising financial health of more countries on the planet should improve the financial status of many of the world's people. In 2015, 2 billion people (of 7.1 billion) enjoyed a middle-class lifestyle.[12] The UN anticipates that by 2030, 5 billion of the 8.4 billion global population will live in the comfort of the middle class, with 2022 predicted as the year when more people on the planet are middle class compared to working class or poor. Of those 5 billion middle-class people, 66 percent will be living in the Asia-Pacific region, 14 percent in Europe, and 7 percent in the United States.[13] While the spending powers of the middle classes vary by country, these statistics paint a clear portrait of a rising middle class, particularly in Asia.

As the middle classes rise, so do the wealthiest classes. In January 2018, Oxfam released a report revealing that in 2017 the world's richest 1 percent (fewer than one hundred individuals) garnered more than 82 percent of increases in total global wealth.[14] Winnie Byanyima, the Oxfam International executive director and one of six co-chairs of the 2015 World Economic Forum, told *The Guardian*: "Rising inequality is dangerous. . . . Do we really want to live in a world where the 1 percent own more than the rest of us combined? The scale of global inequality is quite simply staggering and despite the issues shooting up the global agenda, the gap between the richest and the rest is widening fast."[15]

The same trends that are catapulting billions of the world's citizens into financial health and wealth also risk leaving behind the poorest on our planet, plunging them into increasingly dire predicaments. As the ADB's Kuroda cautioned: "The very drivers of Asia's economic success—new technology, globalization, and market-oriented reforms . . . also create and increase disparities within and among Asian economies."[16]

As the surge in the global middle and wealthier classes takes hold, along with massive progress toward the UN's Sustainable Development Goals (SDGs), the world will witness a surge in demand for natural resources, including energy, food, and water.[17] As pressure mounts on these, the possibility of rising prices will exacerbate the capacity of the poor to access the basic resources. Rising urbanization adds to these pressures, with the high probability of congested cities spawning overflowing ghettos of poverty. For those who remain in rural areas, the urban-rural divide will intensify as financially stretched governments struggle to provide resources to rural regions with small populations.

Despite all of the positive impacts of growth in the next decade and beyond, the numbers of people who will still live in entrenched poverty (people living on less than $1.90 per day, or $700 per year)[18] remains high. Under the most positive of scenarios for poverty in 2030, analysts struggle to see how global poverty can be reduced to the global SDG of 3 percent. World Bank economist Nobuo Yoshida noted, "If each country maintains its current pace of economic growth, population growth, and changes in distribution, then the global poverty rate will decline to 8.6 percent by 2030. While better than 2013's 10.7 percent of the world's population living in poverty the projected percentage for 2030 is stubbornly and substantively higher than the UN's extreme poverty target of 3 percent" and involves hundreds of millions of people.[19] This means that while more people will enjoy middle-class lifestyles, poverty will remain an entrenched challenge, with the gap between the haves and have-nots widening, as extremely poor people lose financial ground. In their more detailed analysis, Yoshida and his colleagues warn that to end extreme poverty by 2030, prosperity (or economic growth) needs to be shared not only between the rich and the poor within a country, but also between rich and poor countries.

Developed economies are not immune to the fallout of globalization. The International Monetary Fund (IMF) revealed in 2017 that since the early 1990s, workers in the majority of advanced economies have received a declining share of national income, juxtaposed against a growing share of productivity gains gleaned by the owners of capital. The IMF attributed half of the decline in share of national income to ramifications of technological progress enabling the automation of routine jobs. The study further concluded that because the wealthy own most of the capital, a falling share of income for workers is likely to precipitate even more income inequality in the years ahead. Emerging markets are also vulnerable. The IMF reported: "Global integration, and more specifically participation in global value chains, was the key driver of declines in labor shares in emerging markets."[20]

These predictions paint a picture of exclusionary and unsustainable economic growth, with millions without simple human rights: clean water, safe food, health, education, safe environments, and sustainable livelihoods. Such exclusion from basic human rights can potentially trigger desperate regional, social, and geopolitical challenges, and global ones as well. The health consequences alone are potentially devastating. In some countries, access to health care and the subsequent impacts on health indicators for the poor have actually deteriorated in absolute terms. Lack of access to maternal and child health services, along with failure to thrive, has intensified in 20 percent to 25 percent of countries. In 10 percent of countries worldwide, infant and child mortality have remained the same for decades.[21]

Such socioeconomic disparities have given rise to the "precariat"— growing numbers of precariously employed workers, often members of the middle class whose jobs have been displaced by declining market sizes in industries like fossil fuels and manufacturing, as jobs go offshore or tasks have been automated. In the United States, these people are often called the "squeezed middle"; in the UK, they have been dubbed "the left behinds"; and in France, "les couches moyennes."[22] The numbers of people constituting the precariat have been steadily growing since the first stirrings of globalization in the 1980s. This growth has been compounded by the integration of some two billion workers from China and other emerging economies into the world's labor market, many earning only 20 percent of OECD (Organization for Economic Co-operation and Development) calculations of average pay of workers around the world.[23]

The precariat's growth was accelerated by the 2008 global financial crisis as the loss of economic opportunity became bleak for so many.[24] Dr. Guy Standing of the University of London estimates that the precariat includes 40 percent to 45 percent of the labor force in many countries, and up to 50 percent in others like Japan. Standing asserts that the precariat is not an underclass. They live in debt, often chronic and unsustainable, ensuring that their net income is well below gross income. Their children are at risk of being caught in the same cycle. In the United States, the people in the top 1 percent to 5 percent of national income spend an average of 5 percent of their total expenditures on education. In contrast, the middle class barely spends 1 percent, and working classes even less, rendering the modern meritocracy hereditary.[25] For these lower income earners, just one environmental jolt—in their own family or in their community—can tip them over the edge of financial survival. As governments' own budgets shrink and they apply high thresholds on eligibility for socioeconomic assistance, the precariat falls prey to deepening poverty traps.

Escalating tensions between extremists and mainstream populations, nationalists and elites

It is a well-documented fact that war and conflict are far more likely in areas of entrenched poverty. Inequalities of wealth can contribute to social unrest, marginalization, and even destabilization of entire regions.

The opposite can also be true. Prolonged conflict disrupts economies and decimates infrastructure, including education, and kills people who provide the intellectual and physical skills for growth. Losses from environmental jolts only add to these tensions and instabilities. During this decade of the twenty-first century, mainstream populations of the world are grappling with the rise of precariat-driven populism. Mainstream populations in the 2010s have also seen the rise of brutal extremist aggression, enabled by technologies that recruit the vulnerable to extremist causes.

Surging nationalist populism has been one response to fear. Professor Standing contends that this rise in populist sentiment is fueled by the rise of the precariat—masses of people upset about stagnant wages and the decline of opportunity since the global financial crisis. Standing says precariats are divided into three factions that, if united, create a formidable backlash force against the negatives of globalization:

1. People hailing from working-class backgrounds who see themselves as less well off than their parents.

They are the people listening to populist leaders. They fear foreigners, migrants, refugees, and others who threaten their lifestyles and their livelihoods. They contribute to the collapse by supporting established political parties and voting for the likes of President Donald Trump in the United States, the far right in France and Belgium, the Five Star Movement in Italy, and Brexit.

2. Nostalgic people who feel deprived.

Often migrants and beleaguered minorities, these people have lost their homes and a sense of belonging. They nostalgically pine for a previous existence and past world order.

3. Progressives.

Typically young and educated, but with limited opportunities for the careers and lifestyles they thought their education guaranteed, progressives feel deprived of a lost future.[26]

The common thread among the factions is the sense of deprivation and unequal opportunities precipitated by their uncertain incomes.

The 2008 global financial crisis and consequent economic shocks exacerbated these factions' sense of deprivation and lack of respect for financial and policymaking elites. Combined with a lack of occupational identity or other narrative to make sense of their lives, precariats increasingly feel despair and alienation. Only compounded by "politics as usual" in many Western democracies, precariats do not feel heard. They feel angry. Unless elites listen, precariats will make themselves heard on the streets, in polling booths, or through extreme means.

In the second decade of the twenty-first century, violent conflict was driven more by clashes between ideological and religious extremists and mainstream populations. Of the eleven substantive wars that have erupted around the world in the last few years, the majority (seven of eleven) involve radical extremists fighting in the name of Islam: Israel/Palestinian Territories, Iraq, Syria, Afghanistan, Pakistan, Yemen, and Nigeria. Add other countries with armed hostilities in the last few years—for example, Indonesia, India, Bangladesh, Egypt, Kenya, Lebanon, Somalia, Sudan, Thailand, and Russia—and all but two were associated with extremist Islamic militants.[27] According to the Pew Research Center, roughly a quarter of the world's countries are grappling with high levels of religious hostilities within their borders.[28] Turmoil and unrest in many of these countries and their neighbors (due to increased refugee populations) have deepened economic and humanitarian challenges. This has created ramifications for the Middle East, Europe, and the world.

In our increasingly networked global world, no country or economy is immune. Foreign fighters importing terror to their homelands, local ideologues who kill to make a point, and refugees spreading out across the world usher increased tensions within and between borders. The terror attack by a white nationalist on a New Zealand mosque in March

2019 reflects the irony that extremist militants, whether from Islamic or white supremacist groups, share the goal of ethnic purity in a world that is increasingly intermingling peoples from all parts of the globe. When fear is inflamed by religious or nationalist extremism, or by business and political leaders (some of whom make arms readily available in many countries for their own advantage), it is not surprising that death and destruction are also increasingly democratized.

Ayman Safadi, former deputy prime minister of Jordan, warns that current global strategies will fail if they remain primarily designed and conceptualized in the West. He notes the consequences of little regard to understanding the problems of the region, and Arab complacency: "We have seen Syria deteriorate from a revolution for democracy and freedom from an oppressive regime into a sectarian war, a civil war, a battlefield for a regional war, and very little is being done about it."[29] Safadi predicts that the next decade will be substantively worse if we continue to deal solely with the symptoms of the problems rather than the root causes. He urges the world to consider the ramifications of droves of refugees fleeing war zones and being thrown together in dire refugee camp conditions: "All the talk now is about providing daily subsistence, food and water. But in reality, in Jordan for instance, there are about 1.4 million people, of whom 600,000 are registered as refugees. Among these there are at least 100,000 children below the age of ten. What are those going to be ten years from now if they are not provided with schools, with education, with hope? We are looking at a ready army for what is worse than ISIS to come and recruit."[30]

OTHER FORCES AFFECTING POSSIBLE FUTURES

As individuals, communities, and organizations navigate these fundamental global realities over the next two decades, a whole host of other trends will also dramatically influence how we live, work, and play. While potentially no less consequential in their own ways, these other forces have less knowable, less predictable trend lines relative to the scope or intensity of their impact on economic, sociological, and political environments. These additional emerging trends may influence how effectively we detect, interpret, prepare for, and manage the impacts on our own trajectory or that of our community or organization.

The extent to which individuals and organizational leaders can navigate these intersecting global trends will profoundly shape the course of their trajectories, their organization's innovation and entrepreneurial activities, and the geopolitical, business, and social environments in which they operate. Many of the concepts explored in these next pages originated in work by Jake Dunagan and Stuart Candy undertaken at the Institute for the Future. Their research has been updated and extended.[31]

The Realities of Networked Technologies and People

We have entered an age when abundant data and a network of physical devices, embedded with electronics and network connectivity, enable millions of people to connect and exchange data (this is also known as the Internet of Things).[32] These forces are colliding and multiplying populations' power. When billions of people and hundreds of billions of things (including mobile devices, appliances, and infrastructures) are communicating and working in concert, a more responsive, personalized, controllable world becomes possible. It also means that the central challenge of a networked world shifts from obtaining data about what is going on to real-time making sense of data in this deluge. Individuals, entrepreneurs, organizational teams, and boards of directors will need to decipher how they will use and interact with this network of people and things. Will this technology be yet another tool of control for those who hold the platform strings, or will it offer emancipatory potential to democratize power and access? The answer is likely "it depends" and "probably both." Keeping a sharp eye on how abundant data and smart systems are developed for an organization's advantage is increasingly important for anyone steering themselves or their organizations toward their preferred, optimal future.

The rise of crowd power and the democratization of everything

Robust online platforms are connecting millions of skilled individuals with companies, agencies, teams, and organizations, while also lowering the transaction costs for engaging large numbers of people. Community and organizational leaders of the future can leverage these robust online platforms—from money to brainpower to surplus goods—to create value for their own organizations. The crowd is now a viable source of project funding (Kickstarter), collective brainpower (Wikipedia), a market for surplus goods (Craigslist), and a mobilizer to protect local communities (the grassroots movement of New York City borough Queens to block Amazon HQ2).

Business leaders are coming to recognize the crowd as both marketplace and competition. For example, the hotel industry has been hit hard by the sharing economy and the rise of platforms like Airbnb, HomeAway, and VRBO; the taxi industry by ride sharing; traditional public relations firms by social media influencers. Innovators of all creeds have the ability to access resources and scale activities at previously unattainable speed and cost efficiency. Peer-to-peer marketplaces allow the exchange of products, skills, services, time, or anything else a person or enterprise needs. The classic example of tapping such abundance and the changing nature of capital is Wikipedia, which took a hundred million volunteer hours to develop between 2001 and 2008, while actually employing few people.[33] Some physical manufacturing is becoming extremely lightweight as well, with everything from synthetic biology to 3D-printed materials allowing for speedy ideation, prototyping, production, and distribution of all kinds of new products. For example, HAX Accelerator is a Shenzhen, China- and San Francisco-based incubator, hardware supplier, and technical and financial support system for potential product start-ups, riding the "Hardware is the new software" trend in start-ups. With manufacturing increasingly outsourced to robots or democratized by at-home "printing," calls for the resurrection of manufacturing jobs are a twentieth-century lost dream.

Rise of the "prosumer"

One potent change in the landscape we must all navigate as a result of the collision of globally networked technologies and the Internet of Things is the nature of the marketplace. The divided and defined roles of consumer and producer are becoming much less distinct. Consumers are no longer mere users or purchasers of goods, they are also becoming involved in the design, fundraising, production, and marketing of many products through collaborative design and the sharing economy. Conversely, producers have become more collaborative in how they integrate feedback and interface with customers. It has never been easier to start and fund a business, especially through crowdfunding and other platforms. More and more people are selling, trading, giving, and sharing their creations with others on a peer-to-peer basis. Organizations founded as traditional businesses are working with these "prosumers" to create innovative business models and practices.

Rise of coworking spaces

Networked technologies and changing marketplaces are also ushering in changes to the workplace. As the digital age evolves and enhances our ability to collaborate virtually, the benefits of and need for simultaneous physical co-location become clearer by contrast. Although coworking among freelancers is long established in some contexts, many impact entrepreneurs see beyond merely sharing space to entrepreneurs of all genres amplifying the value of their location and space use in building innovation ecosystems of entrepreneurs with diverse and complementary skill sets.

Rise of adhocracies

Some of the world's most innovative business solutions are applied to some of the world's most intractable problems. These solutions are increasingly triggered by ad hoc comings together of like-minded thinkers and doers whose values, visions, and actions align around issues or problems, current and future. In these cases, values and impact draw people together from all over the planet to enact innovative solutions with little or no organizational structure, a context in which choosing roles and tasks and executing them becomes organic.

As a result of these ad hoc comings together, we are witnessing the proliferation of new organizational forms. While freelancing platforms and microtasking have generated opportunities for people to find part-time, ad hoc work, many workers who rely on these platforms for their livelihoods have begun to organize against what they feel are exploitative measures. Uber's drivers have staged walkouts and boycotts, not surprising given reports of Uber-favorable contracts and contractor mistreatment. Amazon Mechanical Turk workers ("Turkers"—people around the globe doing outsourced menial piecework for very low payment) have protested changes to the algorithms used to assign and monitor their work.[34]

Precarious workers in many industries are voicing their displeasure at a system that claims to promote flexibility but often keeps workers locked in a system with little mobility. Microtasking platforms can be a valuable resource for social entrepreneurs, but accounting for the ethics and dynamics of these systems will be critical. These new organizational forms are creating new challenges for communities, organizational leaders, legislators, and competitors alike.

Individual networks and organizational structures will also be dramatically influenced by new ways of doing work. It is difficult to create strategies for post-transformation systems, but we may be headed toward such a shift. The rise of automated systems, robotics, 3D printing, social production, free and open knowledge repositories, and other technical and economic trends are convincing many observers that our global economy and human civilization are heading toward a condition of post-scarcity.[35] Production of material goods may be distributed and ubiquitous—prototyped and manufactured in a "desktop" model. Many services will be automated or performed by robots. Digital ordering at food retailers like McDonald's and digital self-check-in at airports are already the norm, eradicating the need for human interactions in parts of the "purchase" process. Almost all of our modern institutions, policies, and economic models are built on an assumption of a finite and scarce base of human workers. In these models, that finite base must be managed either by government planning or by the invisible hand of market capitalism, or some hybrid of the two. Peter Diamandis and Steven Kotler, the authors of *Abundance: The Future Is Better Than You Think*, and many others who track technological progress believe that change will continue to accelerate. They argue that such change will usher in more advancements in solving some local and global problems in the next twenty years than we've seen in the previous one hundred.

Rise of daring data streams

Over the next decade and beyond, diverse data streams will be increasingly and commonly used to coordinate how people, resources, and tasks are routed and used for maximum impact and optimal organizational success. Technologies enabling access to stable hierarchies and physical infrastructures are giving way to flat organizations using "just-in-time" logistics. However, some of these automated coordination tools perform poorly at incorporating local understandings, human experience, and tacit cultural knowledge. We are, however, seeing emerging examples of techniques that blend the best of automated efficiency with local knowledge. Drone infrastructure companies like Matternet are using algorithms to coordinate resources, many for social good (e.g., food and medicine delivery), with "on the ground" knowledge, which builds in flexibility and responsiveness at low cost.

Algorithms can parse transactions with speed and accuracy, and may push out organizations that do not optimize for human-machine coordination (while ensuring that biases are minimized). Data will also be critical. Structures and formulas that reward individual contributions to larger projects are advancing. Platforms like Quirky build a granular royalty structure into every part of technical innovation—from ideation to coding to design. So, for example, if six people are involved in the creation of a new turntable design, then each is credited according to their level of contribution to the final product. This move toward more targeted and refined payment and reward schemes is visible in several domains, including education, health, and design.

Entrepreneurs and business managers can optimize their organizational processes by developing and deploying these new means of tracking and valuing contributions by individuals, teams, and organizations in organizational ecosystems, and how these contributions translate into larger success and impacts.

Radical transparency and accountability

The exposure (intended or not) of financial data, processes behind decisions, reputation evaluations, and metrics of success is disrupting traditional relationships between employer and employee, supplier and buyer, investor and entrepreneur, consumer and seller, and donor and beneficiary. Financial data have always been a consideration in the success of an enterprise, but the details of the relationships between stakeholders are being made increasingly visible through "sunshine" principles, proliferating data generation and access, whistleblowers and leakers, and other tools of internal and external oversight. These technologies and media can also reveal other data about the enterprises' activities, including social and environmental impacts. Bad organizational behaviors that have negative social and environmental impacts will be increasingly exposed. How organizational leaders treat their staff, how staff treat their customers, and how organizations treat the environment are becoming more and more transparent, demanding more and more accountability.

As these new dimensions and levels of transparency take hold, new expectations for actions, sharing, and trust are emerging. Decision processes, reputation evaluations, and success metrics are becoming more open—allowing new ways for stakeholders to connect, learn, and lobby for positive change. Conversely, these metrics also open up potential vulnerabilities, the potential for misleading information, and for some, increased anxiety.

Rise of tokenization and digital currencies

Just as we are witnessing a watershed in disruptive enterprise, we are seeing disruption in how enterprises are funded and monitored. Financing an idea or venture for designing, producing, and selling products and services has historically required creating a formalized organizational entity, but this script is rapidly changing. The ease of value exchange on all scales is leading to funding strategies for entrepreneurs that go beyond the traditional business formula. Crowdfunding, bartering, time-banking, sharing and networked action, alternative currencies (e.g., cryptocurrencies like the pioneer Bitcoin), and microequity all offer new opportunities for exchange. These new sources and streams of value and capital are rewriting the rules of value to embed social good, sustainability, privacy, and other goals into the activities of all enterprises. Along with these changes to the nature of capital for designing, producing, and selling goods and services, changes are equally afoot regarding how consumers pay.

In the 2020s, legalized national currencies will be less prevalent. A variety of nontraditional currencies, from digital cryptocurrencies—estimated to be an $82 billion market in 2017—to tokens, time-sharing services, neighborhood bucks, and other forms of barter will be utilized as alternative ways to fund innovations.[36] For example, in the UK, a Good Neighbours' Community Impact Bucks scheme enables local volunteer groups to support vulnerable, older, or disabled residents in local communities. Free, volunteer assistance might include transport to medical appointments, shopping, errands, small household tasks, and gardening.[37]

Some start-ups are turning to blockchain technology (databases that power digital currencies) developed by Bitcoin to fund their growth in the form of "initial coin offerings" or ICOs. Such ICOs are a special digital form of crowdfunding—an auction of "virtual shares" in which firms issue their own currencies or tokens. Investors sell out when they want, converting virtual shares to Bitcoin, Ether, and fiat currencies (currencies declared by governments as legal tender).[38] Private equity and venture capital research company PitchBook reported in 2017 that ICOs raised four times more capital than Bitcoin companies raised in venture capital dollars for the first part of that year ($1.3 billion versus $358 million).[39] While some analysts reckon this form of capital raising will outstrip or replace traditional venture capital, others label the phenomenon a bubble waiting to burst.[40]

Regardless of the long-term sustainability of the cryptocurrency market, what is sustainable is the diversity of potential sources of capital, along with an increasing recognition of all forms of capital—traditional financial, intellectual, human, social, and natural. As impact becomes more integrated into how we think about valuing assets and success, the more these forms of capital will become integrated into our financial statements and gross domestic product figures.[41]

Generational value shifts and the ascent of purpose-fueled mindsets and actions

Networked technologies facilitate the sharing of heartbreaking stories of the poor struggling to survive on less than a dollar a day alongside images of larger-than-life excesses illustrated in the film *The Wolf of Wall Street*. No longer able to escape images of dire poverty, raging conflict, and rivers of desperate humanity crossing borders to escape war, malnutrition, and death, high-income countries are experiencing a burden of unavoidable awareness. Stark realities are rallying the world's citizens against the above extremes. Our planet-wide instantaneous connectedness is facilitating a powerful global conscience and corresponding calls to action. The emergence of this global conscience and increased worldwide action to improve the lot of those less fortunate is being fueled in part by the rise of the Millennial generations—Gen Y and the first wave of Gen Z, a group numbering more than two billion worldwide.[42] By 2025 Millennials will number at least three billion people and constitute 75 percent of the global workforce. Millennials are uniquely situated at the intersection of ubiquitous, connecting cutting-edge technologies, entrepreneurship, and impact.[43]

According to a Brookings Institution analysis, Millennials and their values could upend the traditional bastions of Wall Street and corporate America.[44] Most surveys have indicated that the Millennial generation is the most tolerant, environmentally aware, and diverse generation in U.S. history.[45] Unlike their predecessors, many Millennials are less concerned with individual success and more concerned with advancing the group welfare.[46] They want to work for, invest in, or patronize companies whose missions change the world for the better. Millennials' attitudes demand net positive financial, social, and environmental impacts. Survey after survey reveals their preference to work for or invest in companies and products that pay fair wages to workers, have ethical policies, and have small carbon footprints.

Millennials are the generation attuned to the impacts of the 2008 global financial crisis, a crisis born of poor ethics. As a result, they particularly value good governance and long-term sustainability. Millennials are already putting their time and money where their values are—more are investing away from banks, away from Wall Street and London's financial "square mile" and into the impact sector. Many entrepreneurs and business school graduates are increasingly drawn to impact enterprises and the quest to do good as much as by the desire to make money. Millennials are creating, joining, and supporting impact enterprises in unprecedented numbers. And, as the first wave of Millennials edge into middle age over the coming decade and start to contemplate their own retirement needs, attracting them will be even more important to investment managers.

Whether Millennials' values of empathy, sustainability, and social and environmental good will remain strong as they enter their next life stages is an open question. But if this generation's values and lifestyle differences grow with them as they enter positions of leadership and increased power, then "business as usual" will be transformed. Gen Zers will be even more diverse and even more closely tethered to their networked devices.[47] These "digital natives" already spend far more hours interacting with their peers on their electronic, networked devices than any previous generation, rendering peer influence (in contrast to parental influence) more powerful in shaping values and actions than ever before.

In this decade of the twenty-first century, Baby Boomers are in a process of reflecting on their lives so far, how they want to spend their last chapters, and making changes to their life trajectories. Combine the rise of the more socially and environmentally conscious Millennials with Baby Boomers and other generations reexamining their lives, and we see a surge in the "purpose-driven" life. The result: more people embracing the notion that doing good for others is one of the single biggest contributors to personal peace, happiness, and well-being. Research affirms those perceptions. Many of the people interviewed during our five years of research, regardless of country or sector, were witnessing an upswing of people wanting to do good. From Japan, India, and Australia to the United States and Canada, transformative technologies are spreading positive impact stories and ethos and people are repurposing with energy, passion, and even zeal.[48] Social Venture Partners Tokyo's Takuya Okamoto observed: "Many people not only in Japan but also the world . . . want to make a difference to the world and I believe that . . . every person can make a difference to something in the world . . . not special people but ordinary people doing extraordinary things."

The largest intergenerational transfer of wealth in history is set to occur over the coming decades—with U.S. Baby Boomers alone transferring some $30 trillion in assets to Millennials—and it will fuel this surge in purpose. And women will control some 70 percent of that wealth by 2030. Financial advisors, asset managers, and mainstream corporations in many sectors, particularly finance, are responding. For example, giants like Goldman Sachs and Chase have heads of impact, BlackRock and Vanguard have green funds. Other financial services firms, like UBS, back environmental and social impact bonds with human capital bond funds. These impact bonds are increasingly available, although highly competitive.

ENTREPRENEURSHIP FOR IMPACT INSIGHTS SUMMARY

The challenges of population growth, disruptive environmental jolts, widening socioeconomic inequalities, and tension between mainstream populations and extremists are complex, immense, frightening, and urgent. The effective and efficient delivery of innovations to tackle these and other intransigent social and environmental challenges has never been more critical. The upside: While such challenges may threaten the way that we do things, they simultaneously present opportunities to do things better for enhanced futures for us all.

CHAPTER 12

2030: Four Alternative Futures

As we shift our focus toward the 2030 horizon and contemplate the multiple possible worlds to come, we can't help but wonder what issues will become most urgent. How might innovators and entrepreneurs intent on positive impact identify and take advantage of opportunities for their enterprises, constituencies, and others around the world? Innovation, entrepreneurship, and impact are embedded in complex ecosystems with an array of forces affecting all nested layers. Together these forces and the patterns they create—deep waves of change like geographical and generational population shifts, dire climate events, the rise of precariats, or cryptocurrencies—will shape strategic decisions for entrepreneurs and others intent on positive impact.

In the face of profound uncertainty—a planet-wide ecosystem far too complex for anyone to simply predict outcomes of current dynamics—the set of scenarios we describe reflects divergent, contrasting, yet plausible alternative futures for entrepreneurship and impact over the next decade and beyond.[1] In this chapter, we present four different scenarios for 2030. In presenting these scenarios, we hope leaders and changemakers will evaluate how they navigate global forces in the present and consider how best to steer toward preferred futures. These 2030 scenarios are just four of the infinite possible futures that may await us.

WHY THINK IN THE FUTURE TENSE?

"When you tell stories about the future, even if you're not claiming to forecast, there's some sense . . . that actually, the future is the story you choose."[2]

—**Dr. Betty Sue Flowers,** scenario writer, Shell International, author, former director of the Lyndon Baines Johnson Library and Museum

Futures thinking, foresight, and long-range scenario planning are methods that nudge us into creatively contemplating the future so we can make better decisions about how we act in the present.

Hindsight = foresight

Futures thinking methods are designed to capitalize on the outcomes produced by two different modes of thinking: reflecting and looking back (retrospective sensemaking) and hypothesizing and looking forward (prospective sensemaking). By taking what we've learned and making sense of it retrospectively, we can develop hypothetical bases for prospective scenarios, or stories about the future. The same process also works in reverse: By anchoring ourselves in a future time and place, scenarios enable us to look back from that point and engage in hypothetical retrospective sensemaking. According to social psychologists, when we treat an event as if it is already over, it is easier to write a specific history for the future event based on imagined past experiences that could have generated the scenario's outcomes.

Professor Karl Weick says that future events described in scenarios are more plausible because we can visualize at least one prior set of pathways that may produce the scenario's picture of the future. He argues that when imagining the steps in the scenario's history, it is likely that the person doing the conjuring will have performed some of the steps before. They can then build on the knowledge gained from their own experiences and join those experiences with new possibilities to light pathways forward from the present.[3]

Thinking in the future tense and reflecting back from that visualized future (compared to thinking in the present and projecting forward) has distinct advantages. Because the human brain views the scenario as completed, over and done with, we can picture the steps it took to get there more clearly and explicitly. In contrast, decision-makers who simply look forward relay descriptions that are less detailed, less rooted in reality, more fanciful, less sensible, and shorter than decision-makers who anchor themselves in the future and look back to construct the means to the end.

Futures thinking and scenario planning in practice

"Scenarios encourage disciplined, systematic thinking about the future. A critical role of scenarios is to present different possible pathways into the future to challenge conventional thinking and to encourage debate in a process of learning. . . . Scenarios . . . give the ability to re-perceive reality."

—**Koosum Kalyan,** former senior business development manager of African Exploration Oil and Gas (Shell International) and scenario writer, Shell International

The scenario-planning team at Shell International (the UK subsidiary of global oil and gas conglomerate Royal Dutch Shell) was full of trailblazing innovators of scenario-planning methodology. The ingenious body of work by team members such as Arie de Geus, Pierre Wack, Koosum Kalyan, Joseph Jaworski, and Betty Sue Flowers was instrumental for Shell's successful navigation of global and local challenges for more than forty years. Their advancements in scenario design have been the foundation for creative strategic planning all over the world, including for governments in South Africa, Guatemala, Hawaii, and

South Australia. The Shell team's talent for developing meaningful scenarios is based in careful research identifying future realities and trends.

The pioneering Shell team showed how rich stories woven around the interaction of known future global realities (based on meticulous comprehensive research), with the myriad uncertainties future-seers must face, have compelling force for decision-makers enacting the present. Betty Sue Flowers, as part of Shell's scenario development team, saw firsthand the power of stories to influence thought and action. Flowers believes stories help people "begin to see that the future is what you use to create the present, and that the present you then create will create the future you want."[4] Stories as scenarios set in the future provide a narrative scaffolding for thinking systematically about a range of possible futures, both good and bad. The remainder of this chapter aims to provide individuals and organizations intent on positive impact for the greater good with four alternative scenarios for 2030. The original conception and writing of these scenarios was done by Jake Dunagan and Stuart Candy, with input from Moira Were and myself. Their scenarios have been updated and revised for the book. Scenarios that are in essence a futures-oriented compass for navigating the territory ahead, as well as some key concepts to use in thinking about today's and tomorrow's challenges.

GLIMPSES OF FOUR ALTERNATIVE 2030S

The four scenarios our research depicts are set in the year 2030. When these different scenarios are mapped against each other, they produce four distinct stories and trajectories, each with its own underlying "logic" for how change could unfold. Each scenario has a different set of values driving action, with particular trends amplified or diminished. We avoid the impulse to classify any scenario as a "best case" or "worst case" future. However, each certainly has clear advantages for particular value sets, mindsets, and business strategies. Considering the four scenarios enables deep reflection about how we can adapt our own pathways to enact a future we prefer, depending on our values, core mission, and perceived relative opportunities.

During our research process, including extensive interviews and expert workshops, two of the most commonly invoked critical uncertainties by impact changemakers were the relative degree of actual impact and the intended scale of targeted populations for the impact product or service. Many of our experts and practitioners differed on the degree of impact possible and whether the best strategy was a coordinated global effort or decentralized local solutions. As a result of this input, we have built into our scenarios two critical uncertainties, or key variables: the level of society at which impact is aimed and the scale of impact from local to global. These variables are positioned along a continuum or axis that describes contrasting potential conditions in the future.

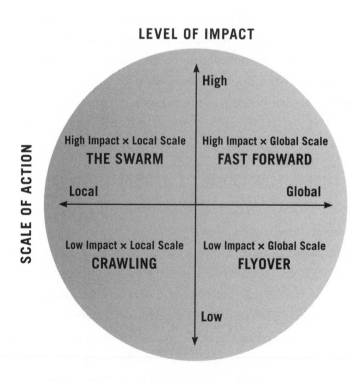

Figure 1: Level of impact versus scale of impact actions

Critical issues such as investment strategies, public perception, education, health, energy, policy, and tech adoption are integrated into each narrative. We have also created original "artifacts from the future" to accompany each scenario. These artifacts, in the genre of magazine covers, express the values, stories, personalities, and events representing each of the four alternative scenarios. It is important to stress that scenario thinking is not about prediction; rather, it is about challenging unexamined assumptions and stretching our minds to incorporate new possibilities. In each of the following scenarios, we have crafted fictional people who are illustrative of the impact changemakers who will inhabit the future. These characters act as exemplars to guide our thoughts.

Scenarios tune our neurons to be able to consider real contingencies and complex, cascading patterns. Merely asking what the future will look like is too simplistic to capture nuances that will inevitably characterize the future. By training our attention toward systems-level changes, scenarios help us anticipate and understand the effects that such changes could have on real people, businesses, governments, other stakeholders, and the planet. Scenarios help us conceptualize alternative possible futures and steer us toward more preferred futures.

2030 SCENARIO 1:
THE FLYOVER (LOW IMPACT X GLOBAL SCALE)

In the *Flyover* 2030 scenario, impact entrepreneurship is dominated by large-scale, ambitious, and highly publicized investment models and business strategies—but very few real and meaningful positive impacts have been achieved.[5] Causes célèbres of the day garner most of the philanthropic and public attention, which always seems to jump from one "crisis" to the next without a high degree of coordination or follow-up.

Still, progress is being made. Extreme poverty rates (those living on less than $1.25 per day) have decreased from 43 percent in 1990 to 18 percent. Fortunately, human-caused carbon emissions never reached the 50 billion metric tons that had been forecast for the 2020s.

Advocates point to these numbers and others as evidence that social entrepreneurship not only saved capitalism, but also that this kind of positively impactful capitalism could save the planet.

There are still critics, however, who claim that these so-called positive impact-oriented businesses are having little effect. The numbers could support them, too: Extreme poverty rates were already down to 21 percent in 2015 and have seen only modest improvements in the fifteen years since. The levels of anthropogenic carbon could also be down because of the persistently sluggish global economy since the Great Recession's onset, *not* because of the heroism of impact entrepreneurs. Milder skeptics point out that impact entrepreneurship as practiced in the 2010s was mostly well intentioned but naïve about its capacity to make a major difference.

A harsher view holds that impact entrepreneurship is merely another ploy of rapacious capitalism, little more than a thinly disguised "goodwashing" campaign or a public relations exercise allowing cynical (or delusional) power brokers to brag about changing the world without really having to address fundamental issues or risk losing their privileged positions.

Such marginal criticism aside, things couldn't be better for the impact enterprise "industry" in 2030. Business is booming in this scenario—for those with the right connections—and impact entrepreneurship has reached stratospheric buzz. The move to a more "capitalistic" social and nonprofit sector was appealing to many and drove an initial wave of investment. In this future, the poster child for this young, ambitious impact entrepreneur is Jerry Cienega, founder of Heal All of Earth Ventures (stock ticker: HAEV). With investments and initiatives all over the world, HAEV addresses critical issues such as water access, internet privacy, and drone-based humanitarianism. Its financial success has been astounding—with a recent market cap at more than $5 billion. HAEV's innovative stock buyback strategies revolutionized the impact enterprise industry. Last year Jerry topped the *Forbes* list of richest impact entrepreneurs and has pledged 20 percent of his total wealth to the recently created Jerry and Elizabeth Cienega Impact Foundation and Fund. As he is fond of saying, "the first duty of privilege is philanthropy."

Like Jerry, many citizens around the world believe in duty and charitable giving. But with countless enterprises now conspicuously positive impact-oriented, the notion that "consumption is charity too" has become popular, and direct charitable giving has receded since its high watermark in the mid-2010s. In the United States, the popular attention lavished on social enterprise returns and "how capitalism can save us" has been blamed by some for the downturn. The United States, long the most charitable nation, slipped to fourth in the world's charity rankings by 2030, paralleling that country's fall in global financial power rankings.

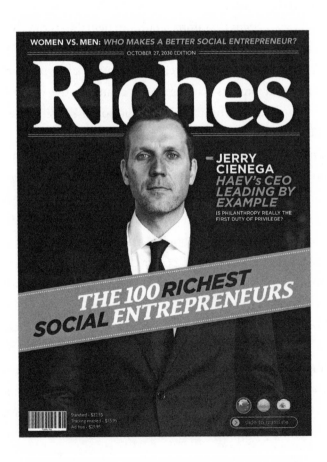

A combination of factors—obscure impact measurements, celebrity-driven publicity, and the lack of effective grassroots collaboration—all conspired to frustrate some of the grander ideas about revolutionary change for "the 99 percent" that had accompanied the surge of social enterprise in the 2010s. Despite the slowdown of momentum for social enterprise, investors were undeterred and continued using a mix of muddled definitions and strategies. Once the "impact investing" model took hold, even organizations with strongly declared social missions were judged on their financial return on investment, and incentives began to skew away from generating social value. Ever since, enterprises founded for their positive impact missions have struggled in the wake of relentless demands for financial returns for investors. Smaller, local, and more experimental enterprises began to be left behind. Tech-driven solutions tended to dominate the discourse, enjoying the bulk of investment. These "sexy" solutions used standard tech industry metrics and key performance indicators to judge success.

Most governments, especially the United States, China, and Australia, kept a laissez-faire attitude toward social enterprise. Other than the few corporate legal formations introduced in the 2010s, there was little momentum for impact industry oversight—notwithstanding the complaints of dogmatic activists. There are still a few "rogue entrepreneurs" who claim that impact entrepreneurship has been co-opted by the same power brokers behind most of the economic, environmental, and political system failures of recent decades. These marginal figures push for much more radical, anti-capitalist strategies. Luckily for the industry, these troubling activists and idealists have been marginalized by the dominant "realist" wing of the social entrepreneurship movement.

For advocates of business for good, as practiced in 2030, the movement has finally grown into a legitimate partner to the global financial sector. Enterprises for good fulfill a noble function by raising awareness of key economic, cultural, and environmental issues for businesses. It remains to be seen if these will gain wider traction, but one thing is clear: The systemic challenges humans face are only getting worse. Few believe we can continue to operate on a "business-as-usual" basis for another generation, as we increasingly experience dire climate events, escalating inequities, and intensifying conflicts over resources and values.

2030 SCENARIO 2:
THE SWARM (HIGH IMPACT X LOCAL SCALE)

In the *Swarm* scenario, business in 2030 is a complex web of local actions and local successes. Positive impacts are achieved, but these are mostly local.

To see the impacts in context, you'd need a satellite view—like a time-lapse of a river re-carving a landscape. From the ground level, it just looks like regular work, but little by little, activities combine into a larger ecosystem. An aggregate positive impact is unfolding globally, but data is tricky to source and verify. While researchers have been actively working on making global indicators more useful, since the 2010s, attention to impact and to measurement of success are closer to home. Financial uncertainty, social unrest, structural trade imbalances, and mass surveillance of leaders and citizens by global superpowers have led many nations to turn inward, eschewing unchecked globalization. They practice deliberate isolationism. In many countries, concerns over energy independence and food security have spurred domestic policies of connecting selectively with the wider system—on their own terms and only where the value of participating is clear and unassailable. In the nine nations that have implemented a basic income guarantee (where all citizens are given a financial stipend)—including Iceland, Canada, Ecuador, and Estonia—local entrepreneurship is booming.

Trends in business, and especially social entrepreneurship, were already pushing companies toward models primed to surf this wave of more grassroots, locally oriented political economies back in the 2010s. It became very normal very quickly. What people twenty years ago had trumpeted as "social entrepreneurship" has become the standard way most governments, companies, and individuals think about business.

Enough people have internalized "doing well by doing good" that the ambitions of certain large companies and philanthropic billionaires for grandiose, centrally coordinated global initiatives enacted for public relations value or white savior guilt-easing gain little traction. Small enterprises are just going about their "business," working closely with customers and communities to craft strategies and share the wealth. Savvy global companies have become much more adept at collaborating with locals, prioritizing community interests rather than exploiting them, and reducing operational costs for working with local partners.

There are fewer calls now to standardize impact measurements for impact-oriented businesses, because clear benefits are emerging from the variety of locally tailored approaches. The potential numbers in this 2030 are promising: Global extreme poverty rates have fallen below 10 percent. Carbon emissions have stabilized at 2020 levels and are on a slow but steady decline. Solar and local renewable energy sources have reached cost parity with fossil fuels in thirty-seven of the thirty-nine Organisation for Economic Co-operation and Development member countries.

But the idiosyncratic nature of impact measurement and the growing use of crypto-equity, distributed collaborative organizations, and other nontraditional forms of value exchange have led some of the more rigorous data-minded types to condemn the current state of affairs as "voodoo entrepreneurialism." Many of the more anecdotal success stories, they say, have to be taken on faith. Technology and big data are being utilized, especially through the rise of distributed autonomous organizations (DAOs) that use cryptocurrency, crypto-equity, and algorithmic management tools that have made centralized bureaucracies a relic of the twenty-first century. Back in 2015, Vitalik Buterin, the Russian Canadian entrepreneur and founder of the blockchain company Ethereum, described blockchain DAOs as armies of accountant robots. The technology enables a corporation to be "distilled to its most basic tasks and operated by little more than code and the logic of *if this, then that.*[6] By 2030 such decentralization tools have allowed investors and businesses to focus less on organizational infrastructure, and more on targeted, locally contextual, and quickly adaptable offerings.

Agriculture has been at the forefront of this movement to use nature and on-the-ground knowledge as guides for running a successful, sustainable, and future-friendly enterprise. In this future, Alisha Obumanu of EcoFlight Farms outside Meru, Kenya, typifies the modern entrepreneur. A former artist, Alisha bought a struggling farm with her family. They implemented new systems of nonindustrial techniques, including "perennial polyculture"—tree planting, composting, and movable fencing—to allow a more natural and self-healing agricultural ecosystem. To further aid the so-called Small Ag movement, EcoFlight has just launched a line of semiautonomous, robotic, solar-powered pack animals to help farmers maintain traditional farming techniques and remain off the energy grid while they do it. These robots do anything from testing the nutrition and readiness of soil for planting to forecasting rain, plowing, harvesting, or drying the produce for storage and later distribution.

All of this local focus is not without limitations. Cities and other municipalities have established their own policies toward taxation, accounting, investment, and other essential functions of impact enterprise. The rise in local government's power has caused what many call a regulatory thicket, and it is blamed for the lack of global streamlining and scalability of many types of impact enterprises.

Advocates argue that the emergent processes of a local orientation are a feature of the overall system instead of a bug. But without a clear understanding of the real mechanisms for change, the movement toward local management of challenges feels somewhat fragile. For many, it feels as if the gains since the 2010s could be lost in a heartbeat if another recession hits, or if climate change were to accelerate unpredictably. Also, while smaller, local businesses are thriving in many places, some economists worry that this model will not be effective in the long term. Although policies in many countries are now more favorable to social business, the global economic system is still fundamentally a capitalist framework that rewards profit. Large companies are currently playing ball with local social ventures, such as Google sharing intellectual property from Big Dog robotics systems with EcoFlight Farms. Other large companies are still taking more of a wait-and-see approach, with many shareholders wary of a full-scale socially minded strategy. It may be too late to stem the tide of socially oriented business practices, but it doesn't mean that the corporate giants are coming along willingly.

2030 SCENARIO 3:
CRAWLING (LOW IMPACT X LOCAL SCALE)

In *Crawling*, 2030 is characterized by minute progress. In this future, minimal positive impacts have been achieved during the 2020s, and those that have been achieved are very local.

This version of 2030 depicts a world where social entrepreneurship has never lived up to its early hype. Large multinational companies found it competitively unviable. There are still some dedicated cottage industries led by Millennials who didn't follow their peers into the "maturity" of financial-based returns. However, impact entrepreneurship came to be regarded as an inherently self-defeating practice—with people having lost focus on core business functions by the distraction of serving a "bigger purpose." The Digital Natives generation derides this notion of social good as naïve and hypocritical, much like Generation X ridiculed the hippie movement of their parents. It may still be too early to pronounce social entrepreneurship dead, although the *Harvard Business Review* famously did just that in a cover story this year. There are occasional signs of social enterprise revival and some promising innovations in local cases around the world, but the odds appear to be against any real systemic change to how business is done. Profit and economic growth remain the Holy Grail. This turn of events has been disappointing to those who care about dwindling planetary resources, increased inequality, and the precariousness of the working class.

In this 2030, extreme poverty has increased slightly since the low of 17 percent in 2021. Anthropogenic carbon emissions have continued their steady climb, surpassing sixty billion metric tons in 2029. Social justice issues are extremely polarized, with women, minorities, and the poor seeing increased rights and support in many wealthy nations, but crackdowns in Brazil, Indonesia, Nigeria, and many Asian nations have left an estimated four billion people living in repressive conditions. Sadly, climbing mortality rates might be the only measurement needed to show how bad things have gotten for the bottom 99 percent of humanity.

On the other hand, there's never been more wealth and prosperity on planet Earth. The top 1 percent has controlled this wealth for a decade. The juggernaut of industrial capitalism rolls on—it had way too much momentum, and too much to lose, to be stopped by rag-tag groups of impact investors and social innovators. Supporters of "authentic capitalism" point to the minimal impact of impact entrepreneurship as evidence that confirms financial profit as the best structural incentive and metric for prosperity. Their opponents argue that with the endless string of half-measures, capitulations, and compromises to prop up an inherently corrupt system, impact entrepreneurship was bound to fail. "You can't solve the problem with the same thinking that caused it," they say. In their view, social business was nothing more than a pretty Band-Aid slapped onto too deep a wound. It will take a revolution from outside the system to make real change, these folks argue, not some dial-turning from within.

Looking beyond the usual ideological battle lines in this world, one must ask why the impact business industry didn't succeed, given its promise and early support. The most compelling arguments can't locate a single point of failure, but rather a cacophony of forces—too few signals and too much noise. Government intervention was a maddening mix of policy contradictions from jurisdiction to jurisdiction. Some nations and cities pushed heavily for regulation and taxation of "regular" for-profit businesses (including true-cost, life-cycle accounting). But the wielding of this punitive stick was met with a major backlash, with companies aggressively forum-shopping for more profit-friendly legal environments. Other municipalities, by contrast, held out the carrot of an incentive-based approach, with tax breaks and low-interest loans for companies meeting their (highly variable) criteria of a social business. Many enterprises claimed positive impact in some areas while failing on other metrics local governments determined irrelevant or misleading.

Collaboration and resource sharing, though initially robust, began to decline as competition increased and long-term economic viability began to wane after the 2010s. The tide that had been expected to lift all boats through reciprocity and collaboration never came, and the dynamic quickly turned to "every man for himself." Companies began to hoard proprietary data, so shared learning never materialized, and everyone started looking for lucrative exits.

In this 2030, impact entrepreneurship finds itself at a final crossroads. Those who share the values and mission of the early impact innovators and advocates must decide: Go back to the source and come up with totally new ways to achieve real social value? Or continue to swim against the tide with the current model and hope there is a breakthrough moment? There may not be consensus on which way to go, but everyone knows that the status quo is not an option.

2030 SCENARIO 4: FAST FORWARD (HIGH IMPACT X GLOBAL SCALE)

Fast Forward is a 2030 in which optimal positive impacts are achieved on a global scale. Successful entrepreneurship requires a good idea, implemented in the right way, at the right time. In Fast Forward, the right time for impact entrepreneurship is in the right now.

Due to the creativity and perseverance of a host of players—including bold investors, savvy policymakers, and talented innovators and entrepreneurs themselves—a tipping point was reached in 2025. Impact enterprise has evolved from the earnest efforts of a band of true believers and trailblazers into a transformative cultural and economic movement. They say it takes twenty years to be an overnight sensation, and that's what it felt like in the impact entrepreneurship space. There are various theories about which factor was decisive in this success, but ultimately it was a combination of obvious trends and more subtle shifts that pulled business practices toward something that looked and acted like true impact entrepreneurship and ecosystem-wide attention and action, maximizing positive impact.

A host of new legal designations and formations generated opportunities to innovate definitions of value and business success with positive impact missions. Openings for innovation were created with for-benefit corporations, positive impact corporations, and other hybrids of profit and nonprofit structures. These first trickles preceded a flood of experiments with types and styles of social enterprise around the world, often at the city level. Some bigger governments began taking notice and leant their momentum to the wave, readjusting funding to match positive impact goals and passing legislation to facilitate investment in them. Nations that provided strong social protections, including basic health care and even income guarantees, were the first to see the possibilities. And overall the values shift—redefining "success" beyond purely commercial terms—paralleled what can reasonably be called an Entrepreneurship Renaissance over the past few decades. Suddenly, people who would have never previously thought they had the capacity to run an enterprise proudly claimed the title and unleashed their passion to build, create, and improve. And they did so to advance the greater good.

Capital flowed as well. Investors actively sought the win-win situation of generating returns and "doing good" at the same time. By and large, the returns were not usually as high as the purely financially optimized business models, but they got close enough to sway many investors to move their money into the positive impact zone and keep it there. There were still risks—both to financial returns and to perceptions about whether a company was making an authentic positive impact. While the highs were never stratospheric, the lows were rarely catastrophic, and the churning middle was quite productive.

The results of this global positive impact momentum were obvious and widely shared. Extreme poverty fell below 10 percent and continues to fall in 2030, even though we are still adding over a hundred thousand people a day to the planet's population. Carbon emissions plateaued in 2022 and have been on a slow decline ever since. Thanks to low-cost technological advances in renewables, manufacturing, and transportation, innovation in business models was joined by innovation in currencies. Complementary currencies flourished, while true alternative currencies and cryptocurrencies gained global traction and stability. These currencies have become recognized by virtually all governments and facilitated and sanctioned via global financial standards. Accountants gnashed their teeth as some organizations cycled through a raft of currency options and strategies.

In addition to currencies, in-kind collaboration—the "shared roots" movement to open talent and intellectual property to potential competitors—and other reciprocity-based innovations made it nearly impossible to generate clear and consistent valuations. CapWeb (aka webby capitalism) typified this new breed of networked positive impact venture. CapWeb strategies involve not only sharing resources, talent, connections, and patents, but also sharing profits with stakeholders.

Pessimists predicted that all of these changes created a tangled web that would soon collapse in on itself, but advocates saw a complex adaptive ecosystem working in productive interdependence. Times of exploration and experimentation are fascinating from the mile-high view, or exciting from the perspective of a distant historian, but for those trying to make a living, take care of loved ones, and make a host of critical decisions, these "interesting times" can be fraught, with equal parts anxiety for every part thrill. And, as always, it is easier to take risks with the security of a safety net—whether private or public.

The upside of impact entrepreneurship remains and is bolstered immeasurably by the sense of being part of a significant moment—with more opportunities than ever for a more diverse group of people to take on the risks and thrills of new ventures. With an increasingly inclusive, long-term, and systemically attuned sense of "wealth" now in view, the tide has gradually begun to turn toward cleaning up the mess of wicked environmental and social problems that had been brewing since the industrial revolution. No one knows how long this moment will last, but all are certain that the old profit-dominated economy is dead and buried, and there is no other way than forward.

ENTREPRENEURSHIP FOR IMPACT INSIGHTS SUMMARY

Having contemplated these alternative futures, now what? What do these four scenarios mean for people working in the innovation, entrepreneurship, and impact arena, or in related fields and activities?

The questions for our age appear to be: Can we continue to build wealth, to prosper as a civilization, and to find delight in life, without destroying the systems necessary for this wealth? Can the present generation prosper and innovate without robbing future generations of their opportunities for prosperity? Our hope is that these four snapshots of alternative futures for our world provide fuel for thought, ideas for deliberation, and motivation for action.

CHAPTER 13

Toward 2030: Insights from Impact Changemakers— Navigating to Preferred Futures

I magine yourself on Tuesday, January 1, 2030. How old are you? Where are you? Who are you with? What do you see has happened in the world in the intervening years, as you look back from then to now? What are you seeing around innovation, entrepreneurship, and impact? Have we arrived at a 2030 that is swarming, crawling, flying over, or enabling freedom of opportunity to more people on the planet than ever before? Or is it some new future we have not yet imagined? What are the signs that the impact space succeeded beyond 2010s ambitions? These are a sampling of the questions we invited impact changemakers to ponder during our consultations.

In the current decade of the twenty-first century, to imagine what future is coming, we can peek back at the four potential alternative futures of the preceding chapter, or we might conjure an infinite number of other possibilities.

When we wake on January 1, 2030, will we have actualized a 2030 in which the flurry of threats in the late 2010s (tensions with North

Korea, the United States, China, and Russia, to name a few) have flung us into a prolonged period of permanent crisis? Is there a twenty-first century cold war with higher, potentially apocalyptic stakes than any war before it? Or a psychological war with the goal of controlling online minds, regardless of national borders? A world in which democracy has given way to puppetry and meritocracy to socioeconomic apartheid, even in the most-developed economies?

Or will we have actualized a much brighter 2030? A year celebrating meaningful progress toward the United Nations' Sustainable Development Goals (SDGs), ratified in September 2015 at the UN's seventieth General Assembly and in effect since January 1, 2016. A 2030 in which the indicators around poverty and mortality have not only progressed, but also the measures of indicators of these challenges have become prevalent, more reliable, more nuanced than ever before. For example, in 2020, up to 1.5 billion people on the planet (mostly women and children from the poorest communities) are estimated to have no official identity, let alone a bank account. People without identification have limited access to basic rights, including health care, education, employment, and credit.[1] If we actualize a preferred, positive impact 2030, everyone on the planet would have an official identity—largely due to collaborative initiatives by nongovernmental organizations (NGOs)—enabling them access to information, education, and health care. If we could improve the world by manifesting one such SDG, imagine what 2030 might look like when we collectively commit to even higher-level goals.

VISIONS FROM CHANGEMAKERS OF POSITIVE IMPACT IN 2030

While they understand the obstacles in the pathways ahead, the impact changemakers we consulted mostly foresee positive versions of 2030. They hold fundamental faith in the collectivity of good intentions to gain momentum through the 2020s. In the 2010s, many of these impact changemakers exemplified in their daily lives how to successfully facilitate more positive futures for all by building positively impacting entrepreneurial trajectories now. They know and understand the global realities of the next decade and beyond. They know that by 2030, global connectivity, pervasive technology-enabled transparency, reputational accountability, and a global surge in purpose will most likely force even the most oppositional individuals and organizations into enacting net positive impacts in what they do on a daily basis. Impact changemakers read these and the signals of other possible futures and approach the future with hope.

For the rest of this chapter, we describe the characteristics of positive futures in 2030 envisaged by impact changemakers, and where relevant, with suggested actions required now for "futures readiness."

Impact thinking and doing are mainstream and integral

In the most positive 2030 futures for impact, the planet, and its people, the changemakers we consulted imagine a time where impact considerations are omnipresent, normal, and ingrained into the DNA of humans and institutions alike. A preferred future in which:

Connectivity Creates Empathy

In our globally networked world, where information about fellow people (rich and poor) is available at the flick of a biometric trigger (fingertips, eyes, voice), there is mainstream awareness of the negative social impacts of all actions, as well as the positive. By sharing the stories of those people in vulnerable and disadvantaged predicaments in real time, technology has transformed the collective consciousness of the world. In a networked world, exposure to such portrayals is unavoidable. When we see another human suffering, it can trigger our mirror neurons, so that many more people feel that pain. In the late 2010s these images come from ravaging hurricanes in the North Sea, the Caribbean, and the Texas Gulf Coast to ruinous flooding in Mozambique or Houston, from earthquakes in Mexico to mudslides in Colombia or landslides in Sierra Leone, from catastrophic wildfires in California to deadly windstorms in Australia. Bound by technology, suffering is no longer disconnected by location. By 2030, with most of the 8.5 million human inhabitants of the planet becoming even more connected, impact innovators envisage that such collective triggering of deep knowing about "the other" will usher in compassion and empathy on an unprecedented scale. Our collective global conscience will compel us to act because such suffering cannot go unnoticed and unattended.

In 2030 omnipresent mainstream awareness demands that we and our organizations minimize negative social and environmental impacts and maximize positive impacts across all levels of society. Acumen's Sasha Dichter believes that by 2030, "social justice values are a mainstream part of the mature ecosystem with widespread social impact role models." Such ideas are echoed by many of the changemakers with whom we spoke. Tom Rippin, CEO of the UK's On Purpose (a leadership program to help people build careers with social impact), noted that in the most positive future, "Mainstream awareness and demand for social impact places pressure on decision makers to ensure positive impact is part of all decision criteria and conclusions." Individuals and corporations will be forced to notice and to act by their friends and family members, employees, employers, shareholders, consumers, and suppliers. Founder of Singapore's first social enterprise incubator (with Impact Hub) and now programs and partnerships lead at Ashoka Singapore, Divya Patel sees social entrepreneurship prevailing as a mainstream phenomenon, rather than as a sector often overcome with doubts as the lesser sibling of business entrepreneurship. Australia's Danny Almagor pictures a 2030 in which impact is not unique to social entrepreneurs, but a part of the fabric of everyday thinking across society, with impact awareness an embedded part of business and political systems.

Connectedness Removes Silos

Argentinian American Mariana Amatullo believes that by the late 2020s impact thinking and doing will be designed into all that humans do. She sees the intersection of design and positive impact as omnipresent by 2030. Design of products, organizations, buildings, communities, public spaces, and processes will all have positive impact at their core. Design for social engagement and innovation will be the norm. As Australian venture capitalist Michelle Deaker observed, these trends will be accentuated as the world moves toward an innovation-dominated economy.

Crowd power and networked technologies will be critical drivers of this mainstream attention to minimizing negative impact and maximizing positive impact. Deniz Gürel Karataş of the Turkish Industry and Business Association described the potent effects of the popularity of the global ice-bucket challenge as it played out in the streets of Istanbul and Ankara. Like her counterparts in other countries, Karataş sees this mainstreaming of individual "for benefit" activity on a global scale by 2030, thus rendering impact as one of the dominant narratives of the time.

In these optimistic renderings of 2030, the "for purpose" economy is seamlessly integrated into all business models. Innovation to minimize negative impacts and maximize positive impacts is woven into all that we do in 2030. The siloing of social entrepreneurs and business entrepreneurs that isolated social impactors in their own sectors in the early decades of the twenty-first century no longer exists. Again, the changemakers' views on this form a chorus: Singapore's Bernise Ang (principal of Zeroth Labs, a systems innovation lab helping cities in developing countries manage the challenges of urbanization) sees a 2030 in which there is "blending of different kinds of methods that traditionally [haven't] come together to tackle development problems and public policy issues, where the blending is informed by science and social science." South Korea's Kwang Hwi Park (an incubation expert at the Asian Development Bank, managing director of Seoul Global

Startup Center, and chair of Social Venture Partners Seoul) also anticipates that "the business sector, the for-profit sector, and the non-profit
sectors are not different. . . . [In the next ten years or so] they are going
forward to meet each other." Social change is no longer the sole domain
of NGOs and nonprofits. As Park adds, "Every combination, every
ownership enterprise will be social business . . . a special concern with
impact innovation."

Connectedness Spans the Globe

The impact changemakers in our research also envisage a 2030 in
which the entire global ecosystem maximizes positive impact. Singapore's Dr. Tan Chi Chiu (chair of the Lien Centre of Social Innovation)
reflected the thoughts of many when he foresaw a world in the late
2020s in which "an impact ecosystem [has fermented] in the preceding
few years, because once everyone starts to get socially entrepreneurial
and understands what needs to be done . . . the linkages have already
been formed and can persist. . . . [The impact ecosystem takes on] . . . a
life of its own."

By 2030 a positive impact ecosystem will be normal, having evolved
as a connected global ecosystem. The global ecosystem—involving
governments, corporations, NGOs, organizations, communities, and
individuals—will exude, as Tom Rippin envisages, "whole of system
impact—policy, advocacy, collaboration." DoSomething.org CEO Aria
Finger noted the enhancing influence of an entire ecosystem being
aware of and intent on impact. Finger foresees late 2020s global conditions facilitating the whole system to support and help enterprise and
impact flourish for the greater good. She also sees consolidation and
streamlining, with more shared resources, so that in the second half of
the next decade "efficient ecosystems eliminate duplication and redun-
dancy." As chair of Social Venture Partners International Lance Fors
reminds us, this global positive impact paradigm will evolve through
whole-of-system learning.

The Popularity of Impact Ensures Legal Standards

Some impact changemakers foresee all organizations in 2030 being accountable for positive and negative impacts by law, both local and international. They foresee professional governance standards requiring public transparency on widespread indices reflecting organizational ratings on financial return on investment (FROI), social ROI (SROI), and environmental ROI (EROI). In the most positive scenarios for 2030, large and small corporations all join the wave of mainstreamed positive impact thinking and doing. As Mariana Amatullo and others noted, in this potential positive reality, "Corporations have moved beyond ticking the corporate social responsibility box and know the good business sense of net positive impact." Impact investment funds started in the first decades of the twenty-first century will have reached full maturity by 2030, with impact-anchored investments now the norm, with investments focused solely on FROI dinosaurs of the past.

As network technologies increasingly intensify connectedness around the globe—facilitating unprecedented shared knowledges and learnings, combined with escalating transparency and accountability—in the next decade, more than ever before, individuals, organizations, and states will learn from what they do, assess outcomes, and adjust their trajectories in alignment with the emergent dominant impact paradigm.

Actions for futures readiness:

- Integrate impact into all thinking and doing.

- Exude thinking and actions that maximize positive social and environmental impact and minimize the negative through the entire value chain of organizations.

- Ensure that individuals, managers, and CEOs embed impact into the organizational DNA.

Danny Almagor and Berry Liberman's Small Giants group in Melbourne, Australia, exemplifies this metamorphosis of embedding impact into individual and organizational DNA. Small Giants is both catalyst and activist, proactively creating, supporting, nurturing, and empowering enterprises intent on positive impact.

Purpose—an intergenerational norm

Millennials constitute 75 percent of the 2030 workforce; their ingrained positive impact values are dominant in boardrooms, courtrooms, classrooms, and living rooms. Abigail Noble of the World Economic Forum and The ImPact sees Millennial attitudes dominating the 2020s. By 2030 many Millennials and some Gen Zers, having inherited their parents' material wealth, are putting their money where their values are so that positive impact is a key consideration in all investments. The impact funds they invest in have become the norm, with FROI just one criterion, perhaps subservient to social or environmental ROIs.

While the pivoting of lives toward "purpose" was noted as a "surge" in the mid-2010s, in the realized positive futures of 2030, all generations display an all-of-life consciousness and intentionality around impact—to minimize the negative and maximize the positive. In 2030 Millennials are not the only generation fully embracing impact. While Millennials and Gen Zers live in ways that exude both consciousness and action around impact, Millennials' parents and grandparents, the Baby Boomer generation, have retired earlier than their predecessors. These retiring Boomers are subsequently enjoying second and third careers geared toward the collective good. By 2030 people are recognizing and cultivating diverse life trajectories, with positive impact at their core. Singapore's Vernie Oliveiro (principal researcher at the Civil Service College) noted: "[In the late 2020s] people see life can be unpredictable, and life has so many more opportunities to provide if [we] just take a little step away from the [traditional] path. . . . We will simply see many more opportunities than we have in the past; it's a bigger world out there."

Actions for futures readiness:

- Enact positive impact actions proactively and share successes.

- Integrate positive impact intentions (with conscious consideration of potentially countering negative impacts) into all thinking and doing.

- Embrace democratization of dialogue and actions.

Collective consciousness keeps organizations accountable

By 2030 only the poorest of the poor and the remotest of the remote will not be connected to the global internet. Confrontations, like calling to account Australia's harmful practices of processing asylum seekers' applications offshore in places like Papua New Guinea and Nauru, or the U.S. government's imprisonment of children in cages at the Mexican border, are no longer the domain of institutions but of the world's people. Collective shaming and calls to action—beamed all over the planet to rally the world's citizens—hold a mirror to policymakers. The information and reputation cascades of the late 2010s are the norm by 2030.

Information cascades result in "hundreds, thousands, or millions of people [coming] to accept a certain belief simply because of what they think other people believe."[2] The interconnectedness of the world means that messages or images that go viral around the planet, regardless of their legitimacy or authenticity, will influence the masses, policymakers, bloggers, and traditional media journalists.

The annals of airline horrors or Hollywood's hall of shame—documented by traditional and social media alike in the late 2010s—are testament to the potent destructive power of reputation cascades. Where negative or embarrassing incidents may have once been noticed days or weeks later by only those interested in watching televised current affairs programs or reading a newspaper, during the 2020s and 2030s, information cascades sharing bad corporate or individual behaviors will be transmitted to billions of personal devices instantaneously, no longer protected by conspiracies of silence or quieted by bullying. Corporations, policymakers, and community leaders are particularly vulnerable to reputational pressures. In 2030 such pressures ensure more positively impactful actions and fewer negatively impactful ones.

These cascades may lead individuals, groups, organizations, and governments to fall prey to psychological and social forces. For example, erroneous judgments occur when our brains naturally take shortcuts, such as the tendency for the human brain to recall events that are most recent or vivid because these stand out in our consciousness and memories.

Networked technologies in 2030 render individuals part of a collective that is more powerful than at any other time in history. A collective that has commanding influence in determining which issues are most salient for communities and nations. Stakeholders of organizations of all kinds, large and small, have the power to expose bad products, services, or behaviors. The collective can make demands for change and enact collective punishment (reputational damage, boycotting products, decreasing sales, profit and market caps). When cascades go awry by spreading inaccurate information, swift countering with authentic evidence ensures collective self-correction.

By setting what information gets distributed and noticed, transformative technologies also set agendas; shape global, national, and community narratives; and make or break reputations, careers, and ROIs. British author Mike Edwards noted that the collective will shape what gets spent globally on social enterprise and impact, rendering the previous domination of impact activities by the mega rich (with zero accountability) somewhat impotent. Acumen's Sasha Dichter was representative of many other impactors we consulted in envisaging the democratization of solution generation to alleviate the predicaments of fellow humans in dire circumstances. Such democratization will potently influence how individuals and enterprises of all genres act.

Actions for futures readiness:

- Embrace democratized global contexts.

- Understand the increasingly distributive nature of power, capital, and influence manifesting as collaboration, partnerships, and networks.

- Embrace and utilize new realities that usher in unprecedented access to information, data records, capital, education, and mentors.

- Develop the skills and knowledges to harness democratized crowds to enact preferred futures for the greater good.

- Develop the art and science of enacting positive information and reputation cascades.

Widespread adoption of a systems thinking mindset

In the most positive envisioning of 2030, the majority of the world's people think systemically about the impact of their decisions and their work in and on the entire system over time. In the late 2020s, systems and network thinking are omnipresent. Communication is the lifeblood of systems learning and facilitating feedback and corrective behavior. Networked technologies are endemic in 2030—with real-time instantaneous sharing of all kinds of information that enables the rapid spread of knowledge, sensemaking, and shared narratives throughout the system. In the second decade of the twenty-first century, Mariana Amatullo of The New School foresees a positive 2030 in which there is ubiquitous "recognition and understanding of the interconnectedness of all things—industry, academia, social impact."

People on the streets or in organizations—using their personal digital devices for research—think systemically about the causes and effects among ecosystem relationships at multiple levels. People everywhere see the relationships, the linkages. They think about how any single action, any single change in one relationship can have a ripple effect throughout the system. They understand the interconnectedness of all of the components of an impact entrepreneurial ecosystem—the ideas generators, the educators, mentors, funders, nurturers, and supporters of innovation and entrepreneurship—that can be synergistic in producing optimal outcomes. People understand that no one element of the system takes primacy. Rather, all elements and the relationships among those elements contribute to either positive or negative outcomes. There is widespread awareness that if you launch an enterprise it may have unintended, unforeseen negative consequences somewhere else in the system, so people are always looking to minimize harm as they build their action plans. There is also increased awareness of impact up and down the chain.

Actions for futures readiness:

- See and think in systems, as an individual and as an organization.

- View Earth as one global system and consider how actions might affect other parts of the system.

- Consider multiple possible impacts: negative, positive, close in, and remote.

- Enact the mantra: Is it good for the people? Is it good for the planet? Does it do any harm anywhere in the ecosystem?

- Systematically and repeatedly ask devil's advocate questions: What are all the ways this act can do harm locally, globally, individually, collectively? Now, later?

Local solutions to local problems become the norm

In the more positive futures envisaged by impact changemakers, the dawning of 2030 sees the abandonment of the "great white hope" do-gooder mentality. Instead of self-serving narratives and the monetizing of everything, a pervasive ethos of collaboration among equals has become common. Today's impact changemakers see the 2020s ushering in deep and intensifying respect for solutions to local problems embedded within global systems thinking. Local leaders drive local processes, cognizant of how local acts impact global contexts.

Impact influencers foresee proactive and deliberate cultivation of and collaboration with local resources as a result of understandings of the multitudinal linkages in the entire system. These understandings are widespread and ingrained into the human psyche by 2030. British journalist Zoe Smith anticipates a time when international development and aid efforts reflect "deep localizations with respect for local context differences—cultures, wealth, women's roles." As *Stanford Social Innovation Review* academic editor Johanna Mair noted: "[In a positive impact 2030] generic trends across geographies are nuanced locally depending on agenda and industry, such as in the UK, Australia, and Colombia." Drawing on decades of experience and evidence accrued in the now global microfinance industry in Bangladesh and beyond, former Grameen America CEO Shah Newaz believes two of the most potent key ingredients for success of the Grameen model are respect for local cultural differences and the building of local partnerships.

Yet other impact innovators interviewed saw "place-based" or city-based strategies as the norm in the late 2020s, where locals are integral to designing and implementing particular solutions to how specific social challenges play out in their place or city.

As designing, producing, and selling goods and services become increasingly globalized, individuals, managers, CEOs, and boards of directors must navigate foreign cultures, workplaces, and markets. In 2030, ever aware of the potential negative impacts of what they do, the leading changemakers in the global impact space go beyond cultural sensitivity and proactively avoid possible exploitation. Not just because they are aware that harm done, even when unintended, can be broadcast around the world in a nanosecond. Consistent with the "local solutions to local problems" mindset, impact innovators have learned to play devil's advocate to their own assumptions about what works and what doesn't in countries that are not their native environments. These successful changemakers go beyond ensuring respect for local people and culture—they build their local/foreign business model strategies with locals who are leading in their communities.

These changemakers know that when people are empowered rather than exploited, everyone has potential to benefit. For example, a large multinational corporation engages the for-purpose enterprise Verb to run a social innovation competition to improve the lives of people working in the corporation's Indonesian factories. As in so many emerging economies, factory workers (typically women) are often tired, sick, and distracted due to challenges in their daily lives. Poor transportation, limited childcare options, and repeated natural disasters affect their capacity to work to their potential. Social innovation competitions empower and reward local impact entrepreneurs to tackle challenges in their own backyard. Local nuances count, whether managing multicultural, multinational teams, designing products, manufacturing in emerging economies, or marketing globally. Western mindsets and solutions may be not only irrelevant but also inaccurate and limiting.

Actions for futures readiness:

- Ensure local partners and local solutions.

- Proactively seek qualified and motivated local individuals and organizations to do the job (at all levels of skill).

- Proactively seek opportunities to contribute to the leadership of locals and build capacity in local communities (at all levels of skill).

continued

- Pivot away from a Western solutions meta-frame and deliberately examine assumptions that fuel individual or organizational behavior around impact, particularly those derived from Western or privileged perspectives.

Collaborations, partnerships, and networks forge better futures

col·lab·o·ra·tion (noun): The action of working with someone to produce or create something.

By the late 2020s, widespread collaborative partnerships for enacting positively impactful initiatives (while mindful to counter negative impacts) will sweep across local and global landscapes, according to today's changemakers. Collaborating: experimenting and creating together. Multilateral agreements facilitating the greater good will be common. Partnerships established in the first decades of the twenty-first century (for example, Global Development Innovation Ventures, a joint initiative established in 2013 between the United States and the UK) will flourish through the 2020s and be emulated by similar partnerships around the planet.

Actions for futures readiness:

- Proactively eradicate white savior mindsets and actions.

- Proactively cultivate and build collaborations (with locals in the lead) across sectors, industries, generations, and countries.

- Join networks like Social Venture Partners International or

Global Impact Investing Network to amplify synergies for potential impact.

- Identify potential collaborative niches and establish organizations and businesses to forge collective positive impact.

Definitions of success are nuanced and expansive

In the most positive of 2030 futures, mindshifts that began with a small minority in the first two decades of the twenty-first century have become entrenched. Many of the impact changemakers we interviewed foresee a definitive broadening and deepening of the notion of success. During the 2010s, so many of the rich or would-be rich defined themselves by their financial net worth and external material things. The rich of 2030 measure and define themselves (and their degree of "richness") by the positive impact they have and the contributions they make to minimize the world's social ills. Impact innovators around the world understand that individual and organizational capacity to pivot across multiple measures of success will be critical as the global surge in purpose dictates actions of the masses.

Actions for futures readiness:

- Explore, operationalize, and embrace multiple definitions and indicators of success.

- Regularly trigger discussions about what constitutes success—as an individual and as an organization—and how those criteria are affected by Western or privileged perspectives.

- Explore and embrace multidimensional measures of success from ecosystem to individual levels.

- Ensure that social and environmental impacts are integral and equal components of success.

Impact measurement is multistoried

As conceptions of success become richer and more complex, measurement of impacts will equally evolve. We draw from the work of Michael White, the co-developer of narrative therapy, and his use of the "life is multi-storied" metaphor.[3] Michael understood that every person's life contains multiple parallel storylines. We often interpret our own storylines from one perspective, one narrow label. That label colors everything we see when we look at our past or toward our future. In narrative therapy, having a "multi-storied" approach helps people understand that life is too complex for one single narrative, that no single story is free from ambiguity, and that our lives can be viewed from the perspective of many narratives. It is up to us to author our own version of the many possibilities, both retrospectively and prospectively.

By 2030 impact will be measured to reflect its multistoried nature at all levels of analysis, from the individual to the global and across the possible range of impacts. Multilayered and multi-nuanced measures of progress against societies' toughest social challenges will be the norm. In 2030 the same technologies facilitating transparency and accountability of governments, organizations, and individuals will facilitate the collecting, analyzing, and sharing of data about impact initiatives' successes and challenges on a local and global scale. At the whole-of-system level of measurement, global, regional, and national social attitude surveys and measures of well-being or gross happiness will be mirrored throughout the system and subsystems.

Actions for futures readiness:

- Explore and embrace multiple measures of impact.

- Embrace and enact transparency and accountability.

- Include social and environmental impacts as critical equal components of success.

- Define and measure positive and negative impacts at all levels of analysis, from the individual to the global.

- Embrace and enact complex multilayered, multi-nuanced measures of progress against society's toughest challenges, including corporate accountabilities and reporting.

- Utilize technologies to collect, analyze, and share data about successes and challenges on a local and global scale, whether as an individual, corporation, government, or NGO.

Capital and sustainability are multistoried

Just as impact in the late 2020s will be enacted and amplified in many ways, capital for growing impact will also involve many diverse forms. As impact entrepreneurship becomes mainstream—as impact talent, products, and services become valued equally, if not more so, alongside business entrepreneurial talent, products, and services—there will be multiple, innovative ways to ensure that impact is sustainable. By 2030 the wholesale shift away from heavy reliance on a grants model of impact enterprise will have taken hold (although there will still be strong acknowledgment that some social challenges warrant unconditional grants). In 2030 multidisciplinary, multi-stakeholder teams will collaborate to ensure the sustainability of the impact as well as the vehicle through which it is enacted. Japan's Social Venture Partners' Takuya Okamoto foresees the long-term sustainability of their organization deriving from "not only the individual partners, but also the government and the company, the business sector . . . coordinating many stakeholders to make a difference or to solve the problems." Connective technologies, crowds, sharing economies—the democratization of everything—will sweep aside old venture capitalist singular, unilateral notions of capital.

Actions for futures readiness:

- Embrace and enact different business models to achieve sustainability.

- Pivot across multiple conceptions of sustainability.

- Leverage strengths to create multiple revenue streams.

- Utilize all of the potential sources of capital in creative ways to contribute to sustainability.

- Conceptualize and enact revenue streams in multiple ways.

- Collaborate and build networks with those sharing the same positive impact missions.

- Apply these skills and knowledge to guide new impact investors as they decide in whom and what to invest.

Scale is multistoried

Just as success can be measured in multiple ways, impact changemakers by 2030 embrace scale as multistoried. They question strictly financial and statistical conceptions of scale reflected in the venture capital model of success—where scale is about growing sales and revenues and scaling production, profits, and financial ROI. The impact changemakers we interviewed see these purely financial measures as outdated through the 2020s. As Tom Meredith, the former CFO of Dell and co-founder of the for-purpose enterprise Verb, noted, scale can be as simple as leaving a footprint from which others spin off. Or, as UnLtd's Katharine Danton observed, scale is not scaling a venture, but scaling impact.

Scale is the ultimate breadth, depth, and sustainability of economic, social, and environmental impact that matters. The movement away from financial and numerical appraisals of scale is exemplified in the work and words of successful entrepreneur Dr. Lance Fors, who founded and grew a leading DNA diagnostics company and has since been focused on venture philanthropy. He sees scale of impact as being central to any enterprise. Fors and other leading impact innovators see scale reflected in the growth of networks, expansion of markets, and increased manufacturing and distribution of products and ideas. Kurt Peleman, the former CEO of the European Venture Philanthropy Association, and Loïc Comolli, co-CEO of NESsT (nurturer of social enterprises in Argentina, Brazil, Chile, Ecuador, Croatia, Czech Republic, Hungary, Peru, Romania, and Slovakia), point out that impact can be increased without necessarily growing the organization. Scale can be many small-scale organizations. With expanded understandings of scale, fledgling impact enterprises like Austin's Multicultural Refugee Coalition, rather than being turned away from some investors or accelerators as they were in 2018, will be feted. Lauded for their vision to deliberately scale by growing the depth and breadth of their services—the depth and breadth of their impact (rather than scaling by the numbers of people passing through their doors). Growing the breadth and depth of their services ensures that their model can be replicated with amplified, meaningful positive impacts across ecosystems.

Actions for futures readiness:

- Explore and operationalize multiple conceptions of scale.
- Think creatively about scale, using the growth of the precariat and the democratization of everything.
- Encourage and reward scale that grows the depth and breadth of products and services.
- Build competitive advantages and successes in nontraditional ways.

Long-term thinking is essential

Thinkers and doers in the impact arena live and breathe long-term thinking. Rather than decision-making time frames dictated by annual report cycles, electoral cycles, or funding cycles, the decision-making

of successful impact innovators is predicated on flexible, pivotal seeing and thinking. They hold one perspective firmly in the present
while the other pivots to the distant future—their mind traversing
the landscape back and forth between immediate and far horizons.
Successful pivoting is like good piloting: When flying, a pilot constantly scans the skies to avoid mid-air collisions, checking multiple
horizons—front, sides, and rear, vertical and horizontal. Pilots are
trained to scan the entire horizon surrounding the plane, not just
the sky in front of the aircraft. When flying under conditions of limited visibility or congested airspace, pilots are trained to adopt even
more systematic scanning techniques while simultaneously constantly
checking back to their instrument panel to ensure that the plane is on
course and flying straight and level. Good pilots do not let distrac-
tions stop the scan.[4] Impact changemakers know only too well that
there will be constant competition for their attention, especially in an
increasingly networked world, and like pilots, they must be vigilant
on all horizons.

Actions for futures readiness:

- Embrace the long term: Live and breathe long-term thinking.

- Constantly scan the past, immediate, and future distant horizons, reading the landscape and noting new landmarks.

- Keep the destination in sight while holding the organization
  steady with its core strengths.

- Systematically scan for, train for, and anticipate opportunities
  and hazards.

NAVIGATING TO 2030: FUTURES-READY PIVOTING

Regardless of which future is ultimately actualized, successful impact changemakers are adept at navigating through volatile landscapes to enact positive impacts wherever they find themselves. Many are able to do this because of their honed capacity to pivot—from current to preferred trajectories, between short- and long-term thinking, between local and global horizons, and between the little picture and big picture, the micro and the macro. Successful impact changemakers hone the skill of pivoting toward their most-preferred future—a skill predicated on an informed understanding of local and global future realities—as well as the capacity to nimbly navigate those realities to their own advantage. This ability to pivot may well hold the key to success, not just for individuals and enterprises intent on positive impact, but for anyone navigating turbulent times. The readiness for successful pivoting goes beyond the capacity for resilience and further than simply being robust under conditions of enormous stress and change. Successful pivoting requires rich understandings of conditions as they unfold and the capacity to be resilient amid rapidly changing contexts. Such skills help individuals and organizations recognize and author their preferred alternative futures.

Examples of successful pivoting in the global business arena abound: Amazon's pivot from online bookseller to being the main online purveyor of everything from clothes to jewelry, furniture, and groceries; or video game designer and manufacturer Nintendo pivoting from techies and teenage male customers playing video games to time-strapped fitness enthusiasts doing in-home sports, from yoga to bowling to golf. Former COO of The Washington Post Co. and general partner at Polaris Venture Partners Alan Spoon described pivoting as a tool for additional growth, growth that might have otherwise been overlooked. He said: "Businesses can grow beyond their initial dreams by reimagining their assets and talents, thinking more broadly about the customer problems they solve, and accessing growth capital to seize the new high ground."[5]

Throughout the 2010s, impact enterprises like DoSomething, IDEO, NESsT, and Verb exemplified skillful pivoting to ensure sustainability and optimal positive impacts. Their pivoting to their preferred futures exhibited all of the hallmarks of successful adaptation to new realities—being opportunistic and going with the flow of their environments without sacrificing their ultimate social impact visions. These impact ventures and the innovators who lead them have honed their organizations' capacity to adapt to volatility, skillfully creating new trajectories and pathways. Impact changemakers understand they might discover new vistas never envisaged when setting out. Rather than adhering to a rigid step-by-step plan, impact changemakers achieve more by having a trajectory with a broad bandwidth in the general direction of their destination. They move toward that destination without rigidly following a narrowly defined route. The key is to both plan and not plan, to have a map and no map.[6]

A wonderful case study, summarized by Karl Weick in his book *Sensemaking in Organizations,* illustrates this capacity for opportunistic forging of future pathways. During World War II, a Hungarian army regiment was engaged in "Outward Bound-type" military training exercises in Switzerland.[7] The young commanding officer sent a troop of soldiers into the mountains. Not long after they were dispatched, a severe snowstorm hit and the troop became lost. When the troop was two days late returning, the commanding officer became gravely concerned, fearing he had sent his soldiers to their deaths. When the beleaguered troop finally arrived at base camp on the third day, the relieved commanding officer asked how the men found their way back without a map. They revealed that, indeed, one troop member did have a map that enabled them to calm down, plan their action, and find their way back to base camp. When the commanding officer scrutinized the map, he discovered it was a map of the Pyrenees mountains. These men were in the Swiss Alps! This story illustrates how maps animate and orient us. Maps are a representation of the terrain that might lie ahead. With a map, any map, the Hungarian regiment was active, had purpose, and manifested a mental image of where they were and of where they were headed. They kept on moving, kept noticing cues, kept updating their sense of where they were . . . and found their way to their ultimate destination.[8] This example also reveals what impact innovators instinctively know: Use the map of the possible terrain (multiple possible futures) as an orientation tool, but improvise along the way, pivoting as circumstances require. The capacity and capability of individuals, managers, CEOs, and boards of directors to pivot their thinking processes and actions while still holding a steady course between past, present, and possible futures is critical.

Pivoting is a way to reimagine and re-tool individual or organizational trajectories, using core strengths to enact strategies that might not have been envisaged when starting out. Impact changemakers pivot by being highly attuned to the contexts and systems in which they operate. They assess their organization's core strengths—whether people, technology, or culture—and how these strengths might be applied to other markets and customers up or down the value chain. They also assess how these adaptations might relate to their products and services, while remaining open to possibilities and mutations that could generate alternative revenue streams. For example, UnLtd USA pivoted from purely nurturing social entrepreneurs to reimagining the products and service possibilities of its organizations. It leveraged its core institutional knowledges to create an income stream. And then UnLtd pivoted again, using institutional knowledges and networks to scale in a way it had not imagined when starting out, by joining the worldwide start-up facilitator Techstars. Like UnLtd USA founder Zoe Schlag, many individuals, managers, CEOs, and boards of directors discover lucrative new landscapes they had not previously contemplated nor envisaged. For UnLtd USA, pivoting toward new local and global landscapes with Techstars financed the nurturing of many more impact enterprises just starting up than might have been possible otherwise.

Actions for futures readiness:

- Hone skills to pivot from past to present to distant futures.

- Hone capacity and skills to detect and seize opportunities, and to forge new pathways as needed.

- Use maps as a rough guide to the possible terrain ahead, but improvise as needed.

ENTREPRENEURSHIP FOR IMPACT INSIGHTS SUMMARY

Ever alert to emerging signals and the nuances of changing global contexts, successful impact changemakers use their capacity to pivot from current trajectories to new trajectories and into preferred futures. Those individuals and organizations with the capacity and capability to pivot—to remain steady in key organizational strengths while simultaneously being ready and able to successfully enact multiple possible trajectories—are positioning themselves and their organizations for thriving through volatile times. Successful impact changemakers think and act with long-term horizons in mind. They think and act with an all-of-ecosystem mindset and embed knowledges of impact, good and bad, into all they think and do. Impact changemakers simultaneously think globally and locally, using networked technologies to collaborate. Then, locals can derive their own solutions or adaptations to their problems rather than have cookie-cutter Western solutions thrust upon them. Impact changemakers think creatively about scale and use the growth of adhocracies and the democratization of everything to build competitive advantage and success in nontraditional ways. Impact changemakers are adept futures navigators; agile pivoters between past, present, and futures; and embody the crucial differences between riding the emergent trends, being swamped by them, or being a trendsetter.

CHAPTER 14

Impact Measurement by 2030

By 2030, according to the most positive scenarios of the impact changemakers we interviewed, entrepreneurship will almost universally be paired with a self-assured determination to do good. This may seem like a somewhat vague description, but it encompasses a mixture of innovating, entrepreneuring, and providing capital for purpose. For positive impact on the planet, on humanity. Impact will be a thoroughly demystified phenomenon by 2030, with the general population and investment companies alike reportedly clamoring over resourcing social and environmental innovations. It is easy to see why.

In the envisioning of impact changemakers around the world, by 2030 the definitional squabbles about what constitutes impact will be long gone. Instead, the late 2020s will be a time in which investing in positive impact enterprise is so vibrant that traditional business investments feel bland in comparison. Rather than debating definitions of impact, optimistic impact innovators picture an ever-growing list of unmissable investments in enterprises doing good *and* making money. Comprehensive impact measurement regimes that rigorously combine qualitative and quantitative tailored data will be common in the late

2020s, replacing stumbles with sureness, murkiness with clarity, and unpredictability with familiarity.

The impact changemakers in our research see market rates of financial return on investment (FROI) in impact enterprises as the norm by 2030. They also see rigorous, widely accepted measures of the social and environmental consequences of an organization's products and services. By 2030 the governance arm of corporate environmental, social, and governance (ESG) assessments of the 2010s will be transformed by technology-driven organizational transparency and accountability across all sectors. The impact changemakers in our study believe that in positive enactments of 2030, a collective awareness and responsibility will be omnipresent—and not just for positive and negative consequences of products and services. Impact can be positive or negative, intentional or unintentional, direct or indirect, immediate or long-term, close to the target population or far removed. By 2030, impact measures will encompass all of these realms, with robust definitive impact data being readily available around the globe in real time. These measures ensure that perpetrators of negative impacts are held accountable: by institutions and the general public.

IMPACT MEASUREMENT FOR THE 2020S

Impact changemakers envisage consolidation and refinement of impact measurement processes and tools between now and 2030.

Metrics reflecting impact as THE way

In the more positive visions of 2030, both financial and impact metrics are part of the holistic lens through which stakeholders—including the general population—view organizations and agencies. In keeping with the expectation of omnipresent attention to impact arriving in the late 2020s, many of the impact innovators we consulted saw impact metrics becoming an embedded and normal component of organizational operations. Impact author Mike Edwards sees a "dramatic reframing of the impact space," even suggesting a revolution of capitalism as we know it, which transforms into a new form of economics with social impact at its core. Along with this revolution, Edwards envisages the impact "field" moving from advocacy to critical self-analysis, self-evaluation, consolidation, streamlining, and embedding. The extent to which these developments occur will be key indicators of the impact field's evaluation of itself. The New School's Mariana Amatullo sees corporations and other organizations adopting an impact mindset—where respect and "thinking human" (Abigail Noble's term) are widespread. Amatullo's ideal 2030 is one in which "corporations have moved beyond ticking the corporate social responsibility (CSR) box [and instead have an innate knowing] of the good business sense of social impact." Indeed, managers, CEOs, and boards of directors will hopefully do far more than oversee organizational policies and activities designed and executed by the CSR department. Instead, organizational leaders and the organizational cultures will engineer the very DNA of their organizations to exude thinking and actions that maximize positive impact and minimize the negative.

Many of today's impact innovators also see the democratization of demand for impact by 2030 with society-wide celebrations of successes (and decrying of failures). The celebrations themselves will be indicators of the impact ecosystem's evolution toward a total embedding of the impact mindset. The *Stanford Social Innovation Review's* Johanna Mair sees a future with a "proliferation of noninstitutional, nonorganizational ways to solve social problems—social movements, virtual organizations, and the blogosphere." The UK's pioneering social impactor Michael Norton pictures a 2030 in which all corporations are social enterprises, with corporate managers, investment firms, and fund managers including social impact and evaluation when considering their investments. Jacqueline Lim (former manager for research at Volans and now a consultant with PivotalShift and She Leads Change in the UK) believes a majority of stakeholders in the late 2020s will want to invest in companies that are socially responsible. And, according to Aaron Horowitz of Sproutel, impact innovators of the 2020s will see the embedded nature of impact reflected in the percentages of corporate budgets that focus on ensuring net positive impact as a normal part of doing business.

Other impact changemakers went further, envisaging all enterprises being accountable by law for the negative or positive impacts emanating from their organizations. They see omnipresent public transparency on widespread indices reflecting organizational ratings on financial, social, and environmental metrics. While they anticipate growing pains of global ESG and other benchmarks, many see impact measurement not only as the norm in words and actions by 2030—integral to all we think, say, and do—but also widely understood. This positive rendering of impact and its measurement is not without caveats. As Sid Myer, Abigail Noble, and others remind us, not all causes warrant rigorous measurement. Some causes just need resources without having measurement to affirm the funds are making a difference.

Clear and intentional impact definitions

Danny Almagor of Australia's Small Giants insists impact is about intentionality. Impact is also about providing clarity around what specifically will be targeted for positive change, how those changes will be assessed, and what those changes look like. This clarity comes from defining anticipated impacts at several levels: individual, target population, and beyond. Some innovators, entrepreneurs, and investors seek positive impact at all levels; others focus on the local.

Our impact innovators see a 2030 in which innovators, entrepreneurs, and investors enact activities with full understandings and declarations of the nature and scope of the consequences of their products and services (intended and unintended). These anticipated impacts must be clearly identified. Many of the people we interviewed emphasized the imperative for any impact organization—designers, incubators, entrepreneurs, investors, and other contributors to the eco-system—to begin with a clear definition of what success looks like, a coherent path of how success will be achieved, and an articulation of the measures that will be used to determine whether success has been achieved. By 2030 impact changemakers will see widespread reporting of these anticipated and unanticipated impacts outside of their organizations due to the ubiquity of connected technology.

Venture philanthropist Lance Fors sees successful impactors in the late 2020s as those whose measurement criteria reflect the selection criteria used to determine whether to invest in the initiative. These selection criteria include whether the organization has a viable model for enacting impact initiatives, a vision of how change will take place, a clear list of organizational activities required to get to the visualized impacts, an understanding of how organizational talent will be developed to contribute to the articulated objectives, and enough revenue to sustain the enterprise. Like Nick O'Donohoe, Big Society Capital's inaugural CEO, Fors says entrepreneurs should distinctly measure what the organization has stated it is aiming to achieve, including the breadth and depth of impacts across multiple realms.

Other impactors recommended using "if/then" statements to reflect the changes an enterprise's activities seek, such as "If we provide microloans and business skills training to women in groups, then more women entrepreneurs will start and grow more small businesses." These statements help organizations set specific, measurable, achievable, and time-related goals—from the individual entrepreneur level to the national and global levels.

Multistoried, unique conceptualizations of success

Many impact thinkers and doers see 2030 understandings of what constitutes "success" embracing both processes *and* products, affects *and* effects, means *and* ends. The means do not justify the ends if either are not good for people, are not good for the planet, or do harm.

Many of the world's corporations in the 2010s have primarily defined success in the traditional manner—by their financial returns, despite growing pressure to measure the "triple bottom lines" of social, environmental, and economic returns. Leading thinkers and doers in the impact space know that success may mean different things to different innovators, entrepreneurs, and investors. For some, success is measured in terms of contribution to positive change on the world's most challenging issues: poverty, equality, conflict, water, and food security. For others, success may be the number of people accessing services, or even just providing a toilet or a computer to an organization in need. The activity in and of itself is impact. Adding to the complexity, the success of an impact initiative varies depending on the level of inquiry—from global, big picture indicators to communities, families, and individuals.

Many thought leaders we consulted envision a definitive broadening and deepening of notions of success at all levels of the ecosystem. First movers who become adept at sharing evidence about how they maximize enhancing social and environmental impacts while minimizing detrimental ones will likely attract the growing numbers of purpose-driven investors, workers, and consumers across the planet. An organization's capacity to pivot across multiple measures of success will be critical as this for-purpose population of investors, consumers, and employees expands.

Some changemakers talked about an "evolved venture capital model" as applied to impact. For example, Acumen's Sasha Dichter sees the late 2020s as a time when the best components of the venture capital model are applied to achieve impact with minimization of the ineffective and inappropriate. Dichter sees widespread appreciation of risk and growth in 2030, with enterprises demonstrating returns on financial and social investment, and impact investing success reflected in breakthrough solutions to problems in new ways. Keys to success in 2030 are about people and sustainable business models for the long term.

In her study of how "design attitude" affects the success of social innovation, Mariana Amatullo showed social innovation success being defined by the degree to which a social innovation design or process pioneered new change, used novel methods, produced novel insights, had potential for significant innovation, met the social aspirations of its stakeholders, addressed the unmet needs of stakeholders, improved stakeholders' needs not met by current conditions, contributed to fulfilling unmet needs, and helped make the world a better place. While we acknowledge that these measures of success were derived from self-reporting survey responses—which have many inherent biases and flaws that can result in erroneous conclusions about impact—they nevertheless provide rich examples of the diverse, interesting, and meaningful ways innovators are assessing impact.

Diverse and unique approaches to measuring impact

Impact thought leaders Johanna Mair and Katharine Danton were upbeat in their conjuring of the late 2020s. They see diverse methods of measuring social and environmental change in place by 2030 that reflect the many ways our society will be *doing* social change. Mair, Danton, and other leading impact thinkers and doers see measures assessing impact in all of its complexity—embracing processes *and* products, affects *and* effects, means *and* ends. Because impact in the late 2020s will be widely understood as a network of interconnecting relationships and feedback loops, impact measures will inherently assess processes, relationships, collaboration, and functionality throughout the ecosystem.

Despite the abundance of tools currently deployed to measure impact, many impact innovators see a positive evolution by 2030 to customized "regimes" of methods and measures that suit the individual needs of organizations and stakeholders. Rather than the field aspiring to one universal measure of social impacts that fits all social enterprise and investor needs, the impact thinkers and doers in our study advocated using the most appropriate standard measure for each particular enterprise as a first step in determining envisioned impacts. This can then be enhanced by complementary customized indicators. Mair, for example, does not see just generic or standard impact measures being applied across sectors or regions. She also envisages individual enterprises defining and measuring success with customized impact measures. Other leading impact thinkers and doers also expect to see enterprises in the late 2020s using both standardized *and* customized measures—their own systematic processes for gathering and analyzing information about impacts. Kurt Peleman, formerly of the European Venture Philanthropy Association, believes the same creativity and innovation characterizing social entrepreneurial initiatives, when applied to developing key performance indicators, will result in rigorous, robust methodologies and measures for gauging the success of impact initiatives.

While our interviewees understood that particular stakeholders—especially investors, government regulators, or the general population—likely want some standardized methods to more easily and effectively make comparisons across impact enterprises and investment funds, some were adamant that the social enterprises author their own impact measurement journeys. Many of our interviewees were cognizant of not burdening impact enterprises with cumbersome reporting requirements. They see impact organizations (from their inception) identifying key impact performance indicators—measures critical to the sustainability of the enterprise and to impact—with tracking of intended impacts over the short term and the long term. And they envision entrepreneurs, investors, and other stakeholders—with the entrepreneur in the driver's seat—collaboratively designing multifaceted measurement regimes appropriate for the enterprise and the stakeholders.

Measures of impact also embrace both the short and the long term, the local, regional, or global, and consider indicators of success beyond the numbers of people directly served, or who does or does not benefit from economic growth. These measures include asking questions like which psychosocial indicators—such as the collective levels of self-esteem or happiness (as in Bhutan's Gross National Happiness Index) or community levels of cortisol (a stress indicator)—might be appropriate. Or, what are the long-term measures of success that may complement or contrast to short-term measures? Other ways to assess long-term impacts require attention to structural elements of an organization or an ecosystem: What does success look like beyond annual reports, say, in five years, ten years, or even twenty-five years? Does the organization, its products, or its services add more value than they extract from a community over decades? Which public policy shifts indicate long-term net positive impacts for the greater good?

Translating learning into practice: TSF's embrace of customized and standardized measures

Determined to translate these insights into internal reviews of our work and investments, our Tingari Group investment team, including the wonder women and men at South Texas Money Management (especially the late Jeanie Wyatt and one of her protégés, STMM partner and executive vice president Christina Lecholop), experimented, tested, and instituted a multistoried approach to assess the impacts of our investments. While an ever-evolving work in progress, our approach includes standardized, publicly available measures, combined with highly customized assessments tailored to our specific impact criteria.

We view the range of available standardized measures as a menu from which to draw. We now routinely reference the following:

- The MSCI indices for ESG and Global Sustainability[1]

MSCI pioneered indices for social, environmental, and governance (ESG) responsibility. Their MSCI ESG Ratings are constructed based on thousands of data points across thirty-seven key ESG issues. These indices screen to exclude companies producing alcohol, tobacco, gambling, civilian firearms, military weapons, nuclear power, adult entertainment, and genetically modified organisms (GMOs) and to include companies demonstrating tangible commitment to positive ESG indicators. The MSCI Global Sustainability Indexes identifies companies that have demonstrated an ability to manage their ESG risks and opportunities.

- Bloomberg ESG data services[2]

We use Bloomberg's Sustainalytics ESG Risk Ratings for corporations. Sustainalytics is an independent research company dedicated to rating the sustainability of listed companies based on their environmental, social, and corporate governance performance. Sustainalytics analyzes at least seventy indicators in each industry to assess the ranking of the listed companies. Other valuable tools include the Bloomberg Barclays MSCI ESG Fixed Income Indices, a partnership between Bloomberg and MSCI ESG Research to develop and implement social responsibility indices (SRI), sustainability, ESG ratings, and green bonds. In 2019 Bloomberg added the Bloomberg Gender-Equality Index (GEI). The first of its kind, the GEI is a much-welcomed source of data on gender equality of some two hundred and thirty companies from ten sectors headquartered in thirty-six countries and regions. Bloomberg collects and shares ESG data for some 11,500 companies in eighty-three countries, building this into its user platform. Bloomberg practices what it measures and publishes an annual Bloomberg Impact Report.

- Equileap Gender Equality Global Report and Ranking[3]

Equileap is a global research firm that researched and ranked 3,206 public companies with a market cap of more than $2 billion in twenty-three developed countries, as of January 2018. Equileap assesses the progress of public companies toward gender equality based on nineteen criteria.

While we particularly draw from the standardized tools described above, others are also available, including the Dow Jones Sustainability Indices, Thomson Reuters' ESG research data, Institutional Shareholder Services, RepRisk, and Corporate Knights' Global 100.[4]

For customized indicators, the investment team conducts comprehensive research—whether online or through extensive interviews of fund managers, CEOs, or other investors. We assess many of the same criteria (both negative and positive screens) in the standardized indices. If these are not available for a particular investment, we use gender and minorities in decision-making roles as a first screen.

We also take into account the organization's status or intent regarding certification as a B Corp. And we note whether ESG-oriented funds like San Francisco-based and employee-owned Parnassus Investments are investors. Parnassus and other funds like it engage directly with potential investment recipients to rigorously assess a range of impact measures so they can invest in "companies that consider their environmental impact; treat their employees well; have good relations with local communities, customers, and the supply chain; and have strong corporate governance policies and ethical business dealings."[5] Recent research affirms the positive ramifications for assessing companies against these more composite ESG impact indices as more and more investors demand this accountability.[6]

Diverse definitions and measures of scale

One of the biggest dilemmas the impact investing and venture philanthropy sector faced during the 2010s is reflected in attempts to measure impacts in nonmonetary ways while applying a venture capital model of growth and success to social enterprises. In the venture capital industry, as Draper Richards Kaplan Foundation CEO Jim Bildner pointed out, success is about scale: scaling production, scaling revenues, scaling profit, scaling financial returns on investment. Such conceptions of success and scale can be restrictive in the impact context. Kurt Peleman reminds us that most small-scale civil society innovations are not incentivized to scale. And yet such innovations are successful by many other measures.

Scale demonstrated by growth in numbers is often touted as the ultimate measure of entrepreneurial success. The scale equals success mindset prevalent in the first two decades of the twenty-first century, while a good starting point to thinking about amplifying impact, is a carryover from the venture capital model of success. In contrast to this one-dimensional financial interpretation of scale, many leading impactors see financial scale as just *one* possible measure of success. Johanna Mair, for example, is wary of widespread overexcitement about the need to scale and welcomes new conceptions of scale beyond the purely quantitative. Mair and other impact leaders see conceptions of what constitutes scale in the late 2020s as also being multistoried and not reliant on the financial growth model as the sole indicator of scale.[7] As Verb co-founder and former Dell CEO Tom Meredith noted, scale can be as simple as leaving a footprint from which others spin off. Or, as Katharine Danton (UnLtd UK and Purpose to Impact) observed, scale is not scaling a venture, but scaling impact. Problems being solved in large-scale ways to aid the poor.

The movement away from financial and numerical appraisals of scale is exemplified in the work of Lance Fors, who now views scale of positive impact being at the core to any enterprise. He and other leading impact innovators see scale reflected in the growth of networks, the expansion of markets, and the increase in manufacturing and distribution of products, services, and ideas. It is the sustainability of economic, social, and environmental impact that matters. Peleman and NESsT's Loïc Comolli point out that impact can be increased without necessarily growing the organization. Scale can be a lot of small-scale organizations, as well as a lot of copycats. If a movement of copycat activities ignites, copycats have the capacity to create and shape an entire industry. In the networked global world of the 2020s, organizational leaders who think creatively about scale and utilize the growth of the precariat and the democratization of everything can build competitive advantage and success of their organizations in nontraditional ways.

Multileveled measures encompass ecosystems

In the late 2020s measures of success automatically extend through all levels of the ecosystem—from the individual to the global—and the measures go far beyond the financial. Impact influencers in this research envisage vast improvements in impact measurement and anticipate the combining of standard statistical measures with more nuanced understandings and assessments of "what change have we made in that person or that society?" They see improved measures that balance the needs of shareholders, stakeholders, and enterprise managers.

By 2030 these improvements will enable positive and negative impacts to be measured at all levels of analysis, from the individual to the national and the global and from the enterprise to the industry and the ecosystem. CEO of Australia's Centre for Social Impact (a collaboration of three Australian universities), Andrew Young, believes that by the mid-2020s a whole-of-system measure of social outcomes will be more salient. His vision is shared by others who believe, for example, that the rising global attention to the United Nations' Sustainable Development Goals is part of this wave.

Recall Kurt Peleman urging for big-level measures that embrace the quality of psychological life—macro measures of societal happiness, depression, and suicide. Curiously, suicide rate is currently the only measure for mental health on the international Social Progress Index. In 2030 nonmaterialistic, nonfinancial measures of success will reverberate throughout the system. Efforts by social science pioneers like the late Sir Roger Jowell (responsible for the British Social Attitudes Survey), Martin Seligman and Ed Diener (Well-Being Index), Michael Green and colleagues (Social Progress Index), and Bhutan's Gross National Happiness Index all illustrate an increasing movement toward more complex multilayered, multi-nuanced measures of progress against societies' toughest challenges. By 2030 such measures will not be unusual, and instead will be reflected through all parts of the global system, including corporate accountabilities and reporting requirements—demanded by both laws and stakeholders.

Impactors saw a convergence of these efforts complementing expanded definitions of success at the highest levels of the ecosystem. They believe that the same technologies facilitating transparency and accountability (of governments, organizations, individuals) will also facilitate the collecting, analyzing, and sharing of data about successes and challenges on a local and global scale. Many impact changemakers believe that by 2030 a majority of corporate, government, and nongovernment organizations will be part of this wave of more complex and nuanced thinking and doing around impact.

Impactors of today believe the whole-of-ecosystem measures will be capturing these aspects of doing impact in a decade or two—measuring levels of collaboration within a system and its subsystems, in cross-sector partnerships, and measuring ripples of impact throughout the system as well as patterns within and across systems.

Collaboration and partnerships = success

In the spirit of circuits, networks, and circles, and of verbs, means, and processes, some of today's visionary impact changemakers see a world in the late 2020s in which constructive collaborations and partnerships are the norm. Kurt Peleman sees global and local connectedness aiding impact. Jim Bildner envisages widespread local–international collaborations. Others picture a surge of space-sharing accelerators, hubs, and incubators that facilitate increased collaboration and preparation toward scale. Lance Fors sees impact communities evolving through these local and global networks—connecting people to facilitate greater impact, a world in which collectives are the dominant places, hubs, and containers in which to do positive impact.

The new and evolving global partnerships, like the Global Development Innovation Ventures or even Social Venture Partners International, will face demand in the 2020s to measure the effectiveness of their collaborations from both a means and an ends perspective, and consequently, from a system-learning perspective. Mariana Amatullo sees the focus on human connectedness, empowerment, and collaboration resulting in a further expansion of qualitative methods and measures. Journalist Zoe Smith pictures collaborations and consortiums as the norm by the late 2020s. Some visionary impactors suggest we will be measuring the effectiveness of these collaborative hubs, accelerators, and incubators in contributing to change in some of the planet's toughest socioeconomic issues. If the number and effectiveness of collaborations and networks are signs of impact success in a positive 2030 (at the ecosystem and subsystem levels), measuring extent and effectiveness will be important components of measuring impacts in the late 2020s.

Integrated impact measurement regimes

In the most optimistic versions of 2030, the showdown between financial ROI, environmental ROI, and social ROI fades away as democratization of demands for impact takes hold; silos disappear and positive impact awareness and action become mainstream. This will be a time when the "for purpose" economy is omnipresent and integrated. Globally connected citizens of 2030—many Millennials hitting their life's stride and Gen Zers becoming increasingly vocal and active—contribute to the surge in action and work for purpose, blurring boundaries between silos. According to the most positive scenarios, 2030 ushers in a world in which making money and doing positive impact are conflated. Our impact influencers see a preponderance of organizations reporting combinations of financial, social, and environmental metrics.

In the most positive 2030, large and small corporations alike join the wave of mainstreamed impact actions and measures. All stakeholders will know the good business sense of positive impact, reflected in widespread corporate and popular demand and action. As DoSome-thing's Aria Finger suggests, companies will internalize realities and both do *and* measure impacts by the late 2020s. Nick O'Donohoe envisages calculated approaches in which organizations will weigh how far they can go along the impact spectrum and still get financial ROI. Others imagine companies being held accountable by law and public transparency on widespread indices reflecting organizational ratings on financial ROI, social ROI, and environmental ROI. Johanna Mair, Jim Bildner, and the late Pamela Hartigan pictured a 2030 with ecosys-tem-wide recognition that entrepreneurial and management skills used for sustainable impact enterprises are the same, regardless of business model. A world in which positive impact is an ordinary part of what is done by everyone and every organization. UK impactors Michael Norton and Jacqueline Lim foresee a 2030 in which shareholders and stakeholders demand socially responsible metrics, with all investment firms and fund managers including impact selection and evaluation in considering and reporting investments.

Locals in the measurement driver's seat

Impact leaders of today see a 2030 in which locals are in control when it comes to deciding what impact they desire and how it will be mea-sured. Western do-gooders looking for Western indicators of "success" will take a back seat. This deference to locals will be accompanied by a trend toward "place-based," city-based, and user-based impact strate-gies, where locals are integral to designing and implementing particular solutions to how specific challenges play out in their place or city, or how success is gauged.

Hannah Chung and Aaron Horowitz at Sproutel exemplify this wave of user-centered design, as do the faculty and students at Designmatters at the ArtCenter College of Design in California. Their "innovations for good" are being designed *with* the people who will most use and benefit from them. A natural outcome of growing rebellion against Western-imposed solutions to non-Western issues, user-centered design contributes to a rising demand for locally designed strategies to abet local problems. The rise in user-centered design will likely be accompanied by increasingly widespread comfort with qualitative measures like those Mariana Amatullo deployed in her research. Her constructs, like tolerance of ambiguity, engagement with aesthetics, systems thinking, connecting multiple perspectives, creativity, and empathy, are prescient of measures that are likely to be endemic by the late 2020s.

Lance Fors, Michael Norton, Katharine Danton, and Michael Traill (founding CEO of Social Ventures Australia) all foresee local and user-driven design and implementation of social and environmental change. In this 2030 scenario, the town or city becomes the driver and place of change, as well as the "container" for measuring change. These impact leaders believe that by the late 2020s, measures of impact innovation ecosystems at the city level will be commonplace. As impact awareness and measures are integrated, measurement of positive impacts (and negative) will evolve with the ecosystem. Today's measures of the success of innovation ecosystems—numbers of start-ups, entrepreneurs, incubators, accelerators, hubs, investors, collaborative networks, successful enterprises, second- and third-generation entrepreneurial ventures—will be applied to impact innovation as well.

Simultaneously track the short-term and the long-term

It may be a cliché, but timing *is* everything when measuring outcomes and impacts. In the more positive renderings of 2030, impactors focus on both the long view and the short view. With an inherent and widespread knowing that much impact occurs over decades, not within quarterly or annual reporting cycles, or election terms, by the late 2020s, impact measurement will be targeted and tailored to capture both short- and long-term impacts reflecting the concerns of impact thought leaders and doers like Sid Myer and Abigail Noble.

ENTREPRENEURSHIP FOR IMPACT INSIGHTS SUMMARY

Successful impact innovators of the late 2020s embed knowledge of impact, good and bad, into all they think and do. They know when and when not to measure. They think and act with an ecosystem mindset with long-term horizons in mind. Successful impact innovators collaborate with locals to co-design local solutions and monitor progress. They embrace both standardized and nuanced, customized measures of success, impact, and scale. Creative actions now to develop adaptable methods, measures, processes, and standards to assess activities, outcomes, and impacts will reap dividends by the late 2020s.

Forthward: Everywhere, Everywhen

We end this book where we began: at an extraordinarily critical juncture—for humanity and for planet Earth. Intense and frequent calamitous events like hurricanes, floods, droughts, earthquakes, windstorms, and bushfires are our daily siren call to change course and do something new. The waning cachet of the United States and the unraveling of Europe, the rise of China and Asia as the world's epicenter of financial and geopolitical power, and the rising up and hunkering down of nativists in their homelands (fending off waves of immigration) are signs that what awaits us on the other side of this decade needs attention and action now. We end this book where we began, but we know so much more. We end with a sense of urgency and a shout-out for the imperative to act definitively. To act decisively. To facilitate more positive impacts and less negative impacts for more people on our planet.

We end this book where we began as humanity. Literally. Forty to sixty thousand years ago. Yet time, like so many other aspects of our existence in different parts of the world, is a cultural concept.[1]

Western notions of time are predicated on the modernist progress myth, in which the future is by definition brighter and more enlightened than the past. In Western cultures, time is a separate entity, a resource gone forever once consumed. Chronological time is marked by the sun rising and setting, the passing of the days and the seasons, and is distinct from and different to the eternal. That is, the temporal, natural world is distinct from the nontemporal, eternal world of ideals.[2] There are exceptions to discrete, measurable, linear, Western conceptions of time. For example, satellite global positioning systems rely on measurements of time beamed from satellites that are orbiting the earth. The earth, in turn, orbits the sun. These synchronicities of nature and the logistics of quantifying and relaying measurements take into account the scientifically documented relativity of time—that is, time is more fluid than we believe in our daily lives. Time dilates—slows down, stretches out.[3] Other cultures have more fluid, all-encompassing understandings of time.

When we renamed our foundation to include the word Tingari, we did so with reverence for the values of ancient Aboriginal Australians. These values are reflected in their songlines—their tellings of past, present, and future and their conceptions about and ties to the land, to every living thing on the planet. Australian Aboriginals are the longest continual civilization on earth. We also humbly acknowledge our generalization of Aboriginal cultures and beliefs that belie the immense diversity of Aboriginal Australians. We equally acknowledge our own learning curve in understanding the richness and complexity of Aboriginal knowledges. Our intent, in our foundation name and our work, is to honor the Aboriginal notion of the interconnectedness of all living things in one vast network of relationships: the confluence of people (currently living, as well as ancestors and descendants), place, land, animals, fish, plants, water, air, space, time.

Aboriginal Australian multidimensional concepts of time inform our thoughts and actions around impact, around intending good and not doing further harm. In ancient Australian Aboriginal cultures, past, present, and future are all bound up in the eternal now. In traditional Australian Aboriginal culture, time contains no innate or inherent importance. No chronological, linear sequences of events stretching out behind us and ahead of us on a continuum. The eternal, all-encompassing now is captured in Aboriginal understandings of the Jukurrpa, Manguny, or Ngarrankarni (the names given by different Aboriginal language groups, inadequately translated as the "Dreamtime" or "Dreaming" in English).[4] An Aboriginal elder from Arnhem Land, Djawa "Timmy" Burarrwanga, described Jukurrpa as "not . . . simply the case that the individual is a fixed point in a temporal flux or continuum, for one's self is, was and will be in the Dreaming."[5] Humans (and all living things, including the planet itself), whether living or ancestors or descendants, are as one in time.

Jukurrpa is grounded in the land itself, with humans and nature equal partners, with continuity between peoples and the landscape. Land is a second skin, critical in sustaining life. We are the land, which must be nurtured and cared for as our own bodies are cared for and nurtured.[6] Aboriginals come to know the land by deep and practiced listening. They are schooled in listening to the land and to stories of the continuity among all living things from their earliest days, having passed on this way of listening for more than forty thousand years.[7] For Aboriginal peoples, the land, or "country," is the central occasion, place, space of learning. Burarrwanga says, "We know everything there—the trees, animals, plants. . . . It's been handed down by our ancestors. . . . [The land] is just like a big book to us. . . . Over the years, people been tearing pages out of our book. . . . We've taken out a whole guts of our book. . . . It would be hard for teaching to carry on after that point."[8] Burarrwanga worries that if we don't sustain the land, when we only take without giving back, we are destroying our place of learning, destroying our life sustainer, destroying ourselves.

In ancient Aboriginal cultures, time works *for* a person, family, or community, for the land; it is not something that has to be adhered to.[9] Australian anthropologist W. E. H. Stanner coined the term "everywhen" to describe Aboriginal conceptions of time (past, present, and future) as "everywhere at all times." Stanner and others use the example of the Aboriginal custom of not disclosing names or allowing photographs of deceased people, because deceased individuals are only considered dead in a physical sense. Those people are still alive spiritually and play important roles in the daily lives of the living. All ancestors and descendants are "everywhere at all times." Everything that happens "in time" is elaborately interconnected and has implications for eternity.[10]

Aboriginal conceptions of the interconnectedness of all things, of circularity, of everywhen encompassed in the now have much in common with modern systems thinking. In highly interdependent 2020s ecosystems, ancient and modern understandings that every action by every person and organization ramifies, with far-reaching consequences in the everywhen—everywhere, anytime—are critical. It is imperative that a significant mass of the world's peoples move to more all-encompassing everywhen, everywhere, everyone understandings of the impacts of what we say and do.

With knowledges of what likely awaits us on the other side of the 2020s, with understandings that for every action there are consequences and reactions in other parts of the ecosystem, no matter how delayed or remote, the potential for innovators and entrepreneurs to enact positively impactful initiatives, to do good, has never been greater or more needed. This book is about different ways of seeing and acting in the now to enact optimal paths ahead. The ideas shared were meant to serve as grist for the curiosity mill, to trigger thinking about what we must do now to enact the futures we want in the next decade and beyond: optimal futures for ourselves, our children, their children. For our planet. Futures in which access to clean air, water, local food, health care, and education are evenly distributed across the planet.

We finish the book with four sections. First, we share a summation of the issues that drive our own sense of urgency. Second, we describe the mindsets that will facilitate capacity to change trajectories for the better. Third, we identify actions—small and large—that can be taken now to enact futures that maximize positive impacts and minimize the negative. We hope the insights illuminate some plausible next steps for you and your organization. Add your own steps to achieve momentum to facilitate trajectories that yield the most beneficial answers to the questions: Is it good for people? Is it good for the planet? Will it do harm anywhere in the ecosystem? Finally, we conclude with a "Forthward" challenge. Poet, philosopher, and author Mattie Stepanek, who died just weeks before his fourteenth birthday, wanted the final chapter of his last book, *Just Peace: A Message of Hope*, to be a "Forthward." Mattie told his co-author, former President Jimmy Carter: "A foreword was when you write something before a book text. A 'Forthward' is where do we go from here? After you read my book, after you read my poems. After you consider all the exchanges of information concerning me and Jimmy Carter and other famous people, then where do we go?"[11] As in *Just Peace: A Message of Hope*, we use a Forthward to illuminate modes of thinking and acting that facilitate realization of more positive futures for all.

ON THE OTHER SIDE OF THE 2020S

Throughout this book, we've relayed evidence about what scientists and other analysts know with considerable certainty lies in wait for us and our planet in the decade or two ahead. What awaits us if we sustain the same rates of consumption—of water, food, energy, air. What awaits us if we continue to discard the same levels of waste—into the earth, the oceans, the atmosphere. We've also relayed exciting and potent developments in technology that can mitigate or exacerbate some of the realities that lie ahead. Most experts agree that on the other side of this decade, we will see:

- **Extreme climate events**. Massive losses of property and life ride on the back of gigantic tidal waves and brute-force winds, in the wake of intensifying hurricanes, tornados, earthquakes, and catastrophic bushfires, endangering the planet's finite resources and access to clean water, food, and air.

- **The richest people on the planet widening their lead over the poorest**. Elites clash with the disenfranchised, nationalists gain power, political parties feed on fears of threats to local lifestyles by "the other," as locals hunker down to protect their psychological and geopolitical territories.

- **Asia becoming the epicenter of the world population.** America's global cachet continues to wane, while China's power rises in this Asian century. Populations in "Western" parts of the world grow ever more tired of politics as usual, ensuring that identity politics pervade and paralyze Western governments.

- **Democratized and empowered crowds ensuring transparency and accountability.** Information cascades prove a potent force for ensuring consequences for bad individual and organizational behaviors. Crowds use their power as adhocracies and prosumers—selling, trading, giving, and sharing their creations with others peer-to-peer—while alternative currencies and crowd funding render twentieth-century-style financing through banks and corporations almost obsolete.

- **Cultural shifts and information cascades ushering in a rise in women power.** No longer willing to stay quiet about being excluded from positions at the highest levels of decision-making and access to working capital, or suffering at the hands of men who've been previously protected by conspiracies of silence, women come into their own through the 2020s. Controlling 70 percent of global wealth and over 80 percent of consumer decisions by the end of the decade, women translate their financial power into successful innovation entrepreneurship, investment, and positive impact.

- **A global surge in purpose even as the world's population mushrooms and resources become further depleted.** With Millennials constituting 75 percent of the global workforce by 2025, they want to work for, invest in, or patronize organizations whose missions change the world for the better. Millennials' (and the Gen Zers who are hot on Millennials' heels) attitudes and actions demand both business and impact, as they put their time and money where their values are, investing *away* from banks, *away* from Wall Street, and *into* impact entrepreneurship.

Understanding the likely and possible global realities of the next two decades will be instrumental—not only in helping make sense of the context in which we will all live, work, and play between now and 2030, but more important, in facilitating how to plan, prepare, and respond to the opportunities and challenges ahead. In the next section, we chronicle suggested mindsets and actions designed to build competence in anticipating and managing future trends and realities so that, globally, more people can collectively share the responsibility of managing finite planetary resources in ways that ensure more positive and fewer negative impacts. Individual and collective mindsets and actions that contribute to the greater good.

ENACTING POSITIVE IMPACT FUTURES

Our journey into the future of innovation, entrepreneurship, and impact revealed that by 2030, global challenges demand we be more mindful of the impacts—negative and positive—of all we do for all time. For everywhen. Our challenge is to be innovative and entrepreneurial in designing and enacting products and services that help mitigate some of the world's most intractable challenges without doing harm somewhere else in the planet-wide ecosystem. Being innovative and entrepreneurial in our impacting. Being impactful in our innovating and entrepreneuring. Mindsets for successful navigation of the territory ahead require us to:

- Think and act like an ancient Aboriginal Australian.

If we all think in terms of everywhen—adopting notions of the interconnectedness of time, place, and us from some of the planet's earliest systems and ecosystems thinkers—we will understand how all of our actions impact futures for each one of us. Such understandings can inform actions in the now to ensure the least harm for the planet and its peoples in the everywhen and the everywhere.

- Think and act like a futurist.

When we think in the future tense—anchoring our minds in richly detailed alternative futures, thinking and acting from a futuristic everywhen mindset, we:

  ○ Welcome uncertainty and get comfortable with ambiguity.

  ○ Strengthen futuristic imagining and fantasizing as an everyday tool.

  ○ Simultaneously think long-term and short-term, understanding that the short term has ramifications for the long term and vice versa.

  ○ Simultaneously think big picture and little picture, understanding that actions are always accompanied by reactions.

- Think and act like an author or an artist in creating our own futures.

Authors and artists constantly scan their environment, paying punctilious attention to every encounter, every incident, and every aspect of their surroundings. Their observations inform how they think, feel, and act. Authors and artists actively look for explanations of why and how current events link to past and future events.[12] Authors and artists create the futures they envision.

- Think and act like a capabilities-centered designer.

When designing solutions to challenges, we typically search for problems to be solved. However, as Italian designer Ezio Manzini and Nobel

Prize-winning economist Amartya Sen have exemplified, if we adopt a capabilities-centered approach, we search for *capabilities to support* instead of problems to be solved. In focusing on capabilities, especially *local* capabilities, knowledges, and expertise, those closest to the challenges can be resourced to meet those challenges. A capabilities-centered mindset involves:

- ○ Cultivating attention to signals that can inform thoughts and actions.

- ○ Cultivating empathy and humility.

- ○ Using words and language that do not inadvertently diminish the people with whom we work.

- ○ Thinking in terms of capabilities, not problems, and partners, not recipients of aid.

- Think "space = place = systems = impacts."

When we consider all of the possible ramifications (positive and negative) of what we do in the context of everywhen and everywhere, we are thinking in terms of systems, of impacts—both intended and unintended. Successful impact changemakers apply an impact lens to all thinking and doing. They enact policies and initiatives reflecting a "maximizing positive while minimizing negative impacts" mission, including transforming investment strategies and conceptions of return on investment.

- Think in circles, not lines.

- ○ Think what goes around comes around.

- ○ Adopt a mindset of impactful entrepreneuring.

- ○ Adopt a mindset of entrepreneurial impacting.

- Think in verbs.

This book has been about innovating, entrepreneuring, and impacting as verbs rather than nouns. As social psychologist Karl Weick reminds us: "Verbs capture the action that lays down the path for sensemaking. Verbs keep things moving . . . verbs point to the actions that are available. . . . To change a verb is to take the first step to change a process."[13] Adeptly preparing for, responding to, and enacting alternative futures requires action words along with attention to and skill in process.

- Think collaborators, partners, capabilities.

Ezio Manzini said: "We can look to the people of the planet in two ways. We can see seven billion people on the planet today or nine billion people tomorrow as the biggest threat and the biggest problem, because we are a little planet. But given that those seven billion people are you, me, my friends, and the people we know, we see them not as problems but as people with capabilities, intelligent operators. . . . What does it mean to enable all the potentialities of so many intelligent people?"[14] When we think capabilities, we search for people to support and collaborations to make. We respect locals' innate understandings of their own situations.

- Think holistically and complexly.

If we are to collaboratively meet the realities awaiting us on the other side of this decade, we must move beyond the meta-frame of Western solutions to every global or local challenge. We must seek to comprehend each part of this great big ecosystem in which we live and embrace its complexity; we must try to understand the interconnectedness of all things; and we must try to act with the knowledge that every act, small or large, can have ramifications for the everywhen. Our actions now affect someone, something, somewhere, sometime.

- Conduct a brutal audit.

Assess all thoughts, words, and actions that could inadvertently harm. Enact changes to minimize harm.

- Engineer our own preferred futures.

Be prepared (with knowledge and skills) for volatility, uncertainties, connectivity, transparency, accountability, and impact.

- Master process.

  o Cultivate and hone listening and observation skills.

  o Embrace simultaneously simple and complex definitions of success.

  o Define what is acceptable and not acceptable, and draw a line in the sand.

  o Carry expectations lightly.

  o Test expectations regularly.

- Understand and attract generational impactors and influencers.

The world is witnessing the biggest generational transfer of wealth in history as Baby Boomers retire or die. Money managers around the globe are meeting demands for positive impact to navigate the changing capital currents. Organizations of all kinds can embrace "do no harm" values for better futures for all.

- Actively ensure diversity, especially women.

Women are on the rise—embrace it. Having women involved in decision-making is good for all returns on investment. Globally, women are poised to control 70 percent of the world's assets by 2030. Women are more inclined to positive impact, and they'll have the financial power to enact their inclinations.

- Understand and utilize the democratization of everything.

Use the distributive nature of power, capital, and influence, which are expressed through collaboration, partnerships, and networks.

- Embrace the new technology-driven era of transparency and accountability.

Get ahead of the curve. Own up. Accept responsibility for wrongdoing. Squash conspiracies of silence. Proactively do no harm. Expose harm being done.

- Develop the knowledges and skills of pivoting.

Hone individual and organizational capacities for changing trajectories within the general bandwidth of an organization's mission.

- Expand definitions and metrics of success.

Go beyond economic impact and financial returns. Be creative and expansive in what constitutes "success" and what constitutes "rich." Share stories of success.

- Comprehend, build, and enable scale in multiple ways.
- Comprehend and enact the multistoried nature of sustainability.
- Apply a "do no further harm" lens to all thinking and doing.

Ask: Is it good for people? Is it good for the planet? Does it do harm anywhere in the ecosystem?

OUR FORTHWARD CHALLENGE

As we neared the conclusion of this research journey, Australian organizational psychologist and colleague Michael McGregor—in the skilled way of a good psychologist—asked piercing, probing questions about the essence of our research, both the journey and the results. His most fundamental question: "What is the future of entrepreneurship?" Our unhesitating response: "Impact." His next question: "What is the future of impact?" Again, our unhesitating response: "Entrepreneurship." Our hope is that the insights shared throughout this book have caught your imagination. Inspired you to think and do innovation, entrepreneurship and impact that will benefit the greater good. We hope these insights invite you to reframe the way you think and act in the now and in the future. The same big challenges gripping our planet in the 2010s will convulse our planet even more in the 2020s if left unchecked. Is that a legacy we want to pass on to our children and grandchildren?

As we turn to face the future, think of time folding in on itself. It is both 2020 and 2030. The oldest Millennials are forty years old, now fifty. The oldest Gen Zers are twenty-three in 2020, now thirty-three in 2030. The youngest Baby Boomers are fifty-five, now sixty-five. Our world population is seven billion people, now nine billion. In 2020 more than a billion people live on $1.90 a day, split 50/50 between middle-income and low-income countries.[15] In 2030 those statistics are much the same, although the balance is tipped to more poor in middle-income countries than low-income countries. In 2020 fish in our oceans are navigating through toxic swirls of plastic debris the size of Texas, choking on petrochemicals. In 2030 the choking is a tight stranglehold, a poisonous death knell. It is 2020 and our planet screams out about the precarious state it is in. Now in 2030 the screams are reaching a crescendo.

In 2017 Nobel Peace Prize winner and former U.S. vice president Al Gore delivered an impassioned plea: "The next generation would be justified in looking back at us and asking, 'What were you thinking? Couldn't you hear what the scientists were saying? Couldn't you hear what Mother Nature was screaming at you?'"[16] Or will we deprive the next generations of hope? Will the legacy we leave for future generations on planet earth force them to fight over access to clean drinking water or fresh nontoxic foods, as they witness the power of the top 1 percent of the wealthiest people on the planet while the bottom 10 percent languish in abject poverty? The preponderance of evidence, whether believing in climate change or not, is on escalating climate events that threaten our very survival. As alarmist as it sounds, the very survival of our species, of our planet, means we can no longer keep our heads in the sand about the global realities we will inevitably face in the 2020s.

So much of what happens in 2030 rides on what we do now. One of the best features of the future is its glorious unpredictability. Do we want to wake on the morning of January 1, 2030, with rationalizations and justifications—an "It's not our problem" abdication of responsibility? Are we going to let humanity stumble into a less than optimal future? Follow a tumultuous path to inevitable conclusions? We have an infinite number of possible futures ahead of us—from the blistering to the blissful, from voices replete with desperation to those exuding hope and joy. It would be so easy to ignore the screams. Or maybe pretend we don't hear them.

Why bother with an interminable odyssey to some faraway future? The evidence about the challenges awaiting us on the other side of this decade is incontrovertible. It is patently clear that the emerging trends and realities, if ignored, will cause extreme social, environmental, geopolitical, and economic damage over the long term. We cannot look away. We cannot ignore. We must act. The most immediate, controllable, consequential means to act, to authoring your own and your organization's trajectory, is to start with small thoughts, small acts.

We hope the stories and actions we shared enhance your ability to think futuristically. To contemplate present actions that might steer you and your organization toward your preferred, most optimal futures. When we connect an entrepreneurial impacting mindset with impactful entrepreneurial doing, we don't have to wait for a future to happen to us. We happen to the future. Immediate change to our trajectory is within our control. Innovating, entrepreneuring, and impacting are about juxtaposition: mixing, matching, contextualizing, comparing, discovering, rediscovering, enacting, and remaining open to the unexpected. Impact is hidden in the everyday. It is already in our work, our play, what we drive, what we drink, what we eat, what we breathe. All we have to do is pay attention. And do something—without harm.

Acknowledgments

L
ike the nested ecosystems described in the preceding chapters, conducting research and writing a book about entrepreneurship and impact creates its own micro-ecosystem. Like so many of the impact changemakers highlighted and quoted throughout the book, our *Impact Imperative* team—who worked tirelessly to bring five years of research to the typed page—exudes all the qualities of impact changemakers, often working their magic behind the scenes, subtly and humbly. Our *Impact Imperative* team members, like their counterparts in ecosystems around the world, simultaneously think micro and macro, big picture and little picture, long-term and short-term. They understand that impact amplifies, rippling up and down and throughout. They think about everywhere, everywhen. They enact their own and their organization's futures accordingly. They approach challenges with a capabilities-centered mindset, respecting individual and collective local knowledges and capacities. They hone their own skills for pivoting and adapting to the jolts they know will unfold as the future unfolds. They trust the process to deliver a positive end product. And above all, they are dedicated to doing no harm. This book would not exist without them.

Our Tingari Group Chief Renaissance Woman, Melissa Abel, quietly makes things happen from the minutiae to the momentous. A Tingari Foundation director, editor, strategist, thinker, and doer, Mel has multiplier impacts on individuals and communities that are far more substantial than she ever imagined.

Futures facilitator extraordinaire and grower of gardens small and large, Moira Were (formerly Deslandes), also works magical positive impacts from the individual to the international. She is often the unassuming impact maker—strategically planting seeds, connecting, brokering, mentoring, and role-modeling. She is always thinking everywhere and everywhen, outside everybody's box. Moira brings all of this positive impact together in South Australia's Chooks movement for women. Her contribution to *Impact Imperative* is immeasurable!

Betsy Thorpe, the author whisperer, has been a calm guiding light throughout the book-writing process. Betsy's sharp, yet gentle probing and editorial insights *always* make for a better sentence, paragraph, book.

The Greenleaf publishing team, especially editors AprilJo Murphy and Judy Marchman, also exuded patient professionalism, adroitly placed questioning, sensitive cutting, and much-appreciated meticulous attention to detail. They have astutely curated these words to a more positively impactful end product. Designer Neil Gonzalez creatively translated the essence of the book into an apt cover (the future of our planet and humanity is in all our hands, and time for meaningful positive impact is running out). And huge thanks to Tyler LeBleu, herder in chief, who kept us all on schedule.

Susan Engelking—with her ever-creative mind (a humble recipient of Austin's [f#*#ing] Communicator of the Year Award when the city was building its foundation for growth)—was chief cheerleader for this book. With her unwavering belief in the power of the written word to change the world for the better, Susan worked tirelessly to help make it happen. Susan's colleague, Sue Kolbly—summarizer, editor, feedbackgiver, and head of marketing in the ride-share community—has been invaluable, not least with her intent on positive impact, one passenger at a time.

Designers, ideas generators, futurists, and contributors Jake Dunagan and Stuart Candy blazed a futures trail in Hawaii as enthusiastic PhD students. They've been firing imaginations with their skillful futures processes, scenarios, and artifacts from the future ever since. Our work together started with a collaboration with the Institute For The Future in Palo Alto, California, but given our Austin and Aussie connections, hopefully it will last well into those 2030 futures we imagined.

Others in our research team toiled long hours interviewing, editing, inputting data, transcribing, brainstorming, and sharing insights. Thank you to Ann Deslandes, Kelly Bandy Young, and Sophie Ryan-Wood for these often anonymous but necessary tasks. And thank you to Riley Ryan-Wood for applying her inspired photography skills to a headshot!

Huge gratitude goes to my international sisterhood and brotherhood—for everything: from championing and modeling positive impact, to pointing out commas in the wrong places, and providing creative feedback on cover designs; for nourishing and sustaining year after year; and nurturing our four-legged family members! Y'all know who you are. You are cherished beyond words.

To both Sophie and Riley—for their piercing questions, their relentless reminding of what is important, and their lifelong unquestioning acceptance of walls in our home being endlessly lined with ideas-filled flip-chart paper. For daily exemplifying how the Millennial generation is a source of hope for better futures for all.

To all the organic tea-makers and baristas in Adelaide (Organic Café, Fleurieu Bites, Pickle in the Middle), Austin (The Steeping Room and Mozart's), and Brooklyn (Neighbors Café), whose wide-grinned welcomes at all times of the day positively impacted the writing process day in and day out. With their gracious smiles and gentle inquiries of "how's it going" and "let us know when it comes out," they daily create an ambience for thoughtful creativity and productivity, and hours of writing! Particular thanks go to Lee and Nicole, the impactful entrepreneuring women at the Organik Café at Glenelg, and Amy at The Steeping Room in Austin, who each make the world a better place, one sustainably sourced ingredient at a time.

To all of the impact changemakers around the world who shared their stories, challenges, insights, and visions of alternative, more positive futures: Thank you for all the ways you contribute to the greater good—of humanity and the planet. Not just in the here and now, but in the everywhere and everywhen.

Forms of Capital for Innovation, Entrepreneurship, and Impact

The 2020s will witness a growing utilization of alternative sources of capital:

Accelerator incubator capital: Whether government, university, corporate, or independent, accelerators and incubators are sprouting all over the world, many international in focus. For example, 500 Startups and Techstars Impact deliberately target international entrepreneurs and offer four-month residential and then virtual accelerator support. Incubators and accelerators provide material support like office space, mentoring, and consulting, and often connect first-time entrepreneurs with serial entrepreneurs and angel investors.

Advocacy campaign capital: For example, Red Nose Day—started in the UK by screenwriter Richard Curtis and comedian Lenny Henry via their Comic Relief nonprofit in 1985 to raise funds for the famine in Ethiopia—now raises funds globally to "help people living tough lives." DoSomething's campaigns also exemplify the power of mobilizing awareness and funds via public advocacy.

Angel capital: According to the Global Entrepreneurship Monitor, angel investors constitute up to 5 percent of funding for early stage companies. Angel investor networks like AngelList (USA), Angel Investment Scout (UK), SyndicateRoom (Europe and UK), and Seedmatch (Germany) are sprouting all over the world.

Awards, competitions, and prize capital: As we noted in the introduction, after almost a decade of operations, our Social Entrepreneur of the Year Award tended to be viewed as just another funding source by many social service providers. The award applicants were right. Impact entrepreneurs can gain majorly from entering award competitions— if the effort dispensed is worth the rewards, both financially and in generating attention. The regional, national, and international Moot Corp competitions and the University of Texas Dell Social Innovation Challenge create opportunities for changemakers, innovators, entrepreneurs, and funders to come together in one place to forge connections, collaborations, and knowledge sharing. **Entrepreneurs beware:** While competitions undoubtedly unleash creative energy, they can also produce a great waste of effort for the "losers."

Bridging or growth loan capital: Our own Tingari-Silverton Foundation is often tapped for bridging loans to finance growth when companies use loans rather than equity to avoid all of the inherent challenges of equity investments. For example, Austin nongovernmental organization EcoRise Youth Innovations (a school-based program empowering students to tackle real-world challenges in their communities by learning about sustainability, design, and social innovation) sought a $250,000 social impact loan to finance expansion of its highly successful program.

Crowd capital: Crowdfunding, on platforms like Crowdcube, GoFundMe, Indiegogo, Kickstarter, Patreon, and Teespring, will grow by almost 90 billion dollars between 2018 and 2022. Equity crowd-funding holds huge disruptive potential for innovation ecosystems. As the power of the crowd rises, lines are blurring across the early stage investment ecosystem, with some equity crowdfunding platforms effectively becoming venture funds. Now often used in conjunction with angel investment networks, crowdfunding enables angel investors to harness more funds than they could alone while allowing smaller investors to "tag along" with experienced entrepreneurs. Some crowdfunding organizations are more selective than others: UK-based SyndicateRoom has a minimum investment of £1,000, and a large entry price. It is an exceptional model, as all ventures have an experienced lead investor who conducts due diligence and negotiates terms, although all other investors receive the same class of shares, on the same terms as the lead. Crowdcube also enables individuals to invest alongside professional investors in start-up, early stage, and growth businesses through equity, debt, and investment fund options.

Corporate venture capital: Corporate investors in entrepreneurial ventures (like Google, Rakuten, Alibaba, and Comcast) are the largest funders of start-ups outside of traditional VC funds. Many corporations are choosing to invest in small companies to inspire their own innovation processes. In 2015 corporate venture funds participated in about one out of three deals in Asia and in one out of five deals in the United States or Europe. Impact entrepreneurs in the life sciences space, which includes biotechnology and medical device companies, represent almost 15 percent of all venture dollars deployed and almost 25 percent of all deals in life sciences investing. The caveats: Corporate venture funding, with different motives from VC peers (and different criteria and measures for assessing and structuring deals), can contribute to historic ("frothy") overvaluations, distorting the market.

Digital/token/cryptocurrency capital: Rather than accepting money in exchange for equity stakes, some advanced start-ups issue their own digital currencies, or tokens, that anyone can buy in a crowd sale. Proceeds from the auction of these virtual shares help fund the business. Over the next decade, cryptocurrencies will expand to other asset classes such as stocks and real estate, pointing to a future in which ownership of everything is recorded on the blockchain and previously illiquid assets, like art and start-up equity, can become as liquid as cash, particularly as infrastructure for trading and storing tokens expands. Some companies are now distributing U.S. Securities and Exchange Commission-compliant cryptocurrencies that represent stakes in businesses or residential developments.

Direct equity or venture capital: These investments can be derived from a mainstream venture capital (VC) fund whose sole aim is return on financial investment, or a niche impact fund (the venture capital strategy for funding for-profit businesses with a social or environmental mission). According to Crunchbase, the number of companies starting out receiving venture capital is very small—whether in Australia, the United States, Europe, or the Middle East.

Endowment capital: An endowment is a donation in which the principal amount is invested so that a social enterprise can benefit from the income on a long-term basis (in perpetuity if sustainably managed), and for some, can help the very activities that no one else is willing to fund. For example, many universities rely on endowments to fund needs-based scholarships or academic research. Harvard University has an endowment of more than $35 billion, the largest in the United States. Some of the world's richest billionaires provide endowments, including duty-free shopping empire founder Charles Feeney, who has funded more than one thousand buildings worth almost $3 billion across five continents, on top of the $8 billion donated to multiple social enterprises; and Sulaiman bin Abdul Aziz Al Rajhi (cofounder of Al Rajhi Bank), who transferred much of his wealth to an endowment holding company, supporting educational, religious, health, and social causes, including the Arab Institute for Arabic Language and National Guard Health Affairs.

Friends and family: The majority of initial start-up funds come from family and friends and others in an entrepreneur's extended network.

Grants capital: Many agencies, such as the United States' National Institute of Mental Health, provide research funding to test psychosocial innovations and apps that might contribute to evaluations of products and services. Universities also have potential funding for research projects that may benefit students, particularly those in PhD programs looking for interesting, practical projects.

Growth capital: A one-time infusion of money. Donors and investors prefer this option where funds are used to develop infrastructure and/or operations that can generate increased impact after the growth capital is spent.

Intermediary capital: Financial intermediaries such as Social Venture Partners or NESsT that aggregate and strategically deploy resources are advantageous for many deploying funds, due to their economies of scale, pooled expertise, learning, efficiency, and teamwork.

Network or alliance capital: Industry associations, sector collaboratives, networks, and so on can all be instrumental in contributing to capital to impact entrepreneurial ventures. Examples include the European Venture Philanthropy Association and Social Venture Partners International—both of which connect entrepreneurs to various forms of capital—financial, intellectual, and social. Member networks like Social Venture Partners that mobilize multiple capitals are often first movers in their field. For example, the global vaccine alliance Gavi received initial funding from the Bill & Melinda Gates Foundation and the Global International Impact Investing Network.

Physical (assets) capital: Over the years, even from our grants budget, our Tingari-Silverton Foundation has provided funding for infrastructure, buildings, or long-term assets. For example, projects include playgrounds at community centers in the Australian outback and the Palestinian Territories, an outreach hospital in Ethiopia for fistula patients, a community village for patients whose fistula injuries prevent them from returning home, a food truck for Austin's Mobile Loaves and Fishes, and a laundry truck for Australia's Orange Sky mobile services for the homeless.

Shadow capital: Some VC firms invite existing Limited Partners (LP) in their funds to co-invest alongside the pooled fund investment for later rounds of financing in an existing portfolio company. These shadow investments are made under the same terms, but are not part of the general pooled VC fund. Shadow investors are adjunct investors. For VC firms with an eye toward social and environmental impact, shadow investors are fast becoming a growing opportunity. With an abundance of LP capital available, the rise of such shadow capital over traditional fundraising may expand as other investors look to bring the pace of deploying capital in private equity under their own control.

"Sweat" capital: Sweat equity is the nonmonetary investment in hours of hard work—physical and intellectual—that owners or employees contribute to a business venture. In the 2020s bartering economy, sweat investment can be expanded beyond owners and employees.

Traditional philanthropic capital: Grants from foundations, government agencies, and corporate philanthropic funds (conditional or unconditional) are applied to specific organizational initiatives or to fund ongoing operations.

Notes

INTRODUCTION

1. "Reward Work, Not Wealth," Oxfam International, January 2018, https://www-cdn.oxfam.org/s3fs-public/file_attachments/bp-reward-work-not-wealth-220118-en.pdf.

2. Author's note: We expand on this definition in a 2019 journal article, "Innovation and Entrepreneurial Ecosystems for Impact: Toward Definitional Clarity."

3. Author's note: Quotes are from personal communication and interviews unless otherwise specified.

4. "World Population Ageing 2007," United Nations Department of Economic and Social Affairs (2007), https://www.un.org/en/development/desa/population/publications/pdf/ageing/WorldPopulationAgeingReport2007.pdf.

5. Larry Elliott and Ed Pilkington, "New Oxfam Report Says Half of Global Wealth Held by the 1%," *The Guardian* (January 19, 2015), http://www.theguardian.com/business/2015/jan/19/global-wealth-oxfam-inequality-davos-economic-summit-switzerland.

6. Richard Wilkinson and Kate Pickett, "The Spirit Level Authors: Why Social Is More Unequal Than Ever," *The Guardian* (March 9, 2014), https://www.theguardian.com/commentisfree/2014/mar/09/society-unequal-the-spirit-level.

PART ONE

CHAPTER 1

1. "Our Impact," Grameen America, http://www.grameenamerica.org/impact.

2. Author's Note: Our discussion of verbs and nouns in the impact context is informed by Karl Weick's insightful analyses in *The Social Psychology of Organizing*. 1979 (p. 44) and *Sensemaking in Organizations*. 1995 (p. 188).

3. P. M. Ryan, T. E. Skiadas, and D. C. Seyle, "The Psychology of Microfinance: The

Evidence," paper presented at the Global Microcredit Summit, Valladolid, Spain, 2011.

4. "Measuring and Managing Impact—A Practical Guide," EVPA, January 7, 2019, http://evpa.eu.com/knowledge-centre/publications/measuring-and-managing-impact-a-practical-guide; and "TRASI: Tools and Resources for Assessing Social Impact," Foundation Center, http://foundationcenter.org/gain-knowledge/foundation-ideas/trasi.

5. Kai Schultz, "In Bhutan, Happiness Index as Gauge for Social Ills," *The New York Times,* January 17, 2017, https://www.nytimes.com/2017/01/17/world/asia/bhutan-gross-national-happiness-indicator-.html.

6. Kate Cooney and Kristen Lynch-Cerullo, "Measuring the Social Returns of Nonprofits and Social Enterprises: The Promise and Perils of the SROI," *Nonprofit Policy Forum* 5, no. 2 (2014): 367–93, doi:10.1515/npf-2014-0017.

7. Ivy So and Alina S. Capanyola, "How Impact Investors Actually Measure Impact," *Stanford Social Innovation Review,* May 16, 2016, https://ssir.org/articles/entry/how_impact_investors_actually_measure_impact#.

8. Throughout the book, when we are discussing alternative futures, different possible 2030s, we use grammar and tense in the narrative as if we were in 2030. This use of language and tense is intended to anchor readers in the future. In 2030.

CHAPTER 2

1. Ivan Illich, "To Hell With Good Intentions," address at the Conference on InterAmerican Student Projects, Cuernavaca, Mexico, April 20, 1968.

2. Excerpts from *Known and Strange Things: Essays* by Teju Cole. Copyright © 2016 by Teju Cole. Used by permission of Random House, an imprint and division of Penguin Random House LLC; The Wylie Agency; and Faber & Faber Ltd. All rights reserved.

3. Teju Cole, "The White Savior Industrial Complex," *The Atlantic,* March 21, 2012, https://www.theatlantic.com/international/archive/2012/03/the-white-savior-industrial-complex/254843/.

4. Ibid.

5. "Inside the White Saviour Industrial Complex," *New African,* January 6, 2015, https://newafricanmagazine.com/opinions/inside-white-saviour-industrial-complex/.

6. Courtney Martin, "The Reductive Seduction of Other People's Problems," January 11, 2016, https://brightthemag.com/the-reductive-seduction-of-other-people-s-problems-3c07b307732d.

7. Jacob Kushner, "The Voluntourist's Dilemma," *The New York Times Magazine,* March 22, 2016, https://www.nytimes.com/2016/03/22/magazine/the-voluntourists-dilemma.html?_r=0.

8. "Secret Aid Worker: 'It's Time to Talk about the Dark Side of Development Comms,'" *The Guardian*, June 14, 2016, https://www.theguardian.com/global-development-professionals-network/2016/jun/14/secret-aid-worker-development-communications-officer-outreach-projects.

9. Firoze Manji and Carl O'Coill, "The Missionary Position: NGOs and Development in Africa," *International Affairs* 78, no. 3 (2002): 567–84, https://doi.org/10.1111/1468-2346.00267.

10. Barbie Savior, 2016, http://www.barbiesavior.com/.

11. Ibid.

12. "Insight Report: Impact Investments 2015—Global Opportunities," *PR Newswire*, November 10, 2015, https://www.prnewswire.com/news-releases/insight-report-impact-investments-2015--global-opportunities-300176537.html.

13. Ryan et al., "The Psychology of Microfinance: The Evidence."

14. PlayPumps, http://www.playpumps.co.za.ney

15. "Smart Focus," REAP, http://reap.fsi.stanford.edu/docs/learning-focus.

16. Jennifer Pryce and Katherine St. Onge, "4.1 Catalysing the Market of Socially-Conscious Retail Investors," *World Economic Forum*, http://reports.weforum.org/impact-investing-from-ideas-to-practice-pilots-to-strategy-ii/4-democratizing-impact-investing-for-retail-investors/4-1-catalysing-the-market-of-socially-conscious-retail-investors/?doing_wp_cron=1562091063.01969909 66796875000000.

17. Mary B. Anderson, *Do No Harm: How Aid Can Support Peace—or War* (Boulder, CO: Lynne Rienner, 1999); Michael Wessells, "Do No Harm: Challenges in Organizing Psychosocial Support to Displaced People in Emergency Settings," *Refuge* 25, no. 1 (2008): 6–14; Carlos Martín Beristain, *Humanitarian Aid Work: A Critical Approach* (Philadelphia: University of Pennsylvania Press, 2006); and P. M. Ryan, R. C. Silver, J. Fairbank, and P. Watson, "Addressing the Values and Challenges of Working in War-Torn, Violent, and Disaster Affected Regions," symposium presentation at the annual meeting of the International Society for Traumatic Stress Studies, Los Angeles, CA, 2012.

18. Ethan Watters, *Crazy Like Us: The Globalization of the American Psyche* (New York: Free Press, 2011).

19. Michael Wessells, "Do No Harm: Challenges in Organizing Psychosocial Support to Displaced People in Emergency Settings," *Refuge* 25, no. 1 (2008): 6–14.

20. Rolf Straubhaar, "The Stark Reality of the 'White Saviour' Complex and the Need for Critical Consciousness: A Document Analysis of the Early Journals of a Freirean Educator," *Compare: A Journal of Comparative and International Education* 45, no. 3 (2014): 381–400, doi:10.1080/03057925.2013.876306.

21. Shawn Humphrey, "The 10 Promises of a Social Good Sidekick," *Shawn Humphrey* (blog), April 5, 2016, https://shawnhumphrey.com/dos-and-donts-for-do-gooders/10-promises-social-good-sidekick/.

22. Ryan et al., "Addressing the Values and Challenges of Working in War-Torn, Violent, and Disaster Affected Regions."

CHAPTER 3

1. Ryan et al., "Addressing the Values and Challenges of Working in War-Torn, Violent, and Disaster Affected Regions."

2. Shawn Humphrey, "Do-Gooder Duel," *Shawn Humphrey* (blog), May 22, 2014, https://shawnhumphrey.com/dos-and-donts-for-do-gooders/do-gooder-duel/.

3. Psychology Beyond Borders, "Managing the Psychology of Fear and Terror: Strategies for Governments, Service Providers, Communities and Individuals," compilation of presentations given at the International Assembly on Managing the Psychology of Fear and Terror, Austin, TX, August 2004.

4. Anthony J. Marsella, Jeannette L. Johnson, Patricia Watson, and Jan Gryczynski, "Essential Concepts and Foundations," *Ethnocultural Perspectives on Disaster and Trauma International and Cultural Psychology Series* (2008): 3–13, doi:10.1007/978-0-387-73285-5_1; and F. H. Norris and Margarita Alegría, "Promoting Disaster Recovery in Ethnic-Minority Individuals and Communities," *Interventions Following Mass Violence and Disasters: Strategies for Mental Health Practice* (2007): 319–42, https://psycnet.apa.org/record/2006-02067-017.

5. Michael Wessells, "Do No Harm: Challenges in Organizing Psychosocial Support to Displaced People in Emergency Settings," *Refuge* 25, no. 1 (2008): 6–14.

6. InterAgency Standing Committee (IASC), *Guidelines on Mental Health and Psychosocial Support in Emergency Settings* (2007).

7. "How Portable Light Began," *Portable Light*, http://portablelight.org/history.

8. *Portable Light*, http://portablelight.org.

9. Rose Etherington, "Spaza-De-Move-On by Doung Anwar Jahangeer," *De Zeen*, March 6, 2009, https://www.dezeen.com/2009/03/06/spaza-de-move-on-by-doung-anwar-jahangeer/.

10. A flagship program of the International Development Research Centre's Urban Poverty and Environment.

11. "Indonesia," UN Global Compact, https://www.unglobalcompact.org/engage-locally/asia/indonesia.

12. "Shelter Associates: Inclusive Planning for the Urban Poor" (Maharashtra: Shelter Associates, 2014), video, https://youtu.be/csAQimd1Ndg.

13. Ezio Manzini, *The Material of Invention* (Cambridge, MA: MIT Press, 1986); Ezio Manzini, *Artifacts: Towards a New Ecology of the Artificial Environment* (Milan: Domus Academy, 1990); and Ezio Manzini and François Jégou, *Sustainable Everyday: Scenarios of Urban Life* (Milan: Edizioni Ambiente, 2003).

14. Muhammad Yunus and Alan Jolis, *Banker to the Poor: Micro-Lending and the Battle Against World Poverty* (New York: Public Affairs, 2003).

PART TWO

INTRODUCTION

1. Author's note: Definitions like this one are sprinkled throughout the book. Adopting creative license, these definitions are mostly hybrids devised by combining definitions from: *The Merriam-Webster Dictionary*, online edition; and *The Oxford English Dictionary*, online edition.

CHAPTER 4

1. David M. Ewalt, "The Modest Tycoon Behind America's Biggest Woman-Owned Business," *Forbes*, May 27, 2015, https://www.forbes.com/sites/davidewalt/2015/05/27/thai-lee-shi-international/#5ae519a74dda.

2. Duncan Green, "Why Social Entrepreneurship Has Become a Distraction: It's Mainstream Capitalism That Needs to Change," *From Poverty to Power* (blog), August 4, 2015, http://oxfamblogs.org/fp2p/why-social-entrepreneurship-has-become-a-distraction-its-mainstream-capitalism-that-needs-to-change/.

3. Michele Glaze, "Announcing the Winner of the 2012 Dell Social Innovation Challenge," *Direct2Dell* (blog), June 14, 2012, https://blog.dell.com/en-us/announcing-the-winner-of-the-2012-dell-social-innovation-challenge/.

4. "Solar Conduction Dryer Wins Grand Prize in 2013 Dell Social Innovation Challenge," Sustainable Brands, May 15, 2013, https://sustainablebrands.com/read/press-release/solar-conduction-dryer-wins-grand-prize-in-2013-dell-social-innovation-challenge.

5. Julie Tereshchuk, "Suzi Sosa: Changing the World, Forging the Next Generation of Entrepreneurship," *Austin Woman* (Austin, TX), February 27, 2012, https://issuu.com/austinwoman/docs/03_mar.

6. Anisha Sekar, "The Top 5 Austin Startups to Watch in 2016," *DataFox* (blog), 2016, https://blog.datafox.com/fastest-growing-companies-austin/; and Colin Morris, "50 Austin Startups to Watch in 2016," Built in Austin, January 31, 2016, https://www.builtinaustin.com/2016/01/25/50-austin-startups-watch-2016.

7. "World Water Crisis," George Barley Water Prize, https://www.barleyprize.org/.

8. Fred Dews, "11 Facts about the Millennial Generation," *Brookings* (blog), June 2, 2014, https://www.brookings.edu/blog/brookings-now/2014/06/02/11-facts-about-the-millennial-generation/.

9. "Solar Conduction Dryer Wins Grand Prize in 2013 Dell Social Innovation Challenge."

10. "Entrepreneurial Behavior and Attitudes: India," GEM Global Entrepreneurship Monitor, 2018, https://www.gemconsortium.org/country-profile/69; and "The GEM 2014 Global Report," Global Entrepreneurship Monitor, 2015, https://www.gemconsortium.org/report/49079.

11. "Global Startup Ecosystem Report 2015," Startup Genome, 2015, https://startupgenome.com/all-reports.

12. Shalina Pillai, "Global Startup Accelerators Hit the Gas in India," *The Economic Times* (Mumbai, India), March 27, 2016, http://economictimes.indiatimes.com/small-biz/startups/global-startup-accelerators-hit-the-gas-in-india/articleshow/51569331.cms.

13. Anjli Jain, "The Rise of India's Entrepreneurs: How to Cultivate Their Spirit and Success," *YourStory,* December 22, 2015, https://yourstory.com/2015/12/rise-of-india-entrepreneurs/.

14. World Bank Group, "India's Poverty Profile," May 27, 2016, https://www.worldbank.org/en/news/infographic/2016/05/27/india-s-poverty-profile.

15. Vaibhav Tidke and Supriya Thanawala, "Young Dreams: Bringing Technology to the Masses," *Rediff,* February 21, 2011, https://www.rediff.com/getahead/slide-show/slide-show-1-career-young-dreams-bringing-technology-to-the-masses/20110221.htm.

16. Ibid.

17. Vaibhav Tidke, "Science for Society Techno Services Pvt. Ltd.: Solar Food Processing to Improve Economic Situation of Farmers & Food Security," *Changemakers,* 2011, https://www.changemakers.com/discussions/entries/science-society-techno-services-pvt-ltd.

18. Ibid.; and Vaibhav Tidke, "India Has Highest Number of Suicides in the World: WHO," *Times of India,* September 4, 2014, http://timesofindia.indiatimes.com/india/India-has-highest-number-of-suicides-in-the-world-WHO/articleshow/41708567.cms.

19. Megha Mehta, "Young entrepreneurs attempt to solve India's agricultural problems," February 5, 2016, https://www.pagalguy.com/articles/young-entrepreneur-attempt-to-solve-indias-agricultural-problems-4600.

20. Elga Reyes, "Indian Solar Invention Drastically Reduces Food Waste," Eco-Business, August 30, 2013, https://www.eco-business.com/news/indian-solar-dryer-investion-drastically-reduces-food-waste/.

21. Rajeshwari Swaminathan, "The Dry Runners," *New Indian Express,* October 8, 2015, http://www.newindianexpress.com/education/edex/2015/oct/08/The-Dry-Runners-826600.html.

22. "Ashoka Changemakers," Ashoka, https://www.ashoka.org/en/program/changemakers.

23. B. Ekbal, "Reducing Infant Mortality Rate: Kerala Has Its Task Cut Out," *The Times of India,* February 1, 2017, http://timesofindia.indiatimes.com/city/kochi/reducing-infant-mortality-rate-kerala-has-its-task-cut-out/articleshow/56903044.cms.

24. Elosha Eiland, Chike Nzerue, and Marquetta Faulkner, "Preeclampsia 2012," *Journal of Pregnancy* (2012): 1–7, doi:10.1155/2012/586578.

25. "UIDAI," Unique Identification Authority of India, https://uidai.gov.in/about-uidai.html.

26. "Students on a Mission to Save India's Mothers," Yahoo India, September 17, 2013, https://web.archive.org/web/20131004064916/http://in.specials.yahoo.com/news/students-to-the-rescue-of-india-s-mother-075730699.html.

27. Ekbal, "Reducing Infant Mortality Rate."

28. Tidke and Thanawala, "Young Dreams."

29. "About Us," Beyond Type 1, https://beyondtype1.org/.

30. Sheena Lyonnais, "What Jerry the Bear Can Teach Us About Designing UX for Children," *Adobe Creative Cloud* (blog), June 9, 2016, https://blogs.adobe.com/creativecloud/what-jerry-the-bear-can-teach-us-about-designing-ux-for-children/.

CHAPTER 5

1. "By the People: Designing a Better America," Smithsonian Institution, September 30, 2016, https://www.si.edu/Exhibitions/Details/By-the-People-Designing-a-Better-America-6095.

2. "Glass House Collective," Glass House Collective, http://www.glasshousecollective.org/.

3. "LifeStraw," Design Other 90 Network, January 5, 2012, https://www.designother90.org/solution/lifestraw/; and "Design Other 90 Network," Design Other 90 Network, http://www.designother90.org.

4. Entrepreneur Staff, "6 Innovative Women to Watch in 2015," *Entrepreneur*, January 17, 2015, accessed September 26, 2016, https://www.entrepreneur.com/slideshow/240845.

5. Designmatters.edu, accessed August 8, 2016.

6. Mariana Amatullo, Liliana Becerra, and Steven Montgomery, *Designmatters Case Studies: Design Education Methodologies as a Tool for Social Innovation* (March 2011); Fostering Effective Models for Social Entrepreneurship in Design Education: Lessons Learned from the Safe Agua Case Study.

7. Mariana Amatullo, "From the Garage to the Front Lines of Social Innovation," *Huffington Post*, June 11, 2014, http://www.huffingtonpost.com/mariana-amatullo/from-the-garage-to-the-fr_b_5484460.html.

8. http://projectthinktank.info/2016/03/20/mariana-amatullo-of-designmatters/, accessed August 8, 2016.

9. Ibid.

10. Sarah Miller Llana, "Chile Earthquake Relief: How One Priest Provides Shelter for Masses," *The Christian Science Monitor*, March 3, 2010, http://www.csmonitor.com/World/Americas/2010/0303/Chile-earthquake-relief-How-one-priest-provides-shelter-for-masses; and *El Mercurio,* http://iglesiadescalza.blogspot.com/2010/06/controversial-departure-of-fr-felipe.html, accessed June 2, 2017.

11. Julian Ugarte, "SIX Interview Series: Julian Ugarte, Founder of Socialab," Social Innovation Exchange, April 25, 2013, https://socialinnovationexchange.org/insights/six-interview-series-julian-ugarte-founder-socialab.

12. "Julian Ugarte," Ashoka, 2014, https://www.ashoka.org/en/fellow/julian-ugarte#intro.

13. Efizity, http://www.efizity.com.

14. http://innovacionymercado.cl/entrevistas/innovador-disruptivo-julian-ugarte-director-ejecutivo-de-socialab&prev=search, accessed January 24, 2018.

15. Socialab, http://www.socialab.com/.

16. "Safe Agua Water System," Design Other 90 Network, October 11, 2011, http://www.designother90.org/solution/safe-agua-water-system/.

17. Laura Parker, "What You Need to Know About the World's Water Wars," July 14, 2016, https://news.nationalgeographic.com/2016/07/world-aquifers-water-wars/.

18. "Centro de Innovación de Un Techo para Chile junto a Art Center College of Design lanza libro de proyecto Safe Agua," Universia Chile, December 10, 2010, http://noticias.universia.cl/vida-universitaria/noticia/2010/12/10/763812/centro-innovacion-techo-chile-junto-art-center-college-of-design-lanza-libro-proyecto-safe-agua.html&prev=search, accessed June 2, 2017.

19. Ernest Beck, "Safe Agua," *Design Observer*, October 11, 2010, http://designobserver.com/feature/safe-agua/19018/.

20. http://innovacionymercado.cl/entrevistas/innovador-disruptivo-julian-ugarte-director-ejecutivo-de-socialab&prev=search, accessed January 24, 2018.

21. UNICEF Innovation, "9 Innovators to Watch: Julian Ugarte," *UNICEF Connect* (blog), June 30, 2014, https://blogs.unicef.org/innovation/9-innovators-to-watch-julian-ugarte/.

22. Katherine Phillips, "How Diversity Makes Us Smarter: Being around People Who Are Different from Us Makes Us More Creative, More Diligent and Harder-Working," *Scientific American*, October 1, 2014, https://www.scientificamerican.com/article/how-diversity-makes-us-smarter/.

CHAPTER 6

1. "Who Is an Educator?," *American Association of Industrial Nurses Journal* 10, no. 9 (1962): 10, https://journals.sagepub.com/doi/pdf/10.1177/216507996201000902.

2. Patrick Pittman, "Pamela Hartigan Is an Unreasonable Person," *Dumbo Feather,*

April 1, 2012, https://www.dumbofeather.com/conversations/pamela-hartigan-is-an-unreasonable-person/.

3. Ibid.

4. "Volans—The Business of Business Is Change," Volans, http://volans.com/#contact.

5. Pittman, "Pamela Hartigan Is an Unreasonable Person."

6. "Could You Be A Social Entrepreneur?," *HuffPost,* June 4, 2015, http://www.huffingtonpost.co.uk/2015/06/04/could-you-be-a-social-entrepreneur_n_7241662.html.

7. Pittman, "Pamela Hartigan Is an Unreasonable Person."

8. Pamela Hartigan, "Why Social Entrepreneurship Has Become a Distraction: It's Mainstream Capitalism That Needs to Change," *From Poverty to Power* (blog), August 5, 2014, http://oxfamblogs.org/fp2p/why-social-entrepreneurship-has-become-a-distraction-its-mainstream-capitalism-that-needs-to-change/.

9. changemakers.org.uk, accessed September 23, 2014.

10. http://civa.org.uk/who-we-are/.

11. YouthBank UK, www.youthbank.org.uk.

12. UnLtd., https://unltd.org.uk/?s=going+mainstream.

13. https://www.unltd.org.uk/about-us/our-strategy/.

14. http://www.kcl.ac.uk/newsevents/news/newsrecords/2014/January/Kings-partners-with-UnLtd-to-launch-social-entrepreneurship-awards.aspx, accessed September 23, 2019.

15. "About Young UnLtd," Young UnLtd, http://youngunltd.org.uk/about-young-unltd/.

16. Charles Keidan, "Interview: Cliff Prior of Big Society Capital," *Alliance Magazine,* April 5, 2016, https://www.alliancemagazine.org/interview/271358/.

17. "Member Highlight: UnLtd USA," *Impact Hub Austin* (blog), April 25, 2016, https://impacthubaustin.com/blogposts/member-highlight-unltd-usa/.

18. Ibid.

19. "Member Highlight: UnLtd USA," *Impact Hub Austin* (blog), April 25, 2016, https://impacthubaustin.com/blogposts/member-highlight-unltd-usa/.

20. Ibid.

21. Ibid.

22. Macdoch Ventures, "The Start-up Guide," *The Australian Business Review,* http://www.theaustralian.com.au/business/the-deal-magazine/the-deal-startup-guide.

23. Bethnal Green Ventures, https://bethnalgreenventures.com.

24. Impact Hub, http://www.impacthub.net.

25. "The Space," Centre for Social Innovation, http://nyc.socialinnovation.org/the-space.

26. Convene Conference Centers, "Convene Interviews with Centre for Social Innovation (CSI) in New York," September 18, 2014, YouTube, https://www.youtube.com/watch?v=u_5Y2S5eFJs.

27. Adam Stiles, "Social Innovation Builds Its Dream Home In New York City," *Fast Company*, May 2, 2013, https://www.fastcompany.com/2681964/social-innovation-builds-its-dream-home-in-new-york-city?cid=search.

28. Anne Field, "Social Entrepreneurs Grow a Computer Garden at Zahn Innovation Center," *Forbes*, May 30, 2017, https://www.forbes.com/sites/annefield/2017/05/30/social-entrepreneurs-grow-a-computer-garden-at-zahn-innovation-center/#303ba866dd51.

29. Adam Stiles, "Social Innovation Builds Its Dream Home In New York City."

30. "Culture," Centre for Social Innovation, https://socialinnovation.org/culture/.

CHAPTER 7

1. Big Society Capital, "Prime Minister Launches Big Society Capital," April 4, 2012, https://www.bigsocietycapital.com/latest/type/news/prime-minister-launches-big-society-capital

2. Sophie Hudson, "UK's Social Bank Turns Two: Has It Met Expectations?," *Pioneers Post*, April 30, 2014, https://www.pioneerspost.com/news-views/20140430/uks-social-bank-turns-two-has-it-met-expectations.

3. "Big Society Capital Launch," Big Society Capital, July 29, 2011, https://www.bigsocietycapital.com/latest/type/news/big-society-capital-launch.

4. ClearlySo, https://www.clearlyso.com.

5. Leslie Huckfield, "Why We've Got It Wrong on Social Investment—Former MP," *Pioneers Post*, March 6, 2015, https://www.pioneerspost.com/news-views/20150306/why-weve-got-it-wrong-on-social-investment-former-mp.

6. Adrian Brown, "How Governments Are Harnessing the Power of Social Investment." *BCG Perspectives*, The Boston Publishing Group, https://www.bcg.com/documents/file97792.pdf

7. Robin Schatz, "Social Change Through Spit and Thumb Socks: Aria Finger, AB '05," *Washington* magazine, Washington University, October 2013, https://magazine.wustl.edu/2013/october/Pages/Aria-Finger-DoSomething.aspx.

8. Ibid.

9. Heather Wood Rudulph, "Get That Life: How I Became the CEO of DoSomething.org," *Cosmopolitan*, December 21, 2015, http://www.cosmopolitan.com/career/news/a50550/get-that-life-aria-finger-do-something-dot-org-ceo/.

10. Ibid.

11. Aria Finger, "College Students Want to Keep Guns Off Their Campus. Today We're Giving Them a Way to Make That Happen," *DoSomething.org* (blog), March 7, 2016, https://blog.dosomething.org/college-students-want-to-keep-guns-off-their-campus-816bf7f090e0.

12. "Taylor Swift, Miley Cyrus, and Beyoncé Top DoSomething.org's 2015 Celebs Gone Good List," Look to the Stars, January 8, 2016, https://www.looktothestars.org/news/14710-taylor-swift-miley-cyrus-and-beyonce-top-dosomething-orgs-2015-celebs-gone-good-list.

13. "An Interview with Andrew Shue, Actor/Entrepreneur," *Teen Ink,* https://www.teenink.com/nonfiction/interviews/article/5443/An-Interview-with-Andrew-Shue-Actor-Entrepreneur/.

14. "Getting Teens Involved for Good: Interview with Aria Finger of DoSomething.org," *After School* (blog), February 10, 2016, https://medium.com/@afterschoolapp/getting-teens-involved-for-good-interview-with-aria-finger-of-dosomething-org-44845c1e4b60#.91jc9yy16.

15. "Our Team: Here's the DoSomething.org Staff!," DoSomething.org, https://www.dosomething.org/us/about/our-team, accessed February 20, 2017.

16. "Getting Teens Involved for Good."

17. "The World Bank in South Africa," The World Bank, http://www.worldbank.org/en/country/southafrica/overview.

18. Nicolaas Kruger, "South Africa Has a Skills Shortage. How Do We Fix It?," *World Economic Forum*, May 10, 2016, https://www.weforum.org/agenda/2016/05/south-africa-skills-shortage-how-do-we-fix-it/.

19. Rorisang Lekalake, "Post-1994 South Africa: Better Than Apartheid, but Few Gains in Socioeconomic Conditions," *Afrobarometer* (2016), http://afrobarometer.org/sites/default/files/publications/Dispatches/ab_r6_dispatchno82_south_africa_changes_since_1994.pdf.

20. Reos Partners, https://reospartners.com.

21. "Southern Africa Food Lab," Reos Partners, https://reospartners.com/projects/southern-africa-food-lab-safl/.

22. Convened by the Global Leadership Academy (commissioned by the German Federal Ministry for Economic Cooperation and Development) and the Blue Solutions Initiative (commissioned by the German Federal Ministry for the Environment, Nature Conservation, Building and Nuclear Safety).

23. Colleen Magner, "The Invisible Middles," Reos Partners, April 26, 2015, https://reospartners.com/the-invisible-middles/.

CHAPTER EIGHT

1. "Women in Focus," Commonwealth Bank of Australia, https://www.womeninfocus. com.au/t5/Community-Stories/Using-Business-to-Change-the-World-Berry-Liberman/ba-p/1430.

2. Larissa Ham, "Big Ideas to Change the World One Step at a Time," *The Age*, September 24, 2012, http://www.theage.com.au/small-business/entrepreneur/ big-ideas-to-change-the-world-one-step-at-a-time-20120923-26f0z. html#ixzz3QYw3nPfZ.

3. Lucy Feagins, "Interview: Berry Liberman of *Dumbo Feather* & Small Giants," July 19, 2013, *The Design Files*, https://thedesignfiles.net/2013/07/ interview-berry-liberman.

4. Mikki Brammer, "Berry Liberman, Small Giants" profile, *map magazine*, http:// theweekendedition.com.au/mapmagazine/berry-liberman.

5. http://www.generositymag.com.au/danny-almagor-money-is-just-a-form-of-energy-it-can-be-saved-spent-or-harnessed, accessed February 2, 2015.

6. Ibid.

7. "Women in Focus."

8. Mikki Brammer, "Berry Liberman, Small Giants."

9. Lucy Feagins, "Interview: Berry Liberman of *Dumbo Feather* & Small Giants."

10. "STAR Community Rating System: Version 1.1," STAR Communities, January 2014, http://www.starcommunities.org/uploads/rating-system.pdf.

11. "About," Impact Investment Group, http://www.impact-group.com.au/about.

12. http://www.generositymag.com.au/danny-almagor-to-impact-investment-naysayers-call-me-i-see-plenty-of-places-to-make-money-and-impact/, accessed November 27, 2017.

13. "About B Corps," Certified B Corporation, https://www.bcorporation.net/ what-are-b-corps.

14. "Home," Certified B Corporation, https://www.bcorporation.net.

15. Lucy Feagins, "Interview: Berry Liberman of *Dumbo Feather* & Small Giants."

16. Ibid.

17. http://www.generositymag.com.au/danny-almagor-money-is-just-a-form-of-energy-it-can-be-saved-spent-or-harnessed, accessed February 2, 2015.

18. Mikki Brammer, "Berry Liberman, Small Giants."

19. Ibid.

20. Karl Weick, "Careers as Eccentric Predicates," *Cornell Executive* 2 (1976): 6–10.

21. Claerwen O'Hara, "Children's Ground: A Model that Could End Intergenerational Poverty in Australia," Castan Centre for Human Rights Law, April 16, 2013,

https://castancentre.com/2013/04/16/childrens-ground-a-model-that-could-end-intergenerational-poverty-in-australia/.

22. James Eyers, "Unclaimed Deposits to be Directed at Social Impact Investing," *The Sydney Morning Herald*, October 28, 2014, http://www.smh.com.au/business/unclaimed-deposits-to-be-directed-at-social-impact-investing-20141028-11czn3.html.

23. Rosemary Addis, "Harnessing Private Capital for Public Good," *Acuity*, January 25, 2017, https://www.acuitymag.com/opinion/harnessing-private-capital-for-public-good.

24. Christian Seelos and Johanna Mair, "Social Entrepreneurship: Creating New Business Models to Serve the Poor," *Business Horizons* 48, no. 3 (2005): 241–46.

25. Johanna Mair and Ignasi Marti, "Social Entrepreneurship Research: A Source of Explanation, Prediction, and Delight," *Journal of World Business* 41, no. 1 (2006): 36–44.

26. Johanna Mair and Ignasi Marti, "Entrepreneurship in and Around Institutional Voids: A Case Study from Bangladesh," *Journal of Business Venturing* 24, no. 5 (2009): 419–35.

27. "Home," Thinkers50, http://thinkers50.com.

28. Mark Hand, "The Research Gap in Social Entrepreneurship," *Stanford Social Innovation Review*, May 24, 2016, http://ssir.org/articles/entry/the_research_gap_in_social_entrepreneurship.

CHAPTER NINE

1. "2016 Preqin Global Private Equity and Venture Capital Report," Preqin, 2016.

2. Anand Giridharadas, *Winners Take All: The Elite Charade of Changing the World* (New York: Penguin Random House, 2018).

3. Joe Manning, "Genetic Profiling: Third Wave Technologies Unravels Mysteries of DNA," *Milwaukee Journal Sentinel*, December 3, 2001, https://news.google.com/newspapers?nid=1683&dat=20011203&id=m7oaAAAAIBAJ&sjid=zj4EAAAAIBAJ&pg=6942,2639373&hl=en.

4. Ibid.

5. Leslie Herzog, "Remodeling: 'Sweat Equity' Could Be the Way to Enter the Housing Market," *Los Angeles Times*, October 13, 1990, http://articles.latimes.com/1990-10-13/home/hm-2064_1_housing-market.

6. Ibid.

7. Arielle Emmett, "Biotech Start-Ups," *The Scientist*, June 26, 2000, http://www.the-scientist.com/?articles.view/articleNo/12898/title/biotech-start-ups/.

8. Ibid

9. Jessi Hempel, "When Givers Get Together," *Bloomberg Businessweek*, March 6, 2005, https://www.bloomberg.com/news/articles/2005-03-06/when-givers-get-together.

10. Lance Fors, "Pledging longer, fewer and deeper bets," *Alliance* magazine, June 2012, https://www.alliancemagazine.org/feature/pledging-longer-fewer-and-deeper-bets.

11. "Transformative Philanthropy Not for 'Rockstars,'" Probono Australia, May 7, 2013, http://www.probonoaustralia.com.au/news/2013/05/transformative-philanthropy-not-%E2%80%98rockstars%E2%80%99#sthash.QU9cUKke.dpuf.

12. Josh Kosman, "Why Private Equity Firms like Bain Really are the Worst of Capitalism," *Rolling Stone*, May 23, 2012, http://www.rollingstone.com/politics/news/why-private-equity-firms-like-bain-really-are-the-worst-of-capitalism-20120523.

13. "Home," The Demeter Foundation, https://www.thedemeterfoundation.com.

14. Tony Walker, "A Rich Diaspora," *Australian Financial Review*, May 27, 2011, http://www.afr.com/it-pro/a-rich-diaspora-20110524-j49ic.

15. Damon Kitney, "Myer Family Restructures Its Investment Empire," *The Australian*, November 11, 2014.

16. Damon Kitney, "Myer Leads Nation on Family Wealth Front," *The Australian*, February 10, 2016.

17. Damon Kitney, "Myer Family Restructures Its Investment Empire."

18. Damon Kitney, "Myer, Baillieu Families Plan Merger of Family Office Operations," *The Australian*, June 9, 2017.

19. "About," Foundation for Rural and Regional Renewal, http://www.frrr.org.au/cb_pages/history.php.

20. Tony Walker, "A Rich Diaspora."

21. Ibid.

22. Anand Giridharadas, "Winners Take All."

CHAPTER TEN

1. Jonathon Moules, "Technology delivers options for entrepreneurs," *Financial Times*, February 8, 2016. https://www.ft.com/content/dbde59b4-4759-11e5-af2f-4d6e0e5eda22.

2. Ben Veghte, "2016 NVCA Yearbook Captures Busy Year for Venture Capital Activity," National Venture Capital Association, March 8, 2016, http://nvca.org/pressreleases/2016-nvca-yearbook-captures-busy-year-for-venture-capital-activity/.

3. Paul A. Gompers and Sophie Q. Wang, "And the Children Shall Lead: Gender Diversity and Performance in Venture Capital," Harvard Business School, 2017,

http://www.hbs.edu/faculty/Publication%20Files/17-103_5768ca0e-9b35-4145-ab02-4a081b71466e.pdf.

4. Kimberly Weisul, "Venture Capital Is Broken and These Women Are Trying to Fix It," *Inc.*, November 2016; and Diane Mulcahy, Bill Weeks, and Harold Bradley, *We Have Met the Enemy … and He Is Us: Lessons from Twenty Years of the Kauffman Foundation's Investments in Venture Capital Funds and the Triumph of Hope Over Experience*, SSRN, May 2012.

5. Ibid.

6. Om Malik, "Silicon Valley Has an Empathy Vacuum," *The New Yorker*, November 28, 2016, https://www.newyorker.com/business/currency/silicon-valley-has-an-empathy-vacuum.

7. "Financial Concerns of Women," BMO Wealth Institute, March 2015, https://www.bmo.com/privatebank/pdf/Q1-2015-Wealth-Institute-Report-Financial-Concerns-of-Women.pdf; and Juliette Fairley, "Women to Benefit from $22 Trillion in Wealth Transfer by 2020," *The Street*, November 17, 2014, https://www.thestreet.com/story/12956116/1/wealth-transfer-some-22-trillion-in-assets-to-shift-to-women-by-2020.html.

8. Aimée Sargent, "Karma Culture," *Ms Entrepreneur Magazine Annual Issue*, Australia, April 2008.

9. "Karma Culture," *Switzer Daily*, February 12, 2010, http://www.switzer.com.au/small-business/women-in-business/feature/karma-culture/.

10. Aimée Sargent, "Karma Culture."

11. *Ibid.*

12. Rose Powell, "The Venture Capital World from the Investor's Point of View: Tips and Insights," Smart Company, June 6, 2013, https://www.smartcompany.com.au/startupsmart/advice/startupsmart-funding/the-venture-capital-world-from-the-investors-point-of-view-tips-and-insights/.

13. Ibid.

14. "Home," Vaxxas, www.vaxxas.com; and Gary Strauss, "Dry, Needle-Free Vaccines Exist and Are Saving Lives," *National Geographic*, November 14, 2016, http://news.nationalgeographic.com/2016/11/mark-kendall-explorer-moments-micro-spikes-deliver-vaccines/.

15. OECD: Organisation for Economic Co-operation and Development and the World Economic Forum, http://www.oecd.org/about/membersandpartners/list-oecd-member-countries.htm.

16. Shaun Drummond, "Venture Capital Funds, Think Tanks Puzzle Over Start-Up Valley of Death," *The Sydney Morning Herald*, April 5, 2016, http://www.smh.com.au/business/banking-and-finance/venture-capital-funds-think-tanks-puzzle-over-startup-valley-of-death-20160405-gnyw09.html.

17. John Backus and Hemant Bhardwaj, "Unicorns vs. Dragons," *Tech Crunch*, December 12, 2015, https://techcrunch.com/2014/12/14/unicorns-vs-dragons/.

18. Business Insider Australia, "Forget Unicorns, 'Dragons' Are the Australian Startup Problem No One's Talking About," *Business Insider*, March 9, 2016, http://www.businessinsider.com/forget-unicorns-dragons-are-the-australian-startup-problem-no-ones-talking-about-2016-3.

19. Kevin Kelleher, "Here's the Major Downside of So Many $1-Billion 'Unicorn' Startups," *Time*, April 7, 2015, http://time.com/3773591/unicorn-startups-downside/.

20. Aimée Sargent, "Karma Culture."

21. Janet Maslin, "FILM REVIEW; A Warrior, She Takes on Huns and Stereotypes," *The New York Times*, June 19, 1998, http://www.nytimes.com/movie/review?res=9C00E3D91E3DF93AA25755C0A96E958260.

22. Sarah E. Ashlock, "The Funding Is Female," *Austin Woman*, May 1, 2017, http://atxwoman.com/the-funding-is-female/.

23. "Home," Global Women's Leadership Forum, https://www.globalwlf.com.

24. Laura Lorek, "True Wealth Ventures' Sara Brand and Kerry Rupp Seek to Change the Landscape of Venture Capital Investing," *Silicon Hills News*, July 28, 2017, http://www.siliconhillsnews.com/2017/07/28/true-wealth-ventures-sara-brand-kerry-rupp-seek-change-landscape-venture-capital-investing/#respond.

25. Sara Brand, *Wednesday's Woman: Sara Brand* (2017; Austin: KVUE ABC), video, http://www.kvue.com/features/wednesdays-woman-sara-brand/466726526.

26. Gené Teare and Ned Desmond, "The First Comprehensive Study on Women in Venture Capital and Their Impact on Female Founders," *Tech Crunch*, April 2016, https://techcrunch.com/2016/04/19/the-first-comprehensive-study-on-women-in-venture-capital/; and "Quick Take: Women in Science, Technology, Engineering, and Mathematics (STEM)," *Catalyst*, January 3, 2018, https://www.catalyst.org/research/women-in-science-technology-engineering-and-mathematics-stem/.

27. Mary Ann Azevedo, "If I Knew Then . . . Sara Brand," *Crain's Austin*, http://austin.crains.com/if-i-knew-then/sara-brand/true-wealth-ventures.

28. Ibid.

29. "The 2017 State of Women-Owned Businesses Report," American Express, 2017, http://about.americanexpress.com/news/docs/2017-State-of-Women-Owned-Businesses-Report.pdf; and "Women's Entrepreneurship," Dell, http://www.dell.com/learn/us/en/uscorp1/women-powering-business#campaignTabs-2.

30. Georges Desvaux, Sandrine Devillard, Alix de Zelicourt, Cecile Kossoff, Eric Labaye, and Sandra Sancier-Sultan, "Women Matter: Ten Years of Insights on Gender Diversity," McKinsey & Company, October 2017, https://www.mckinsey.com/global-themes/gender-equality/women-matter-ten-years-of-insights-on-gender-diversity.

31. Melissa Repko, "Women Behind Texas' True Wealth Ventures Discuss Closing Startup Gender Gap, Female Founder Advice," *Dallas News*, December 2016, https://www.dallasnews.com/business/entrepreneurs/2016/12/19/texas-venture-capital-firm-true-wealth-ventures-bets-big-women-led-startups.

32. Jackie VanderBrug, "Mainstreaming Gender Lens Investing," *Stanford Social Innovation Review*, June 12, 2012, https://ssir.org/articles/entry/mainstreaming_gender_lens_investing.

33. Ibid.

34. Sol Marketing Blog, "Kerry Rupp and Sara Brand from True Wealth Ventures are funding women-led companies for the greater good"; http://blog.solmarketing.com/2016/04/true-wealth-ventures-kerry-rupp-and-sara-brand-funding-women-led-companies-for-the-greater-good/, accessed October 10, 2017.

35. Shari Biediger, "Ventures and Inventors: Annual Startup Week Launches at Geekdom," *Rivard Report*, February 27, 2017, https://therivardreport.com/ventures-and-inventors-annual-startup-week-launches-at-geekdom; and Sarah Ashlock, "The Funding Is Female."

36. Lora Kolodny, "BrainCheck Raises $3 Million for App to Monitor Brain Health," *Tech Crunch*, October 2016, https://techcrunch.com/2016/10/27/braincheck-raises-3-million-for-app-to-monitor-brain-health/.

37. Lori Hawkins, "How Austin Groups Are Working to Bring Diverse Entrepreneurs into a Male-Dominated Tech Industry," *The Austin American-Statesman*, September 24, 2018, http://www.512tech.com/technology/how-austin-groups-are-working-bring-diverse-entrepreneurs-into-male-dominated-tech-industry/hDgYGUWTmNvsZgqjuWjQlK/.

38. Laura Lorek, "True Wealth Ventures' Sara Brand and Kerry Rupp Seek to Change the Landscape of Venture Capital Investing."

39. Mary Ann Azevedo, "If I Knew Then . . . Sara Brand."

40. "LiveSafe's CEO on Having a Job with Purpose," *Quarterlette*, January 27, 2015, http://www.quarterlette.com/propel/live-safes-ceo-on-having-a-job-with-purpose, accessed September 19, 2017.

41. Ibid.

42. "Power Women of DC Tech: Part III," *Bisnow*, August 22, 2014, https://www.bisnow.com/washington-dc/news/tech/Power-Women-of-DC-Tech-Part-III-38132?utm_source=CopyShare&utm_medium=Browser.

43. "LiveSafe's CEO on Having a Job with Purpose."

44. New CEO, $4M in Funding," *The Washington Post*, December 3, 2015, https://www.washingtonpost.com/news/on-small-business/wp/2015/12/03/livesafe-announces-new-ceo-4m-in-funding/?utm_term=.650f756570d0.

45. "Meet the Social Impact Firm That Wants to Change the World," *Free Enterprise*, March 24, 2016, https://www.freeenterprise.com/jenny-abramson/.

46. Barbour Ulrich, "Rethink Impact Invests in DC Companies, Commits to Progress," Federal News Network, April 17, 2017, https://federalnewsradio.com/whats-working-washington/2017/04/rethink-impact-invests-dc-companies-commits-progress/.

47. "Meet the Social Impact Firm That Wants to Change the World."

48. Jenny Abramson, Elliot K. Fishman, Karen M. Horton, and Sheila Sheth, "The Cost of Unconscious Bias and Pattern Recognition," *Journal of the American College of Radiology*, August 2017, https://www.jacr.org/article/S1546-1440(17)30112-6/fulltext.

49. Tanza Loudenback, "Wall Street Alum Sallie Krawchecks Just Raised $34 Million for Her Investing Platform—Here's What It's Like to Use It," *Business Insider*, September 18, 2017, http://www.businessinsider.com/how-to-use-sallie-krawchecks-ellevest-investing-platform-for-women-2017-1.

50. Lynn Langway, Pamela Kruger, P. B. Gray, reported by Susan Garland, Laurie Kretchmar, Beth Kwon, Abby Schultz, and Tara Weingarten, "25 Women Who Are Making It Big In Small Business Smart, Gutsy, Innovative. Without Them the New Economy Wouldn't Look Quite So New," *CNN*, March 1, 2001, https://money.cnn.com/magazines/fsb/fsb_archive/2001/03/01/298108/index.htm.

51. Mike Snow, "SBA Award Boosts Venture Capital Fund for Women," *The Washington Post*, June 22, 1998, https://www.washingtonpost.com/archive/business/1998/06/22/sba-award-boosts-venture-capital-fund-for-women/99e1e355-7adf-492c-bc0b-7ef240474597/?utm_term=.16b8c3819074.

52. Mark Hughes, "'Wonder Woman' Is Officially the Highest-Grossing Superhero Origin Film," *Forbes*, November 2, 2017, https://www.forbes.com/sites/markhughes/2017/11/02/wonder-woman-is-officially-the-highest-grossing-superhero-origin-film/#81323f9ebd9e.

53. George Perez, *Wonder Woman, vol. 1* (California: DC Comics, 1986), https://www.comixology.com/Wonder-Woman-By-George-Perez-Vol-1/digital-comic/409434.

54. Abraham Riesman, "The Untold Tale of the Comics Story That Redefined Wonder Woman," Vulture, June 1, 2017, http://www.vulture.com/2017/06/wonder-woman-revisiting-the-comics-story-that-redefined-her.html.

PART THREE

CHAPTER ELEVEN

1. "World Population Ageing 2007," United Nations, 2007, https://www.un.org/en/development/desa/population/publications/pdf/ageing/WorldPopulationAgeingReport2007.pdf.

2. "Generation 2025 and Beyond," UNICEF, November 2012, http://www.unicef. org/media/files/Generation_2015_and_beyond_15_Nov2012_e_version.pdf.

3. "The State of Food and Agriculture," Food and Agriculture Organization of the United Nations, 2012, http://www.fao.org/3/a-i3028e.pdf.

4. "Generation 2025 and Beyond."

5. "Weather-related loss events worldwide 1980–2017," NatCalSERVICE presentation, Munich RE, https://www.ifat.de/media/website/dateien/pdf/ zukunftsdialog/eberhard-faust-presentation.pdf.

6. Stephanie Chalkley-Rhoden, "Melbourne Water Supply Could Be Under Threat Within a Decade, Water Authority Says," ABC News, July 23, 2017, http://mobile. abc.net.au/news/2017-07-23/ melbourne-water-supply-could-be-under-threat-within-a-decade/8735400.

7. "Worldwide Water Shortage by 2040," *Science Daily*, July 29, 2014, https://www. sciencedaily.com/releases/2014/07/140729093112.htm.

8. "Global Assessment Report on Disaster Risk Reduction 2015," United Nations, 2015, https://www.preventionweb.net/english/hyogo/gar/2015/en/gar-pdf/ GAR2015_EN.pdf.

9. "Developing World's Share of Global Investment to Triple by 2030, Says New World Bank Report," The World Bank, May 16, 2013, http://www.worldbank.org/ en/news/press-release/2013/05/16/ developing-world-share-of-global-investment-to-triple-by-2030-says-new-world- bank-report.

10. "India, China, and ASEAN to surpass combined wealth of West by 2030," May 2, 2012, http://economictimes.indiatimes.com/articleshow/12967527. cms?utm_source=contentofinterest&utm_medium=text&utm_campaign=cppst.

11. Jim O'Neill, "Who Defines the New Economic Giants," *The New York Times*, December 4, 2014, http://www.nytimes.com/2014/12/04/opinion/jim-oneill-who- defines-the-next-economic-giants.html?_r=0.

12. "The World in 2025: Rising Asia and Socio-Ecological Transition," European Commission, 2009, http://ec.europa.eu/research/social-sciences/pdf/ the-world-in-2025-report_en.pdf.

13. Homi Kharas, *The Unprecedented Expansion of the Global Middle Class: An Update*, February 2017, https://www.brookings.edu/wp-content/uploads/2017/02/ global_20170228_global-middle-class.pdf.

14. Larry Elliott and Ed Pilkington, "New Oxfam Report Says Half of Global Wealth Held by the 1%," *The Guardian*, January 19, 2015, http://www.theguardian.com/ business/2015/jan/19/ global-wealth-oxfam-inequality-davos-economic-summit-switzerland.

15. Ibid.

16. "India, China, and ASEAN to surpass combined wealth of West by 2030."

17. The United Nations facilitated working groups of member countries to develop eight Millennium Development Goals (MDGs)—which ranged from halving extreme poverty rates to halting the spread of HIV/AIDS and providing universal primary education, all by the target date of 2015 (http://www.un.org/ millenniumgoals/). In January 2016, these MDGs were superseded by seventeen Sustainable Development Goals (SDGs) adopted by world leaders to mobilize efforts to end all forms of poverty, fight inequalities, and tackle climate change.

18. Nobuo Yoshida, "What Can We Learn from Projecting Poverty for 2030?," The World Bank, January 27, 2014, http://blogs.worldbank.org/developmenttalk/ what-can-we-learn-projecting-poverty-2030; and "Poverty: Overview," The World Bank, http://www.worldbank.org/en/topic/poverty/overview.

19. Nobuo Yoshida, Hiroki Uematsu, and Carlos E. Sobrado, "Is Extreme Poverty Going to End?," The World Bank, January 2014, http://www-wds.worldbank.org/ external/default/WDSContentServer/WDSP/IB/2014/01/06/000158349_2014010 6142540/Rendered/PDF/WPS6740.pdf.

20. "IMF Report," International Monetary Fund, April 2017, https://www.imf.org/ external/pubs/ft/ar/2017/eng/pdfs/IMF-AR17-English.pdf.

21. Adam Wagstaff, Caryn Bredenkamp, and Leander R. Buisman, "Progress on Global Health Goals: Are the Poor Being Left Behind?," Research Observer, July 28, 2014, https://academic.oup.com/wbro/article-abstract/29/2/137/1632142.

22. Guy Standing, The Precariat: The New Dangerous Class (New York: Bloomsbury Academic, 2011).

23. Guy Standing, "Meet the Precariat, the New Global Class Fuelling the Rise of Populism," World Economic Forum, November 9, 2016, https://www.weforum. org/agenda/2016/11/precariat-global-class-rise-of-populism/.

24. Elizabeth Currid-Halkett, The Sum of Small Things (Princeton, NJ: Princeton University Press, 2017).

25. Standing, "Meet the Precariat."

26. Ibid.

27. Steven Pinker, The Better Angels of Our Nature: Why Violence Has Declined (New York: Penguin Books, 2012).

28. "Latest Trends in Religious Restrictions and Hostilities," Pew Research Center, February 26, 2015, http://www.pewforum.org/2015/02/26/religious-hostilities/.

29. "IISS Manama Dialogue 2018," IISS, October 26–28, 2018, https://www.iiss.org/ events/manama%20dialogue/archive/manama-dialogue-2014-3b96/plenary4-6caa/ fallon-72c0.

30. Ibid.

31. Several concepts explored in the next part of this chapter are derived from an IFTF Report for TSF written by our IFTF colleagues, Dr. Jake Dunagan and Dr. Stuart Candy, with imput from Moira Were and Pam Ryan.

32. "Internet of Things: Science Fiction or Business Fact?," *Harvard Business Review*, April 24, 2016.

33. Brian Hoffstein, "Clay Shirky: Unlocking Mankind's Untapped Potential," *Forbes*, August 16, 2012, https://www.forbes.com/sites/singularity/2012/08/16/ clay-shirky-unlocking-mankinds-untapped-potential/#65cd71c421ab.

34. Noah Kulwin, "Amazon's Mechanical Turkers Are College-Educated Millennials Making Less Than Minimum Wage," *Recode*, July 11, 2016, https://www.recode. net/2016/7/11/12148646/amazon-mechanical-turk-college-millennials-minimum-wage; and Miranda Katz, "Amazon's Turker Crowd Has Had Enough," *Wired*, August 23, 2017, https://www.wired.com/story/ amazons-turker-crowd-has-had-enough/.

35. Peter Diamandis, *Abundance Is Our Future* (2012; TED2012), video, http://www. ted.com/talks/peter_diamandis_abundance_is_our_future?language=en.

36. Izabella Kaminska, "Silicon Valley's Cryptocurrency Craze Is a Bubble in the Making," *Financial Times*, July 18, 2017.

37. http://www.communityimpactbucks.org.uk/pages/good-neighbours.html, accessed November 26, 2017.

38. James Chen, "Fiat Money," *Investopedia*, April 10, 2019, https://www.investopedia. com/terms/f/fiatmoney.asp.

39. "PitchBook Fintech Analyst Notes: ICOs," PitchBook, July 21, 2017, https:// pitchbook.com/news/ reports/3q-2017-pitchbook-fintech-analyst-note-icos?utm_medium=nl-na&utm_ campaign=3q-2017-fintech-analyst-note-icos&utm_source=report.

40. "Breaking Down the ICO Phenomenon," PitchBook, July 24, 2017, https:// pitchbook.com/newsletter/breaking-down-the-ico-phenomenon; https://www. ft.com/content/b12dd3ea-6ba9-11e7-bfeb-33fe0c5b7eaa; ibid. from above; and Robert Hackett and Anna Teregulova, "Why Everyone's Talking About 'Initial Coin Offerings,'" *Fortune*, March 31, 2017, http://fortune.com/2017/03/31/ initial-coin-offering/.

41. Jane Gleeson-White, *Six Capitals, or Can Accountants Save the Planet? Rethinking Capitalism for the Twenty-First Century* (New York: W. W. Norton & Company, 2014).

42. Alex Williams, "Move Over, Millennials, Here Comes Generation Z," *The New York Times*, September 18, 2015, https://www.nytimes.com/2015/09/20/fashion/ move-over-millennials-here-comes-generation-z.html.

43. Williams, "Move Over, Millennials, Here Comes Generation Z."

44. Morley Winograd and Michael D. Hais, *Millennial Momentum: How a New Generation Is Remaking America* (New Brunswick, NJ: Rutgers University Press, 2011).

45. "The Next America," Pew Research Center, 2016, http://www.pewresearch.org/the-next-america-book/.

46. Morley Winograd and Michael D. Hais, *Millennial Momentum*.

47. "The Digital Natives Project," Berkman Klein Center, https://cyber.harvard.edu/research/youthandmedia/digitalnatives#.

48. "World Happiness Report 2015," Sustainable Development Solutions Network, 2015, http://unsdsn.org/resources/publications/world-happiness-report-2015/.

CHAPTER TWELVE

1. Robert S. Brumbaugh, "Applied Metaphysics: Truth and Passing Time," *The Review of Metaphysics* 19, no. 4 (1966): 647–66.

2. Robbie Davis-Floyd, "Storying Corporate Futures: The Shell Scenarios in Corporate Futures," *Corporate Futures*, vol. 5, ed. George Marcus (Chicago: University of Chicago Press, 1998).

3. Karl Weick, *The Social Psychology of Organizing* (New York: McGraw-Hill, 1979).

4. Robbie Davis-Floyd, "Storying Corporate Futures."

5. Author's Note: These four scenarios were primarily written by contributors Jake Dunagan and Stuart Candy (for Institute For The Future), with input from Moira Were and Pamela Ryan.

6. D.J. Pangburn, "The Humans Who Dream of Companies That Won't Need Us," *Fast Company*, June 19, 2015, https://www.fastcompany.com/3047462/the-humans-who-dream-of-companies-that-wont-need-them.

CHAPTER THIRTEEN

1. "We Need to Get Digital ID Right," ID2020, http://id2020.org.

2. A trophic cascade is an ecological phenomenon triggered by the addition or removal of top predators or another system-changing element, and involving reciprocal changes in the relative populations of predator and prey through a food chain, which often results in dramatic changes in ecosystem structure and nutrient cycling. Stephen Carpenter, "Trophic Cascade," *Encyclopedia Britannica*, https://www.britannica.com/science/trophic-cascade; and Cass Sunstein, *Risk and Reason: Safety, Law, and the Environment* (Cambridge: Cambridge University Press, 2002).

3. Michael White and David Epston, *Narrative Means to Therapeutic Ends* (New York: W. W. Norton & Company, 1990).

4. Kurt Colvin, Rahul Dodhia, and R. Key Dismukes, "Is Pilots' Visual Scanning Adequate to Avoid Mid-Air Collisions?," Aircarft Owners and Pilots Association, 2005, https://www.aopa.org/training-and-safety/students/presolo/skills/pre-solo-flying-skills.

5. Alan Spoon, "What 'Pivot' Really Means," *Inc.*, August 10, 2012, http://www.inc.com/alan-spoon/what-pivot-really-means.html.

6. Pamela Ryan, *Magic Carpet Flying: The Ride of Your Life* (Toronto: Blue Butterfly Book Publishing, 2009).

7. Karl Weick, *The Social Psychology of Organizing* (New York: McGraw-Hill, 1979). This case study was first related by Hungarian Nobel Laureate Albert Szent-Györgyi, and a poem by Holub in 1977.

8. Ryan, *Magic Carpet Flying*.

CHAPTER FOURTEEN

1. MSCI, "ESG Ratings," https://www.msci.com/esg-ratings#p_56_INSTANCE_WUm9SsNvCpQe.

2. "ESG data," Bloomberg, 2019, https://www.bloomberg.com/impact/products/esg-data/.

3. "Gender Equality Global Report & Ranking," Equileap, 2018 ed., https://equileap.org/wp-content/uploads/2018/10/Equileap-Gender-Equality-Global-Report-and-Ranking-2018.pdf.

4. Davis Polk, "ESG Reports and Ratings: What They Are, Why They Matter?," July 12, 2017, https://www.davispolk.com/files/2017-07-12_esg_reports_ratings_what_they_are_why_they_matter_0.pdf.

5. "Who We Are," Parnassus Investments, https://www.parnassus.com/who-we-are#philosophy-and-process.

6. Nabil Tamimi and Rose Sebastianelli, "Transparency among S&P 500 companies: an analysis of ESG disclosure scores," *Management Decision*, Vol. 55 Issue 8 (2017): 1660–1680.

7. Christian Seelos and Johanna Mair, "The Role of Research in Social Innovation," *Stanford Social Innovation Review*, June 19, 2014, https://ssir.org/articles/entry/the_role_of_research_in_social_innovation.

FORTHWARD

1. William Gallois, *Time, Religion and History* (London: Pearson Education, 2007).

2. Brian Edgar, "Time for God: Christian Stewardship and the Gift of Time," *The Evangelical Review of Theology* 27, no. 2 (2003): 128–46.

3. Daniel Siegel, "The Elasticity of Time," *Humanities* (March/April 2005): 38–41.

4. In this chapter, for the sake of brevity, we use the word of Warlpiri people and other language groups in Central Australia.

5. William Gallois, *Time, Religion and History, (New York: Routledge, 2007).*

6. Sandra Cutts, "Living the Dreaming: The Relationship to the Land for Aboriginal Australians," http://www.bri.net.au/livingbysandra.html.

7. Ibid.

8. Jens Korff, "Meaning of Land to Aboriginal People," Creative Spirits, February 8, 2019, https://www.creativespirits.info/aboriginalculture/land/meaning-of-land-to-aboriginal-people#ixzz51VJUUPC5.

9. Aleksander Janca and Clothilde Bullen, "The Aboriginal Concept of Time and Its Mental Health Implications," *Australasian Psychiatry* 1, supplement (2003): 40–44.

10. Rebecca Walker, "Eternity Now: Aboriginal Concepts of Time," The Salvation Army, August 27, 2010, https://www.sarmy.org.au/Resources/Articles/reforming-society/Eternity-Now-Aboriginal-Concepts-of-Time/.

11. Mattie T.J. Stepanek, Jimmy Carter and Jennifer Stepanek (ed). *Just Peace, a Message of Hope.* (Andrews McMeel Publishing. 2009).

12. Jennie Kermode, "Learning to Think Like a Writer," Explore Writing, January 11, 2018, http://www.explorewriting.co.uk/learning-think-like-writer.html.

13. Karl Weick, *Sensemaking in Organizations* (Newbury Park, CA: Sage, 1995).

14. Amartya Sen, interviewed by Akash Kapur, *The Atlantic*, December 15, 1995.

15. Andy Sumner, "Where Will the World's Poor Live? A Briefing on Global Poverty Projection for 2020 and 2030," Institute of Development Studies, https://www.ids.ac.uk/files/dmfile/AndySumner-BriefingonGlobalPovertyProjections.pdf; and "The World Has Made Great Progress in Eradicating Extreme Poverty," *The Economist*, March 30, 2017, https://www.economist.com/news/international/2171979 0-going-will-be-much-harder-now-world-has-made-great-progress.

16. Al Gore, *An Inconvenient Sequel: Truth to Power* (New York: Rodale, 2017).

Index

About the Author

Dr. Pamela Ryan received her PhD from the University of Texas at Austin with award-winning research on the psychology of decision-making in the U.S. venture capital industry. A dual U.S.-Australian citizen, Pamela has held leadership positions in several international organizations. Her unique skill set and diverse experiences as a psychologist, entrepreneur, investor, business manager, researcher, and author have been applied in business, political, and psychosocial arenas around the world.

Pamela has served as a Limited Partner in U.S. and Australian venture capital firms for more than thirty years and acted as an advisor and consulting psychologist to venture capital firms in Australia and the United States, as well as to venture capital-funded portfolio companies—ranging from semiconductor manufacturing to retail to hospitality. She has advised the South Australian government on building an innovation ecosystem in South Australia, drawing on cutting-edge research from around the world on the characteristics of venture capital firms/funds for optimal success. Pamela serves on the advisory boards of True Wealth Ventures and South Texas Money Management. She has taught entrepreneurship at the McCombs Business School at the University of Texas and the psychology of decision-making at the

Australian Graduate School of Management. Pamela maintains her strong ties with academia as a Research Fellow at the Hawke Research Institute, University of South Australia, and the Center for Australian and New Zealand Studies at the University of Texas.

Pamela is managing partner of the Tingari Group, including the Tingari-Silverton Foundation. She manages a portfolio of business partnerships, organizations, and investments. She chaired the boards of the international nongovernmental organization Psychology Beyond Borders and the international think tank and research institute Issues Deliberation Australia for ten years each. Pamela has authored and co-authored many public policy reports, conference papers, and academic articles relating to diverse projects, including "Why Some Venture Capitalists Escalate and Others Don't," "The Psychology of Microfinance," and "The Future of Social Entrepreneurship and Impact." She has received many awards, including an honorary doctorate from the University of South Australia for her work in the public policy and political psychology fields and the prestigious Order of Australia Medal by the Australian government for her contribution to the field of psychology and to Australia. She has been inducted into the Women's Honour Roll of South Australia and listed in *Who's Who of Australian Women.*

About the Contributors

Moira Were, M.Litt. OAM

Moira Were has worked from the kitchen table as a direct-service social worker through to the cabinet table as a chief of staff to a government minister. She has extensive operational and strategic management experience in diverse organizations at state, regional, national, and international levels. Moira has facilitated interdisciplinary teams for creative and inclusive cross-sectoral work for the design and implementation of change. She has supported enterprises and community development activities in Mozambique, South Africa, Ghana, The United Kingdom, Canada, The United States, Italy, Portugal, Germany, Kazakhstan, and Indonesia. Moira is currently director of Facilitating Futures, a firm dedicated to facilitating futures through strategic engagement and communication support. She is also the leader of Chooks SA, a collaboration of women to build the support and networks to help them get the kinds of capital (financial, social, human, emotional, network) they need to grow their enterprises and positive impact.

Jake Dunagan, PhD

Jake Dunagan is an adjunct professor in the Design Strategy MBA program at the California College of the Arts, where he teaches strategic foresight, tactical media, and social invention. He is also research director at the Institute For The Future, a nonprofit futures research group based in Palo Alto, California. Jake's research examines the role of emerging technologies in transforming individuals, culture, and governance. In particular, he explores how politics, organizations, and societies are adapting to the Neurocentric age, a time of unprecedented ability to view and modify the mind. Jake has worked with governments, businesses, foundations, and nonprofits around the world to create visual media, interactive experiences, and public engagement projects that inject alternative visions of the future into the present.

Stuart Candy, PhD

Stuart Candy is an associate professor in the School of Design at Carnegie Mellon University. A professional futurist and experience designer, Stuart has staged projects cutting across foresight, design, and transmedia storytelling, in settings including SXSW, the California Academy of Sciences, Burning Man, the streets of Honolulu's Chinatown, and online. Working across discipline and industry boundaries, Stuart is often sought for involvement in unusual strategic initiatives. He helped found the Festival of Transitional Architecture in post-earthquake Christchurch, New Zealand; directed the development of the U.S. Centers for Disease Control and Prevention's early games that targeted behavior change in public health; advised the Future We Want project for the United Nations Conference on Sustainable Development (Rio+20 Summit); and designed and ran processes for public co-creation of futures strategies and experiences for the City of Melbourne, University of Oxford, UK National Health Service, Sydney Opera House, *Wired* magazine, State of Hawaii, IDEO, Institute For The Future, General Electric, Australian Academy of Science, UNESCO Youth Forum, and the United Arab Emirates.